THE BOOK OF

DECLARATIONS

THE REMEDY FOR MANKIND'S

DILEMMAS

BY

MICHAEL JEDAIAH

THE BOOK OF DECLARATIONS

Table of Contents

Dedication

This book is dedicated to the greatest Man who has ever lived Yahushuah Hamashiach - and to all the true Believers worldwide who are doers of the Word. I would also like to acknowledge the late pastors, Stephen Darby and Derek Prince, who were my motivation to speak the gospel of the King of kings without conforming myself to the standards of this world. I would also like to say keep up the good work to "Brotha Ray" from Thug Exposed Ministry. Furthermore, I want to salute all my Israelites family spread all over the world from Ethiopia to America. Regardless of our differences, our God is faithful and just, and He has not forsaken us.

To my late mother and my immediate family, despite being brought up in dysfunctional environments, I love you all. I wish you all the best.

Lastly, to all the positive people who the Lord has sent over the years to help shine the way to the path of righteousness, God bless you.

Disclaimer

*T*he *Book Of Declarations* was prepared and accomplished by Michael Jedaiah in his own capacity. The opinions expressed in this article are the author's own and do not reflect the view of any organization, group, or the United States government.

Furthermore, Michael Jedaiah, and any associates of Clarion Ministry are not affiliated with any Hebrews Roots Movement, anti-Semitic groups, religion-based movements, or national hate groups. They are a non-denomination ministry whose goal is to understand, apply, and teach the Word of God without compromise or discrimination. The author does not know any of the individuals whose references have been used in this book, nor do their references personally validate the author's opinions. They are in no way associated with him; nor do they endorse the author. Michael Jedaiah is the sole litterateur behind the message in this book, and he proclaims these messages through the authority invested in him at Calvary by our Lord and Savior, Jesus Christ.

Preface

T his book is intended to enlighten and encourage the children of YHWH (pronounced Yahweh) wherever they may be on this journey of life. It is not intended to provide all the answers of life, for only God knows all things.

The reader is urged to consult the Creator through His only begotten Son, Yahushuah, by the power of the Ruach Hakodesh, as he or she reads through these pages. This book is to be used in conjunction with the Holy Scriptures, for the Word of God is spirit and life, and it is by the Word that we are quickened. This parchment is labeled *The Book of Declarations* because I am sent as a diplomatic emissary with these messages from our King, but ultimately, the overall message in these pages is that Jesus Christ is the one True King and the answer to all our problems. I have tried to be as limpid as possible in my exposé of these heavenly revelations so that the messages may be clear and fluent without losing the substance therein. Some of the initial materials used to reinforce my studies have been either deleted, or the web pages are no longer active; therefore, alternate sources had to be used in the bibliography. Furthermore, some of the materials used in the bibliography were not quoted, but they were still part of the inspiration behind some of my viewpoints. You will find that some of these viewpoints and Bible Scriptures are repetitive; it is because all things are connected to the Vertex of Life, and it is virtually impossible to quote the Alpha without including the Omega. Lastly, due to all the events that took place between 2020 and 2021 and the paranoia regarding the G5 telephone towers and the mark of the beast, I have chosen to use the conspiracy theory platform as my entry point throughout the book. But ultimately, the overlords presiding over any secret societies or cults are just pawns in the game of chess. Jesus holds all the pieces of the game. Be blessed in your reading.

Michael Jedaiah

The Ten Commandments

Exodus 20:1-17

¹And God spoke all these words, saying,

² I am the LORD thy God, which have brought thee out of the land of Egypt, out of the house of bondage

³ Thou shalt have no other gods before me.

⁴ Thou shalt not make unto thee any graven image, or any likeness of anything that is in heaven above, or that is in the earth beneath, or that is in the water under the earth:

⁵ Thou shalt not bow down thyself to them, nor serve them: for I the LORD thy God am a jealous God, visiting the iniquity of the fathers upon the children unto the third and fourth generation of them that hate me;

⁶And showing mercy unto thousands of them that love me, and keep my commandments.

⁷Thou shalt not take the name of the LORD thy God in vain; for the LORD will not hold him guiltless that taketh his name in vain.

⁸ Remember the sabbath day, to keep it holy.

⁹ Six days shalt thou labor, and do all thy work:

¹⁰ But the seventh day is the sabbath of the LORD thy God: in it thou shalt not do any work, thou, nor thy son, nor thy daughter, thy manservants, nor thy maidservant, nor thy cattle, nor thy stranger that is within thy gates:

[11] For in six days the LORD made heaven and earth, the sea, and all that in them is, and rested the seventh day: wherefore the LORD blessed the sabbath day, and hallowed it.

[12] Honor thy Father and thy mother: that thy days may be long upon the land which the LORD thy God giveth thee.

[13] Thou shalt not kill.

[14] Thou shalt not commit adultery.

[15] Thou shalt not steal.

[16] Thou shalt not bear false witness against thy neighbor. [17] Thou shalt not covet thy neighbor's house, thou shalt not covet thy neighbor's wife, nor his manservant, nor his ox, nor his ass, nor any thing that is thy neighbor's.

Declaration

Hear ye; hear ye, all ye inhabitants of the earth. Fear ye the LORD! Fear ye the LORD!

For the LORD is great in power and wonders.

From His Holy Mountain He sees all our deeds.

He searches the hearts of men. He elevates the humble and lowers the proud.

He enlightens the meek and confuses the fools.

Their wisdoms are like sinking ships, and their lifeboats will not see dry land.

The fire of the lake shall consume them, and their evil deeds will haunt them forever.

Hear ye, you wise men of the land, though the land is engorged in flame, thou must not recant your faith.

For the LORD is great in power and wonders, and by His Spirit, He will guide you to the river of living water.

Let not your light be smothered; be wise and consult with the LORD, and be bold and speak the truth.

For thou hast forsaken Me, sayest the LORD.

Hear ye, hear ye, all inhabitants of the land.

Yet a little while, and I will make everything anew, sayest the LORD. Repent; repent you heathen, while the daylight is still here, before the darkness of the night overwhelms you.

For the LORD is great in power and wonders, and He is greatly to be feared!

CHAPTER ONE

JOHN 14:6

The Life of Death

At creation, God made man to enjoy life because He wanted us to have a life full of joy and serenity, a life full of blessings and wealth. A life that is full of liveliness. This life was lost at the fall of man in the Garden of Eden after Adam ate the forbidden fruit, which he substituted for a life of death. This life of death is what we are subjugated to when we do not recognize Jesus Christ as our Lord and Savior. To put it plainly, the life of death is all existence apart from Jesus Christ; it is the absence of any perspective beyond the kingdom of man, which we need to look past and look forward to the afterlife and the judgment to come—because our kingdom is a temporary kingdom; our time is drawing to a close.

Before the birth of Christ, the hope of men was limited to the prophecy of His coming, but since Calvary, our prospect has never been so well defined. He restored what had been lost and provided a clear path to life as originally planned. Jesus is the way to everlasting life in a peaceful kingdom where there will be no pain or grief. This kingdom is within all Believers in the conformation of the Spirit of Christ, which is living in us and guiding us. Life eternal, in God's kingdom, is accessible to all through Jesus. It is not hard to find, but it may sometimes seem very difficult to pursue. It is easily accessible to all, but unfortunately, only a few people will ever make the most of it.

Many believe that this type of life can simply be obtained through financial wealth and material assets, but the truth is all those things have no values of their own, and chasing after them leads to a life of death. The only reason these things are an aim for so many people is because the god of this land, Satan, has said so (2 Cor. 4:4). He has spent millennia creating this belief system, which causes men to hate themselves for not having a twinkle of nothing. Over the years, Satan has mastered the art of deceiving men into selling their souls for a "whoopee moment." This whoopee moment is anything that gives us a temporary sense of validation in exchange for a lifetime of shame. This type of masquerade is very prevalent in the movie business where women are often tricked into sexual acts in return for promise of stardom in Hollywood. Men also are often tricked into cross-dressing by the same industry for that 15 minutes of fame. To maintain this whoopee moment state, these men and women have to keep going back to these movie executives and degrade themselves continuously. This is why most celebrities have to often be heavily medicated to function because they are trying to numb the pain brought forth by their hidden shame.

That kind of hijacking is the same trick the devil used against the first Adam in the Garden of Eden. This fact can be seen more clearly in Genesis 2:16-17 (KJV):

"The LORD God commanded the man, saying, Of every tree of the garden thou mayest freely eat: But of the tree of the knowledge of good and evil, thou shalt not eat of it: for in the day that thou eatest thereof thou shalt surely die."

The devil then ensnared the woman to deceive the man. Now as we continue reading, an amazing fact is presented in Genesis 3:22. We come to find out that the tree of eternal life was also in the garden.

"And the LORD God said, Behold, the man is become as one of us, to know good and evil: and now, lest he put forth his hand, and take also of the tree of life, and eat, and live forever:"

God proceeded to cast them out of the garden. According to the Text, the Tree of Life, which gives eternal life, was there in the garden, and man was not prevented from eating it up to that point. This sleight of hand led to the curse of Earth's civilization and the chain of events that followed.

We often hear preaching about the physical death that the disobedience of Adam brought to mankind, but I would like to invite you to look at that fact from another façade. If we look at that factuality from God's point of view, we can trace ourselves back to our current timeline.

What Adam essentially did in the garden on that day was reject the gift of God, the gift of eternal life; Adam unknowingly traded the universal for the finite, and the eternal for the temporary; he exchanged the gift of life for the curse of death. What is more, this warning of the Creator (in Gen. 2:16) was not directed only to Adam and Eve, but to all of the generations after them until the world ends.

The tree of knowledge being in the garden means that evil clearly already existed before the creation of Adam. Speculation can go on forever, but only God has all the answers. One thing is certain, when God told him not to eat from the tree of the knowledge of good and evil, God warned Adam of the danger of taking part in finitude, of taking part in disobedience. In other words, God said to Adam,

"Choose life, that thou mayest live, because disobedience will bring thee death" (Deut. 30:15-20).

Think about it this way, the Bible says that GOD is the God of life; He is the Creator of life and light and the Giver of everlasting life (Gen. 2:7; Luke 20:38; Matt. 22:32; Acts 17:24-28 and John 10:27-30). Therefore, just like it is impossible for mares to give birth to cows, or a lioness to birth a dog, the God of life cannot create death; death is the result of disobedience to His precepts from Heaven to Earth, and from the iniquity of the serpent to the iniquity of men whom follow the serpent (Deut. 32:12-22).

The inevitable question that arises then in our minds when we read about the tree of the knowledge of good and evil, is why did God place the tree there in the first place?

Well, first, the LORD God Almighty does whatever He chooses to perform. He is above all and before all, and as stated in Deut. 29:29 NIV:

"The secret things belong unto the LORD our God, but the things revealed belong to us and to our children forever that we may do all the words of this law," **that fact is unequivocal.**

However, I personally powdered on this subject for a while, and I developed the following thesis:

The purpose of the tree of the knowledge of good and evil being in the garden was to establish the first principle of love, which is obedience to God.

The omnipotent God placed the tree in the garden to elaborate in man the first principle of love, while simultaneously establishing His identity within us. Because unlike the beast of the sea and the beast of Heaven and Earth, God made us into His image and likeness with the gift of rationality and the right to choose for ourselves. The love of God is called "Agape;" this type of love only emits from GOD, and His desire has always been for His creation to return this love to Him freely (Ps. 86:15; John 3:16; 1 John 3:1; 1 Cor. 13).

Agape is unconditional love and obedient love; it is the love that Jesus demonstrated at the Cross for us, and it is standardized to the obedience that Abraham demonstrated when he went to sacrifice Isaac at the LORD's commands in Genesis 22: 1-18. In both cases, you can hear "nevertheless, not my will but thy will be done," resonate in the heart of each individual. In either case, you may also notice the free will of each individual being given over to the commandment of the Father willingly. Now, GOD does not need to answer to anyone but Himself, and He could have dealt differently with Adam after the fall, but because His Agape love compelled Him to, despite Adam's action, God resolved to exact His predisposed plan of salvation. It is because of His Agape love that despite our many indiscretions through the generations, He has not consumed us.

I praise the name of the LORD God Almighty, for He is not controlled by His emotions. His mercy endureth forever, and even His wrath is subjected to His love.

Once we understand that the Father's love is what has both subjugated and preserved mankind from His wrath, it becomes clear that the only natural response for us to have is gratitude manifested thru our obedience to His commands (Psalm 36:5-12; Psalm 145:20; Proverbs 3:12-18; Genesis 45:4-8). Any other output leads to a circular existence, and to the life of death. Jesus coins it with these words:

"If you love me, keep my commandments," and *"Love the Lord your God with all your heart and with all your soul and with all your strength and with all your*

mind." But He also said, *"Not every one that says to me Lord, Lord will enter the Kingdom of Heaven but only those who do the will of my Father in heaven"* (John 14:15; Luke 10:25-28 and Matt. 7:21 NIV).

He also commanded us, His disciples, to love one another (John 13:34-35); but before we can love one another, we must first have God's love in our hearts, love for God, and for others. The Father knows that it can be difficult at times to get along with one another, but He commands us to give the best of ourselves, and then some more (Matt. 18:21-35; Rom. 12:17-21).

Now let us go back to the tree of knowledge. When the tree was eaten by disobedience, even the knowledge of good in the tree became wicked. This is the primary reason why we have been using our intelligence for evil. The knowledge of the forbidden tree has given us science, and science is an important part of our existence. For without science, Dr. Joseph Goldberger would not have discovered the cause of pellagra, a disease caused by a diet deficiency in vitamin B. This diet deficiency caused the death of many poor Southerners in the early 20th century. Later in that same century, researcher Conrad Elvehjem, through the lense of science, found that niacin could prevent and cure pellagra in both animals and people. This same science, however, has led many to draw away from God and place their hope on eugenics, which is a controlled selective breeding of the human population. People today are trying to substitute eternal life through Jesus Christ with cryonics and transhumanism. Cryonics proponents claim that frozen embryos can be brought back to life, and Transhumanists believe that we can live forever with lifestyle alterations and body part enhancements. People are operating outside the will of God, though it may seem right or even bring forth prosperity for a while (Gen. 3: [6]-19), it is still wrong because of the disobedient aspect starting from Adam. Moreover, at the final stage, all disobedience to God's precepts will be rewarded with bad tidings, specifically in the afterlife.

From the invention of primitive weapons like the sword to the creation of the hydrogen bomb, this tainted knowledge has been the influence behind our self-fueled destruction (Matt. 26:52).

Pertaining to the story of creation, think of it as a newborn baby boy eating steak off his father's plate. The steak itself is not the problem. It is the absence of molars, the risk of suffocation, and the effect on the baby's digestive system, which in many cases will lead to the death of that child. However, once the child is sufficiently developed to treat such food, he is able to eat it and digest it without difficulty. Similarly, Adam and Eve needed to first mature in the garden by obeying the commandment of the Lord concerning the reception of the knowledge of the tree, and then the understanding and knowledge of good and evil would have been given to them.

In comparison, in the book of Enoch, we can see how the 350 years of his obedience led to some of the most marvelous revelations a living man can experience. Mysteries that are unlawful for us to see were shown and explained to him gratuitously. We can also see the position of trust that God gave to those who displayed similar faithfulness throughout the Bible. From His prophets: Daniel while he was in captivity, Elijah who was also taken alive, and Moses' body getting buried by Michael the Archangel himself while his soul was later reinstated for God's use. But also to His servants: Joseph who took control of the whole kingdom of Pharaoh, the young shepherd David who was made king of Israel, and Paul being taken to the third Heaven while he was still in this kingdom.

Through and through the Bible, we see the emphasis that the LORD GOD places upon obedience to His Word and how He rewards those who obey Him with immeasurable gifts. Our God is a jealous God, and He even stresses that point in the first two commands of His Ten Commandments:

"You should have no other gods before Me," and, "You should not make for yourself an idol" (Ex. 20:3-6).

From the beginning of time, the Father reached out to his creation to make Himself known and to make known to us the importance of fidelity and obedience to His Word.

In Genesis, God demonstrated His sovereignty and love for us despite our feeble nature. Through the obedience of Abraham, He gave mankind the blessed hope— Jesus Christ the Savior of the world.

In Exodus, God showed that He was faithful to the covenant He made with Abraham in Genesis 15:13-21, and starting in Exodus Chapter 12 with the Passover, He gave Israel His guidelines through the Mosaic Law.

In Leviticus, He instructed Israel on how to be holy and how to be a blessing to others. In Numbers, God reminded His people of the consequence of rebellion. In Deuteronomy, He reminded them of the terms and conditions of the Mosaic Law. In Joshua, He assured them that obedience to God is rewarded. In the book of Judges, God stressed to the people the importance of remaining loyal to Him. In 1st and 2nd Kings, the Lord demonstrated the value of obeying Him and the danger of disobedience. These are just from the first nine books of the Bible, but there is countless evidence of the first principle of love in the other books as well. With the current state of our communities concerning all the racial tensions and violence, let us look at three more examples of the backlash that failure or refusal to obey God brings.

[1]

Saul is rejected as the first king of Israel because of his disobediences:

It was said to Saul that he should wait for the prophet Samuel, that he, the prophet, might offer the sacrifice before God. Saul, however, gets weary and violates the command. When the prophet Samuel arrived at the location of the camp and saw what Saul had done, he told him that what he had done had just cost him the kingdom (1 Sam. 13:5-14), but king Saul does not repent, and it leads to further disobedience (1 Sam. 15:1-35; Gen. 4:3-7). Saul is then informed of the consequence of his actions, and the kingdom is officially taken from him and given to David. The Spirit of the LORD departs from Saul, and an evil spirit is turned over to him to torment him (1 Sam 16:14-23).

[2]

The young prophet is mauled to death by the lion for not harkening unto the Word of God:

In 1 Kings 13:1-25, we can view the story of the man of God and the old prophet, also known as the story of the young prophet and the old prophet. The young prophet is sent by God to deliver a message to King Jeroboam in the town of Bethel, and God gave him a special set of instructions to follow. He wasn't supposed to spend the night, he wasn't supposed to eat or drink anything, and he wasn't supposed to go down the same road on the way back. The old prophet who lived nearby heard of him and his "exploit" at Bethel, and he was determined to convince the man of God to come to his home. The old prophet told him that an angel had come to him to tell him that the young prophet should come to his home to eat bread instead of leaving the town as God instructed. The young prophet believed him and went with him. Then, while they were both sitting in the house eating bread, the Word of the LORD came to the old prophet against the man of God – verses 21-22 – and he was condemned to death for his disobedience, and he died later that day.

[3]

A Gentile woman named Jael, the Kenite, gets the kill and honor of defeating God's enemy in battle instead of the Israelite judge:

The story in Judges Chapter 4 is about a judge named Barak who was commanded by the LORD to go to war against the Canaanites; the name of the Canaanites' commander was Sisera. However, although the task was given to Judge Barak to ride against Sisera, he demanded for Deborah, the prophetess, to go with him, verses 1-9. Because of Barak's lack of courage and faith in the power of the LORD, the prophetess spoke the Word of God against him saying:

> *"I will surely go with thee: notwithstanding the journey that thou takest shall not be for thine honor; for the LORD shall sell Sisera into the hand of a woman"*
> *(Judges 4:9).*

The fame and honor for killing Sisera and avenging Israel was taken from him and given to Jael the Kenite because she is the one that killed Captain Sisera (Judges 4:18-21). In Judges Chapter 5:24-27, Jael is even included in the song of victory written about that battle. The type of disobedience Judge Barak committed here has to do with hesitation and fear. For God had commanded Barak to draw toward mount Tabor with ten thousand men so that God may deliver Sisera, the captain of the Canaanites's army into Barak's hand (Judges 4:6-7). But similar to the 12 spies that Moses sent to search the land of Canaan in

Numbers 12, Judge Barak was afraid and hesitant to follow the command of the Lord. However, the judgment of the Lord against Barak was relatively light compared to the children of Israel who had to wander for 40 years in the wilderness.

This recurring fact regarding God's stern reaction to disobedience because of our rebellious or hesitant heart is no coincidence; it is God's demonstration of His attitudes towards the value of obedience to Him. The truth is the Father is using us as validation for His judgment against the sons of God, the holy angels, who left their holy habitations for the pleasure of this world (1 Cor. 6:3). Under the counsel of Satan, these holy angels have become fallen angels, even demons, and they have been solely devoted in trying to convince us that their way is the right way, but their ways will only bring about eternal damnation. The Father knows that after the fall we were infected by a rebellious spirit that leads to sin, so He aimed to illustrate His values to us so that we might understand Him and His nature (Ex. 34:14) because walking after His nature is the only thing that will preserve us from eternal damnation. Even Jesus, the Son of God, displayed obedience to the Father throughout the Bible. According to Jude 1:9, Michael, the Archangel, which is Jesus in His pre-Messianic form, did not dare to condemn the devil but said, "The Lord rebuke thee." Jesus could have called for twelve plus legions of angels to deliver Him on that fateful day at Gethsemane when he was crucified, but He knew that escaping death was not the will of GOD for Him. Therefore, He endured the pain and was careful to be obedient to our Father's commands, even unto death (Matt. 26:51-56).

The Father always knows best, and I praise GOD because so does the Son. If the Son had not impelled his final trial, there would not be a blessed hope for us today. The earth as we know it would have been doomed, voided, and returned to the state of formlessness (Gen. 1:2). This is why as Christians, we praise the name of Jesus Christ and dare to carry our cross in a confused world. Our cross is our daily cup, for it is written in Matthew 6:34, "Sufficient unto the day is the evil thereof," and through Christ, we can increase and develop faith to carry it. Similar to Christ, when we face our trials in life and the final cup is given to us to drink at the end, we should take a stand and obey GOD, even if death is the result. Just like Christ at Gethsemane, when we take that stand and obey GOD, Heaven will minister to us and empower us; for to be absent in the flesh is to be present in the spirit, and Believers will not see any jackals when they traverse over (Gen. 25:8). This means that when we die, the souls of the righteous are gathered by holy angels unto their ancestors to rest until judgment day, but the souls of the wicked are drawn by jackals (hellish dogs) into Hades. The Spirit of Jesus Christ is, and will be, the parakletos and guide of the righteous for all time.

The life of death has never been God's desire for us, but it has been brought about through disobedience. To this day, it continues to be the reward for sorcery and idolatry. God created us with free will, so it is up to us if we choose to be disobedient, or to be as Christ was and sound out:

"Father, if thou be willing, remove this cup from me: nevertheless not my will, but thine, be done" (Luke 22:42-43).

My prayer for all of us is for God to build us more like Him every day, so that we may learn to be resilient and confident in our walk with the Lord.

CHAPTER TWO

The Foundational Lies

"In the beginning was the Word, and the Word was with God, and the Word was God. The same was in the beginning with God. All things were made by him; and without him was not any thing made that was made. In him was life; and the life was the light of men. And the light shineth in darkness; and the darkness comprehended it not" (John 1:1-5 KJV).

Jesus Christ is the Alpha and Omega, and without Him, there is no life. Without Him, there is no animation in the beginning or at the conclusion of all things. Without Him, there is no *true* life, even in between those two points in time. We breathe because we exist. We do not live to breathe. Your existence and mine is not simply platonic. We were made in the image of the everlasting GOD, and we are required to acknowledge that reality. As men, we are set aside from any other beings, and just like:

"Plants thus came from the dirt, fish from water and animals from the ground. Furthermore, plants return to the dirt, fish return to the sea and animals return to the ground when they die. All things have the same components and essence

as their source. What God created is, in essence, like the substance from which it came."

- Understanding Your Potential, Ch. 6 by Dr. Myles Monroe

It is impossible for creation to excel or reach its full potential without its pre-existing fundamental value. The origin of all things originates in God, but the substance of everything is different.

So let's discuss man; what is the essence of man? Whence comes the fundamental value of man, and how did we come so far? Well, *"then God said let us make man in our image and in our likeness."* Everything that has breath needs God to live, but each brainchild has to follow their preset directives to operate at top capacity. There's no other way to truly proliferate. Our role for existing is anchored in our Creator's essence and likeness. To understand who we are individually in the Lord, we have to follow the road map that He has provided us with, which is the Bible.

The enemy knows this, and because of its hatred for our Father, it has concentrated its attacks on the destruction of all the tissues of life that glorify God. What is happening today in our generation is a recurring dilemma, and it has brought mankind into a state of blissful ignorance. As it was in the days of Noah with wickedness, sexual perversions, violence, and everything geared toward evil, so it is today:

Eugenics, animal cloning, and transgenderisms are becoming a norm again, and the suppression of the freedom of faith is next. There's even been talk from some of our elected officials in the past to decriminalize pedophilia (see "Sex Bias in the U.S. Code" by Ruth Bader Ginsburg, page 102).

However, God holds all the pieces of the puzzle. He will remake the earth again, and as the time for Our Lord and Savior to come back approaches, the labor-inducing birth is amplifying.

In Revelation 13:11-18, the Bible warns us of "The beast out of the earth" who comes to exercise the power of the first beast (Dagon) that came before him. He comes out of the earth among men in the form of a man to establish the mark of the beast and to cause all who dwell on the earth to worship the first beast (Rev. 13:14-15).

The reason why the second beast is coming in the form of a man is because Satan is attempting to duplicate the work of God; therefore, the anti-Christ must be born of flesh, just as Jesus was born the Son of Man. The beast whose wound was healed in Revelation 13:3, is actually a political, religious, and economics system. This system was made official when Adam gave his authority, through disobedience, to Satan in the garden. Jesus crushed this political, religious, and economics system at Calvary by His resurrection. Then He established His Church on the day of Pentecost, and all those things were prophesied in Genesis 3:15, Isaiah 9:6, Daniel 2:44-45, and Joel 2:28- 29. Moreover, when Christ rose from the dead, He also restored Israel who lost its tenure (Matt. 15:24), and He took the keys of the two major dominions under Satan's commands (Rev. 1:18); He also made a way for all the Gentile nations to be saved, (Acts 13:46-49). After his departure from Earth, Jesus also reassured us with the gift of the Holy Spirit to comfort us, strengthen us, and lead us through these last days until His glorious return (John 14:16).

After the ascension of Jesus Christ, He returned to the Father to prepare a place for us. Satan, who is on a short leash, began to design a way to take back control of the earth. The Lord God, however, is omnipotent, all-encompassing, and all-knowing. He revealed to our brother John the final plans of the enemy within the book of Revelation.

The term "The Last Days" has existed for so long that a lot of people have become indifferent to it. But the last days are merely the period between the time Christ ascended and His second coming. Notice that in the last verse referenced above, our King said, *"I will ask of the Father,"* this shows that although there is no conflict within the Trinity, all things are still done with order and discipline within the house of GOD (see also 1 Peter 1:13-19).

The political, religious and economic system of the beast is simply a repetition of the days of Noah and the days of Lot. Satan has reinstated his foundational lies by corrupting our churches and our governments. Its political, religious and economic principles predate ancient Babylon, which is what Satan wanted to accomplish when he rebelled from God to create a government based on wealth and consumerism, where the rich rules over the meek, do as they see fit, and are exempt from prosecution because of their status and power (Ezekiel 28:1-19).

Satan has changed from the status of guardian cherub (guardian of the law) to that of corrupt politician. All this agitation and murder in our world today is a desperate attempt on the part of Satan to win the cult of men one last time because he is once again reliving his fantasy, or rather, the illusion of a perfect world. Satan wants a world where, "Do as that wilt," is the motto where anything and everything goes, and if we refuse to go along, death or imprisonment will be the outcome. However, although he is granted the power to kill our flesh (Matt. 10:28), he has no authority over our souls unless we grant him permission to rule over our mind, will, and emotions.

This earthly vessel is of this kingdom and has been corrupted since the fall, thus the Father allows the god of this earth to be satiated because we have all sinned (Genesis 2:19; 1 Cor. 15:39-53; Rom. 3:23), but God will preserve the souls of all His elects.

Now to be clear, this last statement mainly pertains to the last test of Rev. 13:15. If you or your loved ones are sick, and you are praying for healing, **do not stop**. Even when we get to the test of Rev.13:15, continue to intercede for divine protection. Some of us will survive and still be alive at the return of the KING OF KINGS. The former is for the skeptics who have been told that there will be no Saints going to the sword at the last tribulation.

Logic alone debunks that lie. If Israel was tested, the prophets persecuted, the apostles decapitated, and Jesus crucified for our sins, how can these wicked generations escape all tribulation?

Now there are four different dispensations of the end of time, but I believe only in the one stated above. Still, even if you disagree, the only thing that matters, as the final test is approaching, is that we stand for Christ, be doers of the Word, and inherit life eternal. The other alternative is to follow Satan into eternal damnation. These are the only two options we have. (Luke 17:26-33; Rev. 13:9-10; Rev. 19:11-21; Rev. 20:13-15 and Rev. 21:3-8).

The system of the beast is restored through those who wear the crown of Dagon, and each one of them calls himself the father of the church of Christ (John 23:9). They are well recognized for their pedophilia practices. Through this creature's political and religious infiltration, the world has come back to the state of mind of the days of Noah and has been under the spell of the beast for quite some time now. Their present king recently declared that all sexual orientation is acceptable to the church. I cannot say how far back for sure, but I believe that its restoration started with the division of the Orthodox and Catholic Church in 1054 CE. It expanded through the Knight Templar in 1119 CE, and finally the Church reformation in the 1500. The devil has been very busy poisoning the Church over the past millennia, and he has wreaked havoc from behind the curtain.

Satan really caught momentum when Copernicus wrote about his heliocentric, astronomic blasphemy of the celestial bodies, followed by Darwin's theory of evolution, and lastly, The United Nations with Resolution 217; and he seems to have maintained this spur up to our present time. These examples are three of the power grab moves Satan has made ever since his head, or political system, was healed and restored by the Roman Catholic Church system. If we really look at every major event since the ascension of our Lord, the list of evil assertions would easily fill up a room the size of the Vatican Apostolic Library.

Satan the beast, the enemy of our souls, by his subordinates, has destroyed the very tissues of every society. The creature has gotten so comfortable with himself that now he openly boasts about those things on live TV through Hollywood, which is also known as the "magic tree." The term magic tree is derived from an actual tree called holly wood in medieval days; that tree was used by wizards to make wands to practice sorcery. Satan runs the airways as "the prince of the power of the air" (Eph. 2:2), and just about every social media outlet is part of his arsenal.

- Heliocentric Astronomy -

With Copernicus, the beast ushered in the belief that the sun is the center of the Universe, which revived movements such as atheism and agnosticism. He managed to dupe men once again into building cities for Baal and Dagon as it was in the Old Testament. Today these false god cities are under different names; they are labeled as UFO cities, the City of Second Chances, or the City that Never Sleeps.

Satan has people mesmerized, chasing after fallen angels disguised as UFOs and convincing them that those little green, cartoonish monsters are our friends, perhaps even a god. They believe these aliens are living 93,000,000 miles away in the sun, and that's why the sun cannot be approached. The devil is turning Sméagol(s) into Gollum(s). He has men and women walking the streets of these urban centers looking for a come up or for a dream that will cost most of them their souls. Sexual dependency is called liberty. The bloods of orgasms (or sperms) are now offered in sacrifices to Beelzebul all over the world through porno addiction or other sexual immoralities, and he has men swearing after Roman gods that are disguised as planets rotating in an infinite galaxy. This lie has opened the doors to infinite inequities. However, nobody can see or prove, even with the most costly telescope, what Nashaw presented to us as the celestial bodies. Nashaw is a Hebrew word meaning to beguile and deceive; this is also the inspiration for the name NASA.

Some might argue that you have to go into space to see it. To them, I say, well carry on.

These lies simply cannot be proven, only regurgitated, and they foster a psycho-semantic system ruled by evil and deceit.

Before the beast established the illusion of a globe earth moving in an infinite space, every culture in the world understood the same thing. We live under a dome, which has been spread as a tent for the Creator's grasshoppers. The only argument that past civilizations used to assert with was: who is the only true God? However, under this new global belief, this "big bang theory" has stolen billions from the prospect of creation, commanding them to regress and worship science-fiction idols, which paved the way for the first Sci-Fi.

"Voyage dans la Lune," by French illusionist Georges Mêliés in 1902, and the "new-age generations" began to be preconditioned to believe in space travel and black holes.

This paved the way for the induction of the false moon landing premiered on July 20, 1969, which was produced and realized by Stanley Kubrick; he was one of the branches of the magic tree. His final film, released in 1999, was named "Eyes Wide Shut," which is a very cryptic movie.

All of the Sci-Fi films, stories and TV shows that follow after 1902 were all part of the master illusionist's repertoire. The beast has built for himself a nice little house of cards, which will soon fall down.

"The conscious and intelligent manipulation of the organized habits and opinions of the masses is an important element in democratic society. Those who manipulate this unseen mechanism of society constitute an invisible government, which is the true ruling power of our country. We are governed, our minds molded, our tastes formed, our ideas suggested, largely by men we have never heard of."

-Opening paragraph of Edward Bernays' 1928 book, *Propaganda*.

Out of this imaginary "Alice in Wonderland" set up, the principalities of the beast and the overlords of this feudal system begin to create secondary levels with their own subcommittees. After the French Revolution of 1789, all they pushed to be mainstream is and always has been part of the manipulative process. They create new trends that make you feel important for some time until the newer trend is created to continue the mass stimulation. The goal of most television ads today is to communicate the importance of engagement and to promote the social stigma of being conservative. These trends all aim to make you feel ostracized, or even excommunicated from your peers, unless you agree to play along with their new standards.

To be part of this perverted system of existence, we have to sacrifice our integrity. In order to integrate, it means that you must rid yourselves of the gift of rationality given to all men by God. It entails that you have to rid yourself of comprehension and compassion; "I just gotta have it, by any means necessary," has become a new standard.

People are ready to steal, kill, and deceive their own mothers, neglect their sons, and prostitute their own daughters to obtain it, but what is it? Nothing! *It...* is just a pigment of the enemy's wicked and twisted imagination; but sadly, **it** is the motto of most people today. The same monsters that control these living conditions now produce many TV programs for their own entertainment and satisfaction. They saturate the airways with shows like *American Greed, Baby Killer, Snapped, Gangland,* and many more. The invisible hands are racking billions while at the same time promoting a state of constant paranoia in the psyche of the populaces.

And would you believe that this whole global belief system started with what scientists refer to as probability theory? "Could it be probable, and isn't it possible" have replaced the definite declaration of the Bible:

"In the beginning, GOD created the heaven and the earth" (Gen. 1:1).

The falsehood of pseudoscience has been repeated over and over again until it pervades the minds of the inhabitants of the earth. It happens so much that now even the church has embraced some of its aspects as norms. Ministers even go so far as to place the globe upon their pulpit in God's temple. They praise God, while honoring pseudoscience at the same time. They demand that the Elects, the people in the church, separate from the world, while incorporating the world into the church at the same time. They also quote the Bible whilst denying the power of God; in one case shouting:

"And on that day the sun and the moon stood still in the midst of the heaven, for the spend of one day before going down" (Joshua 10:12-14).

Still, the same minister in the same message will then talk about the motion of the earth around the sun. I have to ask; which is it? Do we obtain our twenty-four hours a day from the motion of the earth to the sun, or from the sun moving in the middle of the sky over the earth? I trust that it is the latter, not the former. Nietzsche, the so-called atheist madman of 1882 put it better:

"GOD is dead," and "the belief in the Christian God has become unbelievable."

- Friedrich Nietzsche, *The Gay Science*, section 125.

Friedrich Nietzsche made that statement to point out the error made by the church by incorporating pseudoscience into their message. Once the church began to welcome pseudoscience as an appendix to the Gospel of Jesus Christ and to the version of the Biblical creation, they roughly stated that God was not enough. The leaders of the church at the time were filled with excitement and awe, I presume. What a magnificent revelation of something hidden and now revealed many must have believed. They rushed to incorporate this newfound glory in the gospel of Jesus Christ, forgetting the warning of Paul, Peter and James about the doctrines of devils that would enter the church before the end of time. They forgot to check with the Father and seek the spirit through the Spirit

(John 3:6). Unfortunately, even today, many will read this book and continue to deny themselves the privilege of inquiring with God on the matter. The anti-Christ's spirit is upon us, and just like fast food, there is no real concern about feeding healthy food to customers; it mainly focuses on stimulating our taste buds, as the lie can often be more palatable than the truth. Nevertheless, nothing is impossible for the Creator; God is able to work miracles and even stop time to help us overcome our enemies, so be empowered today in the name of Jesus, amen.

- *Darwinism* -

Note: First things first, the word "human" is actually a derogatory term for mankind. It comes from the Latin *humanus*; it's akin to the Latin word *homo*. According to Webster Dictionary, the word *homo* in Latin stands for "any of the genus, hominids that includes modern humans (H. sapiens) and several extinct related species (such as H. erectus and H. habilis); its first known use was in 1591." This word was inserted into our vocabulary to reinforce the attempt from the devil to replace God's natural order of things; God says "son of man," but the enemy says "humankind," which now has evolved into 82 different gender identities. Do not panic, for I myself often use that word in conversation, and I do not stress its origin or intention because I know who my Creator is, and I know who I am in the Lord. This rapid side note was to delve deeper into the devil's tactics and demonic battle plans.

Okay, Darwinism. Charles Darwin states:

"The survival of the human race is based on the origin and perpetuation of new species. He then concluded that those species, whose offspring of a given organism varied, were subject to natural selection, which favors the survival of some of these variations over others."

With Darwinism and his monkey tale concerning evolution, the beast that came from the sea in Revelation 13:5-6 completed the second phase of blasphemy by giving man an alternate reality. The illusion of the "evolution theory" is intended to convince men that God does not exist. He has taken the Lord's creation and replaced it with a "barnacle, turned fish, turned monkey, turned man tales" to satisfy the appetite of anyone still perplexed about the origin of mankind. After the circuit of the evolution theory was completed, the spirit of the beast then expanded even further with "natural selection," which states:

To put it plainly, if you are at the bottom of the food chain, just give up! There is no hope for you, and you will not make it! Darwin, in his theory, posited that those species that best adapted to the environment are the species that survive and reproduce, thus taking away the possibility of hope and faith for a certain group of people. Under Darwinism, perseverance is to no effect, the purpose of prayer is wiped away, and we are simply what and where nature intended us to be. This is an excellent tool to perpetuate racism, fanaticism, sexism, partisanship, and bigotry.

That ideology of adapting or dying is what we will later see become the One World Order, or New World Order. This is intended to enslave all of civilization under the premise of a better world.

In truth, we have more than enough resources to sustain ourselves, but this battle is not a battle of flesh and blood; it is a spiritual battle. The fight between the realm of darkness and the realm of light is a fight for the souls of men. God's hand was made plain at the Cross so that all men could consider. He loves us so much that He took the form of a man. He wrapped Himself in meekness and paid for our souls with His own blood, so that whoever believes in Him would not perish but have everlasting life. He had already given this very gift to mankind in the Garden of Eden, but the gift was stolen from us by the snare of the snake. But Jesus restored it.

The character of God will not allow Him to be an enabler, so He had to curse Adam and Eve for their disobedience. He had already made arrangements for us ahead of time. Before the land was called out of the sea, He prepared all things to become present, past, and future, according to His purpose (Gen. 1:2). The Ancient of Days formed the heavens, the foundations of the earth, and the restoration of mankind. He has foreseen all things.

God's origin is a mystery, and I am but a feeble man, but I will try to paint the best impression possible.

There is no beginning for God. He is, was, and is to come. Through eternity, God exists.

While being God through eternity however, at a certain point of eternity, God said to Himself: Self, here we are forevermore, but we have no discernible form, for we are Spirit. Then God answered Himself, well, let us be a form of our choice to our good pleasure. So God then became a form to Himself. After becoming a form to Himself, behold, He was pleased, and His form resembled the shape of man. God called His form "The Ancient of Days." As God, as The Ancient of Days, stood before God the Spirit, He declared to Himself, "I AM." At the declaration of these simple words, a duplicate magically appears with a burst of Glory; The Son of God was now standing before Him, and God beheld Himself, and said, "SON," the Son answered, "FATHER." The trinity was completed.

The Father then said to the Son, "You are my executive power, everything in Me is in You; let us begin to create a visible world. The first is to be the spiritual realm where we exist throughout eternity. Let us make cherubim and seraphim, slight and great, with various roles and powers in our celestial kingdom. Let us make a topographic point for us, above all, because there is none above us. From there, we will rule all with love, justice, and compassion. Let us have "The Law" to govern our estates so that our kingdom will know our desires towards them; it will instruct them so that order and discipline may rule supreme. Let us have some of the cherubim as keepers of the law and assist in the work of teaching their brethren. The Son conceived all that the Father had commanded and brought His plans before the Father and the Holy Ghost. The Trinity was well satisfied with all that the Son had configured for their kingdom. Out of the Invisible, the visible, only in the realm of the spirit, was created, and all was well (John 4:23-24; Isaiah 43:10; John 5:37; Ps. 103:9; Daniel 7:9-10; John 18:4-9; John 1:1-4; Matt. 12:31-32).

Eons went by and then Yahweh God said, let's create a lesser being to be an extension of Ourselves under Heaven and call it the kingdom of Earth. Let us not only induce them to be spirits, but let us make them closer to our likeness, as a spirit living in a vessel with a soul in between, and we shall call him man (1 Cor. 15:38-41; Ps. 33:6-9). Moreover, the Eternal God said, Let us give him orders concerning the kingdom of the earth and power to procreate as we can. By the use of his vessel, he may also give life.

Let us grant him the power to rationalize, think for himself and be free. When the time comes, we should instruct him in the mystery of Heaven. When he is worthy to know, we should teach him the secret things. And so, the Eternal God began to labor upon His purpose for man and the kingdom of the earth, and all was well.

This completes my reveal on the origin of The Trinity and creation.

Now a guardian cherub of God named Lucifer began to stir with discontent in his heart. He began to question the reasoning of the Almighty and asked, "Why should we, the gods, be uniformly with these commoners? Why should I, the magnificent one, be ever compared to anyone?" He boasted: This Creator must be losing His marbles... I will show Him how it should be done. He then rebelled against God and started a war in Heaven with the help of those initially under Satan's command, and they were all kicked out of Heaven for their insurrections.

- Dilations -

At the start of the Scriptures in the book of Genesis, the Bible tells us that the earth was void and formless. The earth is the footstool of the Eternal, and our magnificent Creator would not have an empty and chaotic footstool. The reason the earth was in such bad conditions was the cataclysmic events that happened here eons ago. These cataclysmic events directly resulted from a battle between Lucifer and his angels, and Michael, the Archangel, and His angels, which also means that scientists and theologians are wrong on the age of the earth. Only God knows the actual age of Earth.

One thing is clear regarding God's Earth. In Genesis 4:8-15, the Bible tells us that Adam was not the first man; he was the "first man Adam" (1 Cor. 15:45). But Genesis 4:8-15, let us know that there were other men, besides Adam and his folk, living on the earth at that time. Jesus, as the Son of Man, is the "last man Adam," sent to restore the order of the first.

Clearly the men alluded to in Genesis 4:14 were wicked and practiced killing as Cain, Adam's son, said, "It shall come to pass, that every one that findeth me shall slay me," and this was the sole reason for Cain to be sorely afraid of an encounter with these men. I believe they were so wicked and murderous that the news of their action reached the ears of Cain, and he eventually followed their paths. God even shows him mercy and gives Cain a mark of protection to help him against these people. The mark of protection he received was an exemption from judgment, which was a spiritual warning to anyone who would come in contact with Cain (see also Ez. 9:4-6). Since John 1:1-4 tells us that Jesus created all things, these cruel men must also be the creation of God. Furthermore, the only way that any of God's creations can know wickedness is through the wicked one. In my opinion, Satan is solely responsible for the condition of these villains as well.

Hence, when God created Adam, He placed him in the garden far from the rest of the world until the fall. God desired a preserved and undefiled version of man for Himself so that He might accomplish His zeal toward us (Gen. 2:7-17; Acts 17:22-31; Rev. 1:5-6, Rev. 5:1-14). This means that the devil has been corrupting and destroying God's creation for longer than initially assumed. Each time God planted a seed, Satan came and said, "Kill them before they grow." (Quoted from Bob Marley, but see also Mark 4:11-20.)

Each time God gave Earth's authority to man, Satan came and tricked man to surrender the deed over to him. He despised the notion of being in a kingdom with inferior creatures, especially if that creature were to rule over that kingdom. He despised the fact that man was made to rule as an extension of God, here on Earth, instead of him. "He should be me," said the demon. "I have the tenure." Where he could have found redemption for his past mistakes, he dug an even bigger hole for himself by attacking man, which is the image of God. The battle that had initially occurred in Heaven before man was made was now upon Earth. Because of his arrogance and stubbornness, Satan was brought low. In the end, his entire kingdom will be destroyed with him forever.

Since Satan would not stop being a pest, after the fall of the first Adam, God summoned the pest and his army to stand before Him. God put on His drill sergeant's hat and established a new order. As the sovereign ruler of all the realms, God could not just have this poison running loose willy-nilly, and it was clear that Satan would not atone. Consequently, God set up the meeting, and at that meeting, He set up all the rules of battle to follow. At that meeting, authority was officially given to Satan and his henchmen (the fallen angels that followed after him) over the realm that he had stolen from Adam. To Satan's second general, God gave command over the power of death. To his right hand, God gave authority over the souls of man who would live and die in sin; his name is called Hell.

From the highest to the lowest, Satan's regiments were formed; and afterward, the battle for the souls of men started. To those who fall for the traps of Hell, Satan is rewarded with their souls to repay them accordingly. Hell is ordered to be fair and to set up various degrees, or levels in Hell, to match the actual lifestyles of the poor souls that would succumb to Satan's trickery. The same goes for Death and all the other minds that work against men. This was the standard until the Son of God took the configuration of a man, went down unto the belly of the earth, defeated them at their own game, and rose again on the third day victoriously with the keys to their kingdom (Colossians 1:12-18; Rev. 1:18; 1 Cor. 15:53-58).

In the New Testament, Jesus speaks about Hell more than Heaven not to make us fearful of Hell per se, but to warn us of the danger of eternal damnation, which is the outcome of getting cast away from God. Since Hell is under the authority of Heaven, he must do what the Father dictates until his time comes to an end (Rev. 20:13-14).

Satan was so excited at the prospect of getting the free wheel of motion to operate in the daylight, that he took the bait. He did not know that God's plans were from before the commencement of time. God, the omniscient, has always been a step ahead of the enemy. By getting Satan to agree to the terms and conditions, He led Satan to plant his own fate. Satan's own actions condemned him, and since the Bible is completed, his end is now inevitable.

Hell is a state of condemnation or eternal separation from God; but at the end, even Hell (the henchman), gets cast into Hell (the lake of fire).

Some may ask, *how are the rules concerning the battles for the souls of men fair to us?* Well, let us look at things from this angle. I don't think anyone in their right mind would spend 20 years working for McDonald's on the frying pan then expect to receive an executive retirement package on their last day from JP Morgan. It does not work that way in this kingdom and the other because everyone must reap what they sow. Even if some are able to fly under the radar in this realm, we all have to pay premiums according to our work in the end.

According to the Scriptures, even demons are cast into hell for their insubordination. Angels who left their habitation for the lust of the world are also subject to the fate of Hell (Gen. 6:1-4; Jude 1:6; 2 Peter 2:4). For the Ruler of the universe is a fair and righteous Judge, and there is no partiality in His fairness (Eccl. 3:15- 20). He gave us the Bible so that we could be informed, armed for combat, and have a fair chance on the journey (Prov. 30:15- 16). It was written at great costs through blood, pains and sorrows; therefore, we must spend time studying the Holy Scriptures.

The beauty of life is that we have the free will given to us from on high from the Father Himself. Without free will, we would be like zombies walking without brains. However, unless we obey God, our free will may lead to rebellion and eternal death.

Moreover, although the Father could have destroyed the devil at the time, He wished to accomplish what He had already planned in His heart. God created all things for His good pleasure, and because His desire is that, every living being should have full enjoyment of life, according to the parameters of His directives. He set the rules for the battle of our souls to give the world time to be fruitful and multiply so that myriads of us through the ages may come to know Him one day and live the life He initially meant for us all (Matt. 13:24-30; 2 Peter 3:9).

The law was for our benefit, not our judgments or condemnation. Although God loves us, He will not compromise His integrity and values (Ex. 19:3-5). If He would ever do such a thing, we can forget about the fabric of society because the core values of the universe would be tainted, and all of creation would derail. The omniscience of the Father dictates that He foreknew the possibility of rebellion; but the Father is not weary, and His omnipotence makes Him fearless. Nothing is too great for Him to do. He is not restricted by time; time was constituted for us at Earth's creation. His omnipresence guarantees that He is with us until the end of time; He will never leave us nor forsake us.

- Resolution 217 -

Under The Universal Declaration of Human Rights (UDHR), Resolution 217 was signed at the United Nations on December 10, 1948 at the Palais de Chaillot in France, Paris.

Following the Second World War, the newly formed United Nations burst into action to supposedly help prevent a repetition of the atrocities of the Second World War. They conveniently forgot to mention that Jesuit priests and the Kazharian lineage were the ones behind every war since they were established. They were also the ones behind the foundation of the United Nations.

The declaration is composed of 30 articles affirming an individual's right, which was the first step in the process of formulating the International Bill of Human Rights. This Bill of Rights was completed in 1966 and came into force in 1976. Though the Declaration itself is not in and of itself part of domestic law, it is the predecessor of a one-world system of government, which slowly but surely prepared the way for the anti-Christ.

A French jurist by the name of Rene Cassin, who introduced the second draft of the Declaration, compared it to the portico of a Greek temple and a pediment. Porticos are pillars usually placed at the entrance of a temple in ancient cultures. The Greek temple was dedicated to the goddess Artemis, also known as Diana in Rome, Ashtoreth in Semitic cultures, Semiramis or Ishtar in ancient Babylon, Isis in Egypt, Queen of Heaven in Israel in Jeremiah 7: 17-19, and Ekwensu or Columbia in America.

Our nation's capital was literally dedicated to a pagan whore from ancient Babylon, while they simultaneously popularized the term "Christian Nation" to keep the American people in blindness. The people of the land even celebrate her every summer in Buffalo, New York with their "Queen of Heaven Carnival."

These are all the same person—one pagan goddess with different names for different eras and cultures. America has been a blessed nation because of a few faithful men and women. The 50, turn 40, then 30... now 10. We are running out of numbers. Is there anyone left to hold the line?

According to the Webster dictionary, a pediment is *"a triangular area on the face of a building below the roof, above an entrance, etc."* It goes on to describe the origin of the word as *"probably an alteration of the English word pyramid."*

How ironic that Mr. Cassin, a French Jew or rather a French Jesuit, would use these specific words to glorify the ancient Babylon religion while using the symbol of the so-called "enlightened one" to describe their Universal Declaration of Human Rights.

Before I go forward, if you have not figured it out yet, this book is about Spiritual Warfare, how Satan disguises his craftiness in plain sight, and the remedy for his pathogen. I must reiterate that this is not a book about politics, nor is it intended to entice any groups against one another. It is important that everyone knows the truth so they can make an educated decision moving forward. This is based on The Holy Spirit's revelations to me, and as always, search the spirit by the Spirit.

Although most of the articles from the Universal Declaration of Human Rights seem legit on the surface, I would like to shine some light on some key points. Judge for yourselves.

"The Universal Declaration promises to all, the economic, social, political, cultural and civic rights that underpin a life free from want and fear. They are not a reward for good behavior. They are not country specific or particular to a certain era or social group. They are the inalienable entitlements of all people, at all times, in all places

for people from every colour, from every race and ethnic group; whether or not they are disabled; citizens or migrant; <u>no matter their sex, their class, their caste, their creed, their age or sexual orientation.</u>"

- UNITED NATIONS webpage, UDHR, page 6-7.

Until the underline portion above, everything seems right to me. After considering all the changes that have molded our society lately concerning gender identification, I realized what is occurring has been in the works since 1948. From the feminization of man through transvestigation (Deut. 22:5), the legalization of homosexuality, and the latest gender identity agenda, the devil has been pushing his plan to the forefront. The blueprint of the so-called "Universal Declaration of Human Rights" is now in the application phase.

To be clear, I'm not homophobic, but from a Biblical perspective, I have to put it as it is. The LGBTQ community lives in sin, and unless they repent and turn away from that way of life, eternal death will be their reward. Now, if you belong to any of the above groups, Jesus loves you. He died for you also, and if you confess your sins and repent of your lifestyle today, He will receive you into His kingdom.

"For God so loved the world that he gave his only begotten Son, that whosoever believeth in him should not perish, but have eternal life. *For God sent not his Son into the world to condemn the world; but that the world through him might be saved. He that believeth on him is not condemned: but he that believeth not is condemned already, because he hath not believed in the name of the only begotten Son of God"* (John 3:16-18; also Isaiah 56:1-8).

If you have been feeling miserable or conflicted within your own skin, and you are looking for an answer, give Jesus a chance. He will heal you and make you whole again; besides, what do you have to lose?

I know there has been a great deal of controversy as to whether or not the LGBTQ community can be saved. I think it's because oftentimes, people in the church forget that the battle is not a natural battle but a spiritual battle.

"For we wrestle not against flesh and blood, but against principalities, against powers, against the rulers of the darkness of this world, against spiritual wickedness in high places" (Eph. 6:12).

See, the kingdom of Satan is not in Hell because Hell is one of the principalities as demonstrated earlier in this chapter. Neither does Satan look like a red, hairy monster with cloven hooves, horns and a pitchfork. Lucifer is actually a well-spoken individual with a beautiful outer appearance. The reason many believe the lie about the cloven-hoofed monster with the pitchfork ruling from Hell is because Satan himself has been perpetrating it through motion pictures and cartoons for decades. The kingdom of Satan is actually restricted to Earth (Matt. 4:8-9), but at one point, his seat was somewhere between the first and third heaven. The heavens were made to declare the glory of God and to show His handy works as a sign of His existence and magnificence (Ps. 19:1). The third heaven is considered to be the holy abode of God by many faiths, while some believe there are as many as seven different heavens; only God knows for sure, but I will stick to the former to keep things simple. The second heaven is considered to be the humble abode of the sun, the moon, and the stars (Gen. 1:16-17). These are fixed according to the Lord's purposes within the firmament, and according to The Book of Enoch section 3 Chapters 72 to 80 (I used the version translated by H.R. Charles Oxford published by The Clarendon Press), they travel through various portals in the firmament to provide light for days and nights. The stars are also used as markers to navigate by night, to rule the night alongside the moon, and to uplift the spirits of the people of Earth (Acts 27:20; Ps. 136:6-9; Ps. 8:3-4; Matt. 2:1-2; Rev. 1:20). The sun, the moon, and the stars travel from chambers within the firmament and below the firmament. When they are below the firmament, they are in the 1st heaven right above the clouds. They were set by God to rule over days and nights and to mark the seasons, days, and years (Gen. 1:14-18). These heavenly constellations, as they were called before the word "planets" were inserted in the Bible to describe them, are right above us, and throughout the years, they can clearly be seen moving below the firmament. Not millions of miles away as taught by NASA and the other overlords working for Lucifer. Their placement and purposes are not coincidental; everything that was made serves the purpose of God according to His will (1 Cor. 15:40-41). At the conclusion of all things, Jesus promises to make us in the likeness of their glory, so we are not to worship the hosts of Heaven because they were made for our benefits (Daniel 12:3 and Deut. 4:15-[19]). Satan knows this, and to draw men away from Christ, he has created pseudoscience and invented blasphemous constellations, which lead many to observe and worship Lucifer unknowingly (compare Daniel 7:23-[25] to Rev. 13:1,3-[6]). Now, Satan's kingdom after the fall from Heaven expanded to Earth and the underworld. But when Jesus came down from Heaven, He took Lucifer down from his seat in the heavenlies once and for all, and He also made the underworld surrender the keys to their domains (see Rev. 12:7-12; Luke 10:18 and Rev. 1:18). The Father could have dealt with this matter right after the fall of Adam, but since the jealousy that led to Satan's rebellion was his hatred for man, which is the image of God, the Father wanted to defeat Satan by the hand of a man. Jesus is that Man, and through Jesus, we have the authority and the power to crush Satan as well (Luke 10:18-24).

Since the time he was cast down to the earth, recognizing that his time is near the end, Satan has been causing more havoc and death than ever before (see Isaiah 14:12; Rev. 2:13, 12:10-12, 16:10 and 1 Peter 5:8).

He has since then managed to convince men with the aid of his offspring – shape-shifters – and Kazharian bloodline to occupy the world with radio wave technology and satellites, so that he can reclaim control of the air as the prince of the power of the air (Ephesians 2:2). That is why the airways are saturated with darkness from the Tell-Lie vision to the Internet and social media. Satan has created various channels to promote his doctrines, his filth, and demonic influences. Everything we see today on these various networks promotes sex, violence, drugs, and looseness, including news and video games. This is also the reason why lately, everyone that is questioning the COVID-19 pandemic has been getting censored or blocked. Our 1st Amendment right is being suppressed; meanwhile, can someone please explain to me why these women's skirts on those news channels keep getting shorter and shorter?

Alternatively, why do the video game industries torture and kill live animals then use the recordings of their agonies for their game's characters? This is done regularly in both the gaming and movie industry. For a more detailed breakdown of these evil practices, look up *Why I quit the Industry* by Clint Richardson, a former sound designer and game developer for Hollywood who felt compelled to blow the whistle on the matter. He has worked on games such as *Devil May Cry 4, Resident Evil 5, God Of War 2, Silent Hill:Origins*, and many more. These practices are the work of the devil, and Satan's marching orders have always been to corrupt and dumb down the nations. It is no coincidence that our societies have become mummified, hypnotized, fat, and slothful. Dopamine is the chemical that mediates pleasure in the brain and makes us feel validated. It gets released when we experience pleasurable events and stimulates the desire to regularly seek the activity, or activities, that brought that feeling. Dopamine is good for us, but it must be stimulated through healthy means. There are many things that can release the dopamine chemical which makes us feel good, such as sweet treats, playing sports, or an instrument. However, drugs, alcohol, porn, and video games can also make us feel good, but these cost more than they are worth. They are not worth our time. Moreover, a piece of cake is a sweet treat, which when eaten in moderation, can lower our stress level and give us the motivation to take on the next challenge ahead. When Elijah was running away from Jezebel for instance, an angel of the Lord woke up Elijah and fed him some cake that gave him the strength to run for 40 days and 40 nights to Mount Horeb (1 King 19:4-8; Eccl. 2:24; see also Matt. 4:4). Too many sweets, however, will make us fat and slothful. We must indulge with moderations, and if you are diabetic, look for sugar-free or low-sugar treats. Satan is well aware of the effect and benefits of dopamine, and he uses our own biological make-up as a tool against us. This universal declaration from the United Nations is just another one of his tools (see John 8:44, 14:17, 2 Cor. 4:3-4; Jude 1:11-16, Rev. 13:13-14; Rev. 20:3,8,10; Rev. 12:9 and Rev. 2:9; 3:9).

CHAPTER THREE

Pay Attention to Details

In the book of Revelation 12:13-17, the Bible is talking about Israel being persecuted for giving birth to the Messiah (see also Rev. 12:1-2). Only the Creator has the power to instruct the sun and the moon, as seen in Joshua 10:12-14, and the twelve stars represent the twelve tribes of Israel from which, through Judah, the Messiah was born.

At the sight of Jesus, our Great Hope, wrapping Himself in meekness to come on the earth to redeem mankind, Satan and his army orchestrated their plan of attack and attempted to destroy the only hope for us to ever receive salvation (Rev. 12:3-4).

Nevertheless, as The Eternal GOD lives, unto us, the Child was born. For our iniquity, the Son of God was given, thus establishing a bridge for reconciliation between God and man – through His Church. The government is now upon His shoulder (Matt. 28:18), and His name is forever more Wonderful. He is our Counselor and Advocate. The mighty God. The everlasting Father. The Prince of Peace.

"Of the greatness of his government and peace there will be no end. He will reign on David's throne and over his Kingdom, establishing and upholding it with justice and righteousness from that time on and forever" (Isaiah 9:7 NIV).

The Zeal of the LORD Almighty has accomplished this (see also Hebrews 2:14; Colossians 3:13-15; and Rev. 21:3-7).

The angel is glorifying our Lord and Savior in Revelation 12:10-12 for His victory at the Cross, the destruction of Satan's base of operation in the heavenly, for the overcoming power of the blood of the Lamb, and lastly, for the power of our testimony to the Lord even unto death. The power of our testimony comes from the Blood of the Lamb; moreover, the Blood has and will never lose His power, and this same power was given to the Elects—past, present, and future.

Therefore, be empowered today to know that when you have Jesus Christ as your Savior, your pain and your sorrows are not in vain. Be empowered every day to know that the Blood of the Lamb will never lose His power. Rejoice and be empowered forever more to know that Heaven is our home, and we have the victory in Christ Jesus. Amen and Amen.

As mentioned in Chapter Two, the mortal wound of the beast, which is the corrupt political, economical, and religious system of the world has been healed. However, let me pause here to say that our Father for the purpose of one last test, which is the last tribulation mentioned in Matthew 24:4-44, has regulated and sanctioned it all (see also Rev. 13:9-10).

The red dragon, which is Satan, has restored the three spirits of Rome, which are swiftness of conquest (manipulation, infiltration, and assassination), tenacity (strength, pride, and arrogance), and voracity (greed, gluttony, and consumerism), just to see them destroyed for the last time at the final judgment, which is to come.

Satan gives his authority to those who wear the crown of Dagon to help them exercise spiritual wickedness and to keep the people nourished with religious treats. These religious treats include praying to "The Blessed Virgin Mary" for help, praying to the various saints' patrons for guidance and good luck, doing the sign of the cross, which is an upside-down cross, which represents Peter's crucifixion instead of Christ. Their false teachings have spread to the Protestant churches as well with the worship of the goddess of fertility, known as Easther. Some even believe that to be truly touched by God, you have to be slain in the Spirit, which implies falling down and convulsing as if possessed by a demon. All these religious rituals keep the people of the church feeling gratified, while keeping them spiritually dead. As one of the ten kings under the rulership of Satan (Rev. 13:1 and Matt. 23:9), the pope promises the people purification while pouring a little water on their foreheads and speaking benediction while his clergy are capitalizing on the confessions of their constituents. This is another vague attempt from Satan to imitate the Trinity with him as the essence of this corrupt system, Dagon as "the father," and the false prophet or anti-Christ as "the savior." This is why the anti-Christ, the second beast, comes to cause men to glorify the image of the first beast according to Revelation 13:11-18.

He is imitating the work of Jesus Christ who came to fulfill the will of the Father and to give Him glory. However, there is no possible comparison between the two kingdoms because The LORD God Almighty holds all the chips. This prolonged spanking of the stubborn child, known under the name of Satan, is to our advantage, so that many would have become sons and daughters of God through Jesus Christ and be saved. Satan knows that he is an impostor and that eternal damnation is the result of his treachery. As the son of perdition, he is condemned to the lake of fire (John 17:6-12).

All these treaties and so-called efforts to bring about world peace have been scripted. The truth is, it is all part of the show, smoke screens to help facilitate the takeover. They keep pushing their agendas and speaking of world peace while spending trillions on surveillance and military defenses towards a complete takeover under the Agenda 21 catalogue.

Former President, Donald Trump, declared they would be opening a space force in the near future. They've already started working on it; in fact, NASA has conducted a flight test for space. The name of the space shuttle that was launched is the SpaceX Dragon. This has been happening amid the COVID-19 pandemic and the racial unrest that has been destroying our country. What is really going on? There has been no valid justification for this program; this is a waste of money, especially now amid all the chaos and financial crisis. My surmise is that it will help in the working of those false miracles, those signs of wonders prophesied in Rev. 13:13. This space force can also be a very good platform to stage a fake world invasion—the last major crisis that could tilt the table in the Dragon's favor.

My advice to everyone reading or listening is, if you can afford to do it now, establish a hideout for yourself and your loved ones in the mountains where you can endure the last tribulation. Let it be a place that you can get to if things do not get better, where you can pray and wait for the Lord's return in safety. The test will not be easy, but Jesus will keep you anchored. I also recommend that you start to exercise and eat healthy so that you can be in an optimal state.

The truth is, if the ruling parties really wanted to make the world a utopia, they could. However, their greed and blindness lead their way.

According to Google, the earth land mass is 57,308,738 million square miles; if you multiply that by 640 to convert it to acres (1 mile = 640 acres), it equals 36,677,592,320 acres. When you divide that last number by the earth's population of 7.5 billion, you get 4,890,345,642.67 (or 4.900 trillion) acres per person, so there is no need for population control. We're not running out of living space on Earth, we're running out of love.

The idea of global warming cannot be proven, and Al Gore's propaganda about it has long been demystified. The real reason for all these natural disasters we've been witnessing lately is the wrath of God being loosed on this wicked world. So what is the real reason for the inequity among us?

Here's another riddle. How can one man make $142 billion a year while 3 billion people are living under the poverty line, some with less than $2 a day?

There is more than enough landmass in the world for every one of us to live comfortably for a thousand generations with our families, and more than enough money to make it happen. This Universal Declaration-fueled utopia is based on the beast's plan to have men surrender their lives over to him to take the mark of the beast and to worship him, which will lead to eternal damnation and being cast away in the lake of fire.

- Satan's Fundamental Legality -

Articles 6-11 of Resolution 217 refer to the fundamental legality of human rights with specific remedies cited for their defense when violated.

Now that the beast has set up the foundation, let's see in what kind of scenario it could be used under this new global order.

One of the main stories on the airways for the last eights years was about a gay couple that took a baker to court in Colorado because he chose his faith over money. The gay couple wanted the baker to make a custom wedding cake for their marriage ceremony in order to celebrate their union. The baker informed them that same sex marriage was against his faith and offered to sell them a pre-made cake instead, which the couple could decorate themselves. The gay couple would not honor the baker's faith, so they took him to trial for having a different disposition about marriage. The baker was found not guilty of discrimination against the same sex couple in 2018. According to news reports, the Supreme Court ruling in favor of the baker was marginal, meaning the judges could have easily ruled against him on the matter.

Our 1st Amendment to the U.S. Constitution states, "Everyone in the United States has the right to practice his or her own religion, or no religion at all." Under the Constitution, this should have been a landslide for the Christian baker and businessman. Furthermore, how can, in a Christian nation, a Christian man's desire to practice his faith get marginalized? We are living under a corrupt system, and we have to pay attention to details; not so much that we become paranoid, but so we may be aware of the signs of the time (Matt. 24:3-31). In addition, since June 2017:

"All places within Canada, under the Canadian Human Rights Act, equal opportunity, or anti-discrimination legislation, prohibit discrimination against gender identity."

What this means for Christianity in Canada is there's a law that you can actually be fined for referring to someone by the gender they were born with if they identify themselves differently. This means that our brothers and sisters to the North have to walk on eggshells because man decided to redefine God's creation to fit his own perversion.

It may seem that I'm bashing on sexuality a lot, but you must understand that those so-called liberties are the main ways that Satan creates distance between God and man. Moreover, getting a sex change is a very dreadful act. The sinful consequence behind this act is equal to getting a DNA alteration or a facial change; it makes us unrecognizable to our heavenly peers and our guardian angels.

Similar to Adam after the fall in the garden, if we are walking in rebellion to God's precepts, we will lose our identity, and Heaven cannot see us as we once were. In addition, just like we have ID cards to be identified in this realm, we also have a spiritual ID, a seal for the spirit realm. If we grieve the Spirit of God so much that we squander our spiritual seal, we will lose our boarding pass for Heaven.

Moreover, if we cannot be identified as a member of God's children in Heaven, we will be left behind to die with the devil at the gathering of the Saints. Therefore, do not take God's liberty as a green light to defile His creations and His earthly temple.

Israel was severely chastised by the Father for defiling themselves with foreigners and pagan idols as an object lesson for us not to follow (Hosea 10:1-12).

- Approved Sexual Behavior -

In Genesis 2:23-24, Adam declared, after seeing Eve:

"This is now bone of my bones and flesh of my flesh: she shall be called Woman, because she was taken out of Man. Therefore shall a man leave his father and his mother, and shall cleave unto his wife: and they shall be one flesh."

This declaration from Adam was also the first recorded prophecy spoken from man in the Bible. While standing in the presence of God, Adam understood and just knew the vision of the Father concerning mankind vis-à-vis the purpose of conjugality. The statement *"and they shall become one flesh"* is speaking of the soul tie that is created when a man and a woman mate, which in turn leads to pro-creation as God intended. That prophetic blessing from Adam does not offer provision for any other type of conjugality. When a child is born, they carry characteristics of both parents. Characteristics procure to them through DNA, which also has the attributes of the soul. That process of conception is the only procedure approved by God, and man was blessed by God for that purpose. In Gen 1:28; He makes that clear by stating, *"Be fruitful, and multiply, and **replenish** the earth."*

If Adam had made a mistake in his declaration, God surely would have corrected him. Instead, He blessed mankind beforehand. Likewise, the everlasting blessings of paradise are only for those who are doing what is acceptable to God.

Moreover, concerning sexuality, God Himself makes His standard clear on the matter in the following Bible verses:

"Do not have sexual relations with a man as one does with a woman; that is detestable" *(Leviticus 18: 22).*

In Leviticus 20:13, God says, *"If a man has sexual relations with a man as one does with a woman, both of them have done what is detestable. They are to be put to death; their blood will be on their own heads."*

Romans 1:18-27 declare: *"For the wrath of God is revealed from heaven against all ungodliness and unrighteousness of men, who hold the truth in unrighteousness; Because that which may be known of God is manifest in them; for God hath showed it unto them. For the invisible things of him from the creation of the world are clearly seen, being understood by the things that are made, even his eternal power and Godhead; so that they are without excuse: Because that, when they knew God, they glorified him not as God, neither were thankful; but became vain in their imaginations, and their foolish heart was darkened. Professing themselves to be wise, they became fools, and changed the glory of the incorruptible God into an image made like to corruptible man, and to birds, and four footed beast and creeping things. Wherefore **God also gave them up to uncleanness through the lust of their own hearts, to dishonor their own bodies between themselves: Who changed the truth of God into a lie, and worshiped and served the creature more than the Creator, who is blessed forever. Amen. For this cause God gave them up unto vile affections: for even their women did change the natural use into that which is against nature: And likewise also the men, leaving the natural use of the woman, burned in their lust one towards another; men with men working that which is unseemly, and receiving in themselves that recompense of their error which was meet."***

In the verses above, God shows His disposition on the question of sexual orientation apart from His decree. He also makes it clear that because of man's disobedience, God has judged man, and His wisdom has abandoned them. This is why our generation has returned to the minds of Sodom and Gomorrah. The lack of understanding and tolerance for anything unclean comes from disobedience.

The only way to avoid these damnations is to become attached to Jesus, the King of kings and the Lord of lords. Though we have all sinned, and we all should be put to death, Jesus made a path for us all to be redeemed and to live a life free of the bondage of sins. This does not mean that we cannot sin, but sin does not have any claim over us and cannot hold us (1 Cor. 10:13). The last verse is also where we get the saying, "God won't put on you more than you can bear," and that is true. However, our bearing's meter must match God's will (2 Cor. 1:8-10).

Our due rewards should be annihilation, but *"God so loved the world,"* that He made a way through Christ for us. Even now when we go astray, Jesus stands as an advocate before the Father for His Elects and pleads, *"Lead them not into temptation, but deliver them from the evil one."* As the Creator, He has the right of claim over us all. He bought us back with His own blood, and He holds the keys of the kingdoms of Hell and Death.

In Romans 1:28-32, Paul tells us of the wicked spirits that befall those who reject the Father's rules on the matter of idolatry and sexuality: spirits of wickedness, evil, greed, depravity, envy, murder, strife, deceit and malice; spirits of gossips, slanderers, God-haters, insolent, arrogant and boastful. Those spirits, or curses, also promote evil thoughts, innovations of darkness to commit more evil, disobedience to parents, infidelity, lovelessness, and lack of mercy. Despite all of the Father's warnings of the corollary between sin and affliction and His plea with men to repent, to this day, many continue to descend into darkness willfully.

Satan's modus operandi is to bring these curses upon all men by leading us astray as he did in the beginning in the garden. A little bit at a time, he has been changing the norms set by God and re-defining right and wrong on Earth. It will not be long before the rule of the goddess of ancient Babylon becomes the standard for the whole Earth and righteousness becomes illegal. This is already taking place in every façade of society. From politics to the church, anyone standing for what is right is persecuted. Speaking the truth is no longer a birthright; it has become an abstract and a privilege. Whistleblowers either are suppressed or escorted out of the White House for practicing their 1st Amendment rights. The rich are getting richer; the poor are getting poorer, and they are both being played by the same hand. Repent.

- What Is Next on the Devil's Agenda? -

The last Articles of Resolution 217 that I am going to touch on are 12-17. Those Articles' overall message is: "establish the rights of the individual towards the community (including such things as freedom of movement).

Translation, obey the prescribed New World Order's community guidelines, and you can continue to purchase and sell. Disobey, and you will be confined, restricted, starved or put to death. The recent COVID-19's live training exercise is just a taste of what is to come, and we don't even have to imagine the worst because the injustice that our brethren in China had to endure because of COVID-19 restrictions is a testimony.

Just imagine what it would be like if we were beaten, sprayed with water hoses, and arrested for venturing 5 steps outside of our homes just to get some fresh air like the people of China endured last year. As bad as things have been here in the U.S. since the beginning of the COVID-19 pandemic, Jesus has clearly been fighting to preserve this great land. The United States is not a perfect place, but there are more Christians here, and for the sake of the Elects, the land has been preserved by God. For the sake of the true Believers, the 50, turned 40, then 30...now 10, for if the Lord would not destroy Sodom and Gomorrah for a few potential righteous men (see Genesis 18:24-32). Surely the Lord is fighting for America for the sake of the few righteous men and women present here today.

I know that to some, it may seem like I'm fishing or exaggerating my points, but remember this: there are two sides to a coin. There is nothing free in this world but the grace of God. Nothing is unbiased but the love of God, and the history of mankind—and the evil that we have propagated throughout the generations—speak for itself.

There has never been a government ruled by men based on men's point of views in the history of mankind that was not corrupt. The only way for us to truly succeed in governing ourselves is by agreeing with God to govern our lives (1 Sam. 8:1-[19]).

Any government established apart from Christ's doctrines is a duplicitous system of government, therefore corrupt, and Satan is the head of that said system. Nevertheless, the prince of darkness is not to be feared; you need only to understand his tactics and keep your eyes on Jesus. Through the power of His Holy Spirit, He will guide us into all truth as He promised us. We are, rather we opted to accept it or not, travellers in a foreign country.

We are spirits in the midst of a temporary physical experience, and we are all faced with the inevitable choice of eternal life with God in paradise or eternal life with Satan in the lake of fire. Furthermore, Jesus has consecrated the Church (ekklesia), and given them the power to shut or open Heaven and to bind or lose. Although the enemy is the god of this earth, we have the armies of Heaven at our support, respectfully, and Heaven rules over the earth. Moreover, while God sustains and encourages the pursuit of success while we are still here, it is important to remember that this current earth is not our home. It was destined to be, but we failed to sustain that which was given. We corrupted this world through our unethical, stubborn, and rebellious minds.

This lair will pass away with the heaven above at the great white throne of judgment, and there will be no place left for them at the magnificent presence of God (Rev. 20:11). Then the Lord God Almighty will make a new Heaven and a new Earth. Our abode is the kingdom of eternal joy, for whomsoever will, according to His will - the true land of milk and honey is waiting.

I am not here to create conflicts, but the conflicts are here. Only a few dare to talk about these matters. I merely choose to be one of them, and in these last days, we need more than ever to be of the same Spirit, which is the Spirit of Christ, and not of the beasts or the anti-Christ. It just does not make sense to follow after the beast anyway. As blurry as the road may be sometimes, and regardless of how many times we may fumble, we must push until the end. *"For He that lives in us is greater than he that is in the world"* (1 John 4:4). Therefore, why follow the world (1 John 2:15-17)?

In addition, if you feel out of place in this world because you have chosen to consecrate yourself to the will of God, it is normal (John 15:18-19, 16:20).

Hence, with prayer at the forefront, may those of us anointed to be apostles press on. May the prophets of the Lord stand up. Teachers, keep teaching as instructed by our Lord and Savior, and be ye all faithful to the Holy Spirit's instructions. Where are the sacred wonders of old? Does not the Lord still reign? I hear many speaking in various tongues, but who among us has the gift of translation? Evangelize, you evangelist, for our greatest weapon is the Word of truth, which is the Word of God (John 17:17). Truly, all some of these churches need is a good deacon to stand tall before the Lord and tell the truth (1 Peter 4:10-14).

In addition, everything concerning the application of your *doma* gift must be done with reverence, order, and discipline, without causing conflict within your church.

If it seems that I am bold, it is because I feel led by the Holy Spirit to be completely transparent on all matters. This is despite percussion from my own assembly, but for those of you who are called to the ascension ministry, or the five-fold ministries mentioned in Eph. 4:8-11, follow the Holy Spirit.

"Be ye therefore wise as serpents, and harmless as doves" (Matt. 10:16).

"Go ye therefore, and teach all nations, baptizing them in the name of the Father, and of the Son, and of the Holy Ghost: Teaching them to observe all things whatsoever I have commanded you: and, lo, I am with you always, even unto the end of the world. Amen" (Matt. 10:16, 28:19-20).

Side Note: Bear this in mind also and remember: the second coming of the true Savior will not be a Hollywood production. The one that needs to televise his so-called second coming is a fraud.

One of the other reasons for this profane earthly globe, which was invented by pseudoscience, is to mislead men to accept the staged second coming of Christ. As stated before, this is also why President Trump was talking about "space force," through the use of his technological empire. The red dragon intends to muster a masterpiece, a great show from the sky, to lure Believers and unbelievers alike to crown him as king of the earth and worship him. It is the concluding chapter in the masquerade if you will. Take heed not to be deceived by him.

The return of the KING OF KINGS and LORD OF LORDS will not be televised, nor will it need to be. The return of His Majesty will not be visible on one end of the earth, but not the other. All that exists belongs to Him, visible and invisible; and when the dome is open, His heavenly kingdom will be revealed.

"For false messiahs and false prophets will appear and perform great signs and wonders to deceive, if possible, even the elect. See I have told you ahead of time. So if anyone tells you, 'There he is, out in the wilderness,' do not go out; or, 'Here he is, in the inner rooms,' do not believe it. **For as lighting that comes from the east is visible even in the west, so will be the coming of the Son of Man"** (Matthew 24:24-27 NIV).

On that glorious day, the heaven above will open and the resplendence of God will be revealed to all. No one will have to tell you, "Let us go and see His return or turn to channel 6 to see the Son of God." All eyes will see Him, and all of the saints will rejoice on that glorious day.

CHAPTER FOUR

JOHN 14:6

The Mark of Death

O kay, now let us talk about the "mark of the beast" for a minute. Foremost, let us remember we are dealing with spiritual warfare; what happens in our natural world is a direct influence of the spiritual or astral world. Whether the cause is from the Kingdom of Light or the kingdom of darkness, it is always based on the spirit land, and all final commands come from Heaven.

The consolidation of the mark of the beast is coming really soon, but the disposition of our hearts is what will make a difference in our Christian lives.

Truth be told, the stigma of the beast is part of our daily life and part of our societies already, but Jesus has given us the power to overrule its mandate and application in our daily lives.

After His victory at Calvary, Jesus extended His authority to us to bind and unleash the power of the spirit world. Through His authority, we can now rule over invisible principalities and live a life free of spiritual bondage (Romans 8:11-13).

This does not mean that we will not have trouble in this life. But when trouble comes, we now have the power to rebuke those demons accordingly. However, we must also understand that the authority Jesus has given us does not trump the Father's plan; everything is done according to His will. We ought to utter things that are not as if they ought to be, for we are our Father's children, and the Father knows best (Rom. 4:17). He works in mysterious ways, and sometimes, He may veto a request. Therefore, if you have been dealing with bleeding for 18 years or were born blind, understand that this may just be for the Father's glory (compare 1 Peter 4:12-19; Ezek. 24:15-27).

I would however continue to pray; prayer is just a personal moment with God anyway. Besides, what are a couple of hours among friends?

God recognizes that His anointed power upon men can sometimes cause boastfulness and pride, which leads to corruption; this is similar to when Satan became corrupt with iniquity in his pride. Because of that, God sometimes adds a little extra weight to our cross. This is for our own good and safety. When you inquire of Him on the matter through prayers, He will give you serenity to know His purpose. Be deliberate and wary of preachers who only speak of blessings and prosperity regarding our time in this realm.

For instance, Paul was a man of great power in Christ. To maintain his humility, God allowed a thorn, a messenger from Satan, to curb his natural instinct (2 Cor. 12:7). In spite of this stark reality, Paul remained faithful (see also Psalm 18:30-32).

Regarding our Christianity, one of the reasons for this extra weight upon the righteous man's cross is because we can often confuse the voice of the soul for the voice of the Spirit. The world gives us the lust of the flesh, the lust of the eyes, and the pride of life. The lust of the flesh and the lust of the eyes are self-explanatory, but the pride of life can be hard to spot at times. The pride of life has to do with the desire to be noticed or egotism; it is similar to Balaamrism. The word Balaamrism here is named after prophet Balaam from the book of Numbers Chapters 22 to 24. Balaam was a non-Israelite prophet who was used by God to bless Israel, but he also practiced divination and sorcery. As a result of Balaam's evil practices, he was rebuked by God for using his gift for divination, and he was killed by the Israelites (Joshua 13:21-22).

We are made of three parts: our spirit (the breath of life/Holy Spirit), our soul (our minds, emotions, and will), and our flesh (we all know what the flesh is all about). The spirit feeds off the truth (John 17:17; John 6:63), the flesh feeds off bread and meat (Isa. 22:13; Luke 12:19-20; Matt 4:4), but the soul is fed off whichever of the two we incline to.

If the soul is partially fed with the truth (The Word of God) and partially fed with the lust of the flesh, or the lust of the eyes, we often get a situation where we will speak "the truth" with contention, envy, and misperception. This leads us to the pride of life. This type of set-up leads to the flesh and the soul conspiring together against our spirit to suppress the essence of God living within us. The truth that we speak under the influence of egotism is not pure and blameless; it is a tainted truth; it is the ministry of the soul, and it leads to the divining of lies and conceitedness (Ezekiel 22:24-[28]; Jer. 28:[12-17], 23:21-40). People under that tainted spirit/flesh chemistry often practice the "ministry of condemnations," they love to bring up your pass or flaws to exercise control over you.

When half of what inspires our soul is from God, and the other half is from self-gratification, which the lust of the flesh, the lust of the eyes, or the pride of life bring (Proverb 25:27; Proverb 16:1-9; Luke 18:9-14), we begin to preach lies and declare our desires as God's standards (Luke 9:51-[55] 56). Although no man is perfect and we all have flaws, we have to fight the logic of the soul and should at least try to lean more on Christ than our soulful pride (Eph. 4:27).

We need the Axe Head Anointing to remain sober (2 Kings 6:5). The Axe Head Anointing represents a constant connection with God, and this only happens when we walk in the Holy Spirit daily. The Axe Head Anointing is a greater requirement for those called to the five-fold ministry spoken by apostle Paul in Ephesians 4:11-15, and we must be careful to only use our liberty to glorify God (1 Cor. 10:1-14; James 1:13-[20]); lastly, we must learn to speak from the Spirit-authority point of view. The Spirit is always testifying about God, and *"they that are after the flesh do mind the things of the flesh; but they that are after the Spirit mind the things of the Spirit"* (Rom. 8:5; see also Rom. 8:26-27; 1 Cor. 2:10-16). This is where the real power against the forces of darkness resides because our soul is tainted, because we are all born in iniquity, and there is nothing good in us. Therefore, our soul is tainted, so operating through soul-authority is tainted, and the flesh profits nothing. In life, we go through many things, and the only way we can push through it all is by the strength of Christ living in us. Therefore, memorize the Word of God in your spirit, not just your mind (Proverbs 7:3, 16:2; 2 Cor. 3:2-6; Psalm 119:11).

As the Son of Man, even Jesus Christ had to undergo a test similar to that of Paul, which you can see at His encounter with the legion spirit at the catacomb (Mark 5:1-13). Now, before the skeptical mind takes the lead and weakens your faith, permit me to explain something about this encounter:

During His time on Earth, Jesus was fully man and fully God simultaneously. He is the Son of God and the Son of Man at the same time. As our Messiah, our Father's mission and instruction to Jesus was to establish a blueprint for man using only His manly attributes with the inputted power of God (Luke 4:18-19).

The reason for those specific instructions is that God wanted to set up an obtainable target for His clerics. Therefore, He had to be tested in all things, including the test of humility. If Jesus had not established the foundation of His Church as a man, through the power of the Holy Ghost, then no one could follow Him because only GOD can be God.

Jesus made it an attainable goal for us to be men and women of God when He accomplished His mission as such. Where the first Adam failed, Jesus succeeded by applying the first principle of love, which is obedience to the Father.

Subsequently, once He had fulfilled all things, He also poured out His Spirit, the Spirit of truth, to live within us. Just as the Spirit of the LORD was upon Him on His journey, we also have been equipped for success in this spiritual battle according to each person's task.

The Lord Himself blessed us beforehand when He said:

"Verily truly I tell you, whoever believes in me will do the works I have been doing, and they will do even greater things than these" (read John 14:1-21).

On that day at the catacomb, I can imagine the wheel turning in my Savior's head – Do I go fully God on this sucker!? (My words, not His.)

The command in Mark 5:8 was for the unclean spirit to come out of the man. The evil spirit knew and acknowledged the sovereignty of Christ in verses 6 and 7. Although he was commanded to leave, he insisted on begging for mercy. This is because the spirit realm deals with legality, and they are well aware of the rules. In Matthew's account of this encounter, we discovered that their plea was based upon the fact that the time of their judgment, which was designated by the Father, was yet to come (Matthew 8:29).

Jesus might have made it a personal matter, but he knew that it would enable the enemy (Satan) to have some form of claim to his ecclesiastical church (see also Zechariah 3). What I mean here is spiritual warfare has its own directives, which were set by God the Father, and Jesus, as the Son of Man, was under the rules of those directives, but He fell under these directives willfully for our sake.

When the author of the Book of the Hebrews said that Christ, as our high priest, was tempted in all the ways that we are, he meant in all the ways! Jesus established an eternal and unwavering foundation upon which we can stand (Hebrews 4:14-16; Hebrews 2:14; Hebrews 11; Hebrews 12:2; 1 Cor. 13 and Philippians 4:13). After the fulfillment of His zeal for the earth, the Father then took of the Spirit of the Son and poured it over His Elects, as He did with Moses in the wilderness (Numbers 11:16-17, 25; Numbers 27:18-23; Deut. 34:9; Mark 16:16- 18).

Therefore, it is very important to walk in the Spirit of God because the Spirit of God searches the deep things of God and declares them to His Saints according to our vocations. Even in the Old Testament, we can see occasions where the Lord's instruction or disposition seems conflicting at first (see 1 Kings 20:35-43, 2 Kings 4:8-37 and Hosea 1:1-11), but the Father always knows best; He works in mysterious ways.

In 2 Kings 4:27, I believe the intent of the Lord hiding the exact situation from Elisha is because Elisha needed to be humbler. Elijah had shown humility in that same situation before in 1 King 17:17-24, but with Elisha's double portion anointing, he needed to demonstrate even more reserve.

As Christians, one thing we must understand is that we are living towards eternity, and the LORD is constantly chiseling and perfecting us (Hebrews 12:23).

We can never get too comfortable in our walk with Christ; as someone once said, "There is always a new place in the Lord."

In 1 Kings 20 and with Hosea, clearly the LORD used them to cast curses and exact His judgment on the offending parties.

It all goes back to obedience to God, which is the test that seems to withstand the test of time itself. Reverence to the Father is the key to success in all things from this life to the next. Some may even say that ever since the action of Satan in Heaven, God developed a pet peeve towards disobedience.

Without Christ as our Savior and Advocate, the wrath of God would consume us. Many of us today, inside and outside of the church, are lacking reverence for the LORD because of the atmosphere of the "Age of Grace," also known as the acceptable year of the Lord, or the year of Jubilee.

This atmosphere was set up and paid for by Jesus Christ on the Cross. He did that to allow us to be free of the onus of the law that no one could keep and to give us room to fulfill our mission, "The Great Commission." In Matthew 28:18-20, Jesus gave us The Great Commission by commanding us to go teach all nations His ways and baptize the unsaved in the name of the Father, the Son, and the Holy Ghost. Simply put, it means to spread the Christian message and convert unbelievers with the testimony of our lives.

The Father, the Son, and the Holy Spirit are of one accord and God does not change. He is the same in His steadfast love (Malachi 3:6) and in everlasting faithfulness (Malachi 3:1-5). In the latter, the prophet Malachi speaks of both the first and second coming of Jesus Christ. The first coming was to restore the heritage of Israel, to fulfill God 's promise to Abraham, and to establish a new covenant with men, which extends to all nations (see also Galatians 3:10-16; Romans 2:11-28; Acts 10:34-35 and Isaiah 14:1).

The second coming will be of eternal joy and wonderful rewards to some, and to the remainder, it will be full of terror, weeping, and gnashing of teeth (see also Matthew 24).

- What Is the Mark of the Beast? -

One of the recurring subjects that have been on everyone's mind lately is the mark of the beast. Satan, who is the ancient serpent, along with his beasts are well aware of the scope of divergence in the minds of men, and they have been exploiting this loophole for generations now. Many have been speculating that the mark of the beast will be of technological source. I agree to a certain extent, but I would like to elaborate certain facts. I myself have spent countless hours meditating in the Spirit on this subject, and the Holy Spirit has shared with me the followings:

The mark of the beast in Revelation 13 is not specific to what it will actually be. The angel commands us in wisdom, so the first thing that anyone who meditates on this passage should do is ask the Eternal God for wisdom (James 1:5-8 and James 4:7-8).

We must recollect that "we wrestle not against flesh and blood" (Eph. 6:12). When the intended seal or mark of the beast of Rev. 13:16-18 is made official, it will be demoniacal in its true essence, but disguised in its natural form, so it will not be evident to the naked eyes. However, in Revelation 13:18, the mark of the beast is said to be the number of a man, and the number is 666. The number 6 in the Bible represents pride in the work of man, and 666 represents the hubris/exaggerated pride of man, and the number of Satan. Therefore, we can deduct from the meaning of the number "666" that the mark is directly connected to the work of men. This work represents the various sects, groups, politics, fraternities, sororities, street gangs, and many other guilds. Many people in Europe even go as far as killing each other in order to promote their allegiance to their soccer teams, if their team loses the game. Through these various cults, Satan has been acquiring the allegiance of men and women who feel like they can only live and die according to their affiliation to these guilds. The devil has been planting the hubris seed to keep us divided so that he can easily conquer our minds and thoughts.

The hubris seed in question has been with us for quite some time now and is now coming to fruition. This fact has been more evident the last couple of years with the charade we've been witnessing with the back and forth between our two main political parties. The United States is in the middle of a crisis and both Republicans and Democrats have been more focused about "representing" for their "crew." This hubris way of thinking has been established by the anti-Christ spirits (1 John 2:18-19), and when we get to that chapter of our history in Revelation 13, the devil will simply be consolidating on his long-time investment by making an official seal. It will be the official seal of the new world order. The mark on the right hand, or on the forehead, has to do with the oath of loyalty to Satan.

The supreme mark - the sign of the beast - is the actual denial of Jesus Christ as the Son of God and King of kings through trickery and misdirection. It is paramount that as Christians we stay close to Christ now more than ever before. We must walk with Christ every second of every day in the Holy Spirit in order that He may preserve us from confusion (Rev. 14:6-13, see also Daniel 7:24-27).

We need to spend time with the Lord every day and reflect on His words daily. We need to set aside time for fasting with spiritual growth as the goal. There are many forms of fasting. If you are a person with a certain state of health, search for one that will not make your conditions worse. We can find a lot of healing and empowerment in prayer and fasting.

According to Webster Dictionary, exercising means: *The act to bringing into play or realizing in action.*

The actual anti-Christ, the second beast, will be the one who **exercises** the mark in Rev. 13:11.

Just like the Father exercised His Zeal by the power of His Holy Spirit and through Jesus Christ the Son, the devil and the first beast will be allowed to exercise his so-called vision of a perfect world through the second beast, which will be a world ruled by demons and deceptions. A "perfect world" that leads to eternal damnation. Although the second beast is the actual anti-Christ and the one that will make the seal of Satan official, all those working towards this new world order are corrupt and of the same spirit of perdition, which is the spirit of Satan; therefore, they are not to be approved.

According to Hebrews 8:1-5, the Ark of the Testimony and Tabernacle of Meetings in Exodus 25 was a shadow, or carbon copy, of the foundation of God's throne in Heaven shown to Moses in the mount. As a guardian cherub, Satan was one of those cherubs back in his days as Lucifer. Moreover, in Ezekiel 28:12-19, we get a perfect overview of what led to Lucifer devolving to Satan and the devil and the final verdict concerning his action. He is likened to the ruler of Tyre in verses 1 to 5. We also discover that his heart became prideful because of his beauty, and he corrupted his wisdom. In Isaiah 14:13, the Bible tells us that he was desirous of being God. It is this same foolish desire that leads him to this day.

He knows that it is impossible, but he cannot prevent it; some may even say that he is under the curse of a reprobate spirit. His imperilment for self-gratification, however, has been his motivation. Beginning with the angels under his command in Heaven, until our present day, he has been able to redirect the value of objectivity.

The way the mark in question has been implemented on the earth for quite sometime now is through the indoctrinations of demonic credence. By his anti-Christ spirits, Satan has been dividing and conquering the allegiance of men through the power of suggestion (semantics). What we are seeing now happening in our communities is the fruition of all the work stated in the previous chapters. After the French Revolution of 1789, the enemy, via its Jesuit army, infiltrated the upper and lower levels of all governments and society. From there, they began to complete their final plans for world domination. While the chief goal of these infiltrations was to usher in their one world government for the sake of "the greater good," the underlying goal was to poison the minds and souls of men with various satanic lies and misdirection. Even though some participants were not conscious of the underlying goal, they've all been working for Satan.

Adam became a failed victim of this old crook and agreed to eat the fruit because his desire was to be like God. Adam's reason was innocent in one sense, and his desire came from his awe of God. While standing in the mine of the Almighty, Adam recognized the value of the essence of God as primordial. He recognized that God is marvelous and perfect in all His ways and wanted to experience that actuality; but the test of love needed to be completed first. It was not yet time for men to experience this moment.

This is not to allege that we will ever be equal to God, but rather, He always intended us to be gods (Psalm 82:1-6; John 10:34-36). Just like the first Adam, there are countless men and women today who seek to be validated, and they have been bamboozled into consuming the lies of the devil. These lies have led, most of them unconsciously, to obtaining the mark of the beast as doctrines to live by.

Each day, people of the latest generations spend their day basing the value of life on false objectives. Their interactions within their house and with their neighbors are based solely on the popular trends of the day. The mark of the beast leads the decision-making process of most. They are blindly following or pledging allegiance to trends, which are mass projected through the beast's many channels and avenues of approach.

People today do not value reality, only the trends or the popular illusion of the moment, and they even go about ridiculing anyone who is not onboard or has an individual opinion. We are now in the state of "trending being the norm." In addition, if any questions are raised about these so-called norms, you are instantly castrated from society and labeled a troublemaker. This predisposed "fit-in sentiment" is what Satan is counting on. He knows with that kind of programming in place, the masses will simply just agree to settle and take the supreme seal just to avoid being judged by others. So many Saints have gotten so tired of walking on eggshells all the time, that they've just surrendered and joined the perspective of the masses.

This is the power of the spirits of the anti-Christ, and they are preparing the way for Satan's masterpiece—the staged second coming. The first beast has been busy and has not only orchestrated every major conflict since the coronation of his first king, but he has also been capitalizing on the cause and effect. He first attempted to set the stage after the First World War with the League of Nations and failed, but he succeeded through the United Nations after World War II.

With the heliocentric globe and Darwinism as his foundation, he then began to establish the principles of the mark.

Let us dig a little deeper. For the sake of argument, I will only cover the influence this mark has on the initial three ethnic groups of this great nation.

- Native Americans -

Foremost, the enemy sent his army to invade a nation of hunters. He raped and killed them by the million, then gave them land so they could bury their sorrows and feel ratified. Then he oppressed them, killed them some more, and took back the land given for reparation. He then repeated the cycle, as many times as was needed until they were well broken, leaving them with a spirit of discontent. He then eventually returned some parcels to rebuild but used the empathy of their brokenness to influence a legacy of gambling and alcoholism that haunts the Native American community to this day. These casinos are the equivalent to a compliment from a rapist to the surviving victim. What's more? Alcoholism and discontent are a perfect mix for domestic abuse; they can then be left to police themselves because the scars of their history now mark them. Nobody on their side dares to speak about the scourges that are rotting their communities because they have endured too much. The mockery and the shame will be too much. Besides, where else will they go? They have fought tooth and nail for these parcels. And to this day, they are still fighting to hold on to those plots.

To my Native American brothers and sisters, the answer to all your problems has always been there. Jesus is the way, the truth, and the life. No one comes to the Creator but through Him. There is only one true God. Do not let the idols and the scars of your ancestors cheat you of eternal peace and true justification. The Wakan Tanka god of yours is of the devil and bears no power. The belief that all men are inherently good and should be respected for his decisions has made many of you reluctant to seek Jesus when you should. We are all God's creation, and the will of the Father is that your ethnic group should also come to recognize Him and have eternal life. Just try speaking to Him just once; you will not regret it.

What was taken from you is the chance to know eternal bliss in Christ Jesus. He is not the white man God! He is the only God, the One True God, and He is the answer to all your pain. If you are reading this and have not yet received Him as your Savior, He invites you to do so today.

- Igbos -

For the next victims, divide and conquer was the play. Igbos here represents the Black people taken from Africa and brought to America. The enemy enslaved this group of people and oppressed them to the point of break, and then he turned them against each other using the Willy Lynch principles. He raped some of the women and created mixed-babies that were later given a higher position on the plantation, and then he taught them to hate their half brothers. He raped their women, blindfolded the young slave boys, and made them rape their mothers, then marked them "motherfuckers." He raped the man then branded them "sissy boys."

He let that fire fuel for a while, and then following the Civil Rights Acts, he flooded their neighborhoods with drugs, guns, and liquor stores. The street gangs then followed and then the perpetual hate between them was established. This devil is familiar with the Bible, so he takes great pleasure in knowing that God has sanctioned their punishment; he even attempted to eradicate every one of them with the help of Margaret Sanger (Rev. 12:13-17; 1 Peter 4:17).

Many for the longest considered Margaret Sanger a shero, but recent reports from Planned Parenthood stated that she was in fact working with "explicitly ableist and white supremacist groups." On plannedparenthood.org, the organization has even published a public service announcement called, "Opposition Claims About Margaret Sanger." The organization now acknowledged that:

"Sanger also believed in eugenics — an inherently racist and ableist ideology that labeled certain people unfit to have children. Eugenics is the theory that society can be improved through planned breeding for "desirable traits" like intelligence and industriousness.

Margaret Sanger was so intent on her mission to advocate for birth control, that she chose to align herself with ideologies and organizations that were explicitly ableist and white supremacist. In doing so, she undermined reproductive freedom and caused irreparable damage to the health and lives of generations of Black people, Latino people, Indigenous people, immigrants, people with disabilities, people with low incomes, and many others."

This is what Darwinism in action looks like.

How can a group of people from the same continent spread to the four corners of the earth and the islands of the sea, then be told about it in the history books, and still not understand the love of God? (Deut. 28; Deut. 30:1-3; Isaiah 11:16; Isaiah 14:1; Isaiah 43:5-11; Isaiah 56:1-8; Ezekiel 34:11-24; Psalm 106:21-48 and Malachi 3:6).

It is not because the artists came with the brush and painted all the Biblical characters to look white that they now say, "This is not my God; this is the White man's God;" it is because they are stubborn and blind people. They have gone back to the "queen of heaven," one of the false gods Israel worshipped, and they honor her symbol again (Jeremiah 44:1-22). The moon is her symbol and some even call themselves "The Nation."

Stubborn children, listen up; it was for strategic reasons that The Holy One of Israel was taken to Egypt to be hidden among Africans. The hieroglyphics speak for themselves.

Do not allow your hate for your brother Esau to rob you of any true remedy for the sickness that still plague the black communities today.

Moreover, to those of you who can decipher the Word, do not make this a yoke for yourselves, stubborn Israelites. The seven sons of Sceva used Jesus' Hebrew name and was defeated, so clearly obedience to God is the key to victory. The sons of Sceva were also strategically placed in the book of Acts as an example not to follow. Instead, you should reach out with love to those who are still in deep blindness and connect to those who remain enslaved in psychological plantations that kill each other, then go and rap about it in music videos. Reach out to the brothers who have sold their souls to the industry chasing after the lust of the eyes and constantly bragging to their neighbors for every dollar the beast has given them.

There are just two groups in the universe: one that promotes darkness and eternal damnation, and the other promises eternal life in Jesus Christ. Wearing a "Jesus piece" around your neck does not make you holy, nor does it cover your iniquities. You have to have Jesus Christ as your personal Savior, and you have to renounce the world (Rev. 3:20- 22). Besides, this so-called "Jesus piece" is the portrayal of Cesare Borgia, the son of Cardinal Rodrigo de Lanzol y Borgia (Pope Alexander VI), and this dead – alleged pervert man – is not our Savior.

Furthermore, the "13 Candles Prayer" that some street gang brothers are reciting as allegiance to "the crew" was initially named "The Prayer of Eternal Damnation." It is exactly as it sounds, a declaration of eternal damnation over whomever declares it. Those same secret societies that formed the street gangs and gave them their mark of allegiance also influence this prayer as an oath of death upon oneself. This prayer is a witch's prayer that starts with the declaration, "Blood is the life," and it ends with "And fear not our eternal damnation." It starts with this declaration because the devil loves to twist the Word of God and use it to cause disorder and bring curses (Gen. 3:1-5; Lev. 17:11; John 6:63). This is why you will notice that many Hollywood films that depict witchcraft or voodoo generally have an open Bible in the scene. They are openly declaring their diabolical acts to us, while inciting the oppressed to follow them.

I myself never joined the gang, but I grew up in a violent and obscure environment, and I lived the life of the streets growing up. I also thought it was cool to be a thug for a while and to live by any means necessary. However, it wasn't long until I realized that the street life is purely demonic; we were literally serving Satan while simultaneously proclaiming ourselves as innocent because of the system. I felt justified at first because of the hand I was dealt, but eventually, it became clear to me that this lifestyle was just another form of cult worship and devotion to the system of the beast.

Can Israel please explain to me how every street gang uses the triple six as their logo? Alternatively, why do they all have the same six-point star or rabbits in their emblem? The ancient Babylonian spirit is one of the enemy's best assets. It matters not how you place the mark in your right hand; again, it means allegiance to the beast. How ironic that the secret societies use the same gesture of the hands as the gangs. Wake up Israel!

[For a detailed breakdown of the relation between the gangs, the fraternities, and Satan, look up: THUGEXPOSED.ORG on YouTube.]

- Esau -

Now, to the Edomites. Esau here represents the White American race. The beast used them well. Similar to the Knight Templar, they felt justified in their deeds. They came to America, the land of "milk and honey," and brought some indentured servants with them to help them settle. At first, those pilgrims actually kept their end of the bargain and gave those servants some land to build for themselves. However, the prophecy of Deuteronomy 28 had to be fulfilled. So, here comes the devil to press on the Lord's bidding and pursue after the woman who gave birth to the Son of Man. These Edomites, influenced by the same animal we call Satan, were sold on the concept that the curse was on the Black race, and they believe that they are the superior race and all evil comes from everyone but them.

They believed that the brain of a Black man is closer to the Neanderthal man and the monkeys. These ideals help give birth to Darwinism, which maintains the impetus of hatred to this day. Look at what happened in Minnesota with George Floyd and Officer Derek Chauvin. There is just no validation for Officer Chauvin to casually kneel on George Floyd's neck for 9 minutes and 29 seconds, choking him to death, while being video recorded. This is what the concept of natural selection leads to.

Many of these perpetrators who taught race superiority and ableism were community leaders, pastors, and scholars. Some were even thought of as pillars of our society. Many of these pastors taught the justification of slavery from a biblical point of view. They used every chapter and verse they could find, except those that would contradict their evil inclination (see Exodus 21:1-27; Deut.

23:15-16). America is getting soused with many curses because of all the violations of the Law that Esau has committed (Deut. 21:22-23; Isaiah 55:10-11).

Dazed by the spirits of the anti-Christ, most of the White folks in those days inadvertently graded God's creation, mankind, based on the color of their skin and social stigmas. Black men were considered three fifths of a man, Native Americans were considered savages, and poor white men were called white trash. To this day, the mark of the beast, which is based on the hubris of man and the various sects we have cultivated as a form of validation, remains predominant in the minds of many. Although America has accumulated many enemies over the years due to international conflicts, the biggest concern of this great country remains the pigmentation of the skin. For those who are hardened fanatics, such as White supremacist groups, the devil gave the Hitler's salute and the swastika as a mark in their right hand or in their foreheads as a symbol of worship. They are also referred to as "The Nation."

Sadly, those who are under that demonic trance would rather see America burn and overrun by foreign forces than learn to love and treat all people equally. They feel like they have too much to lose, and they can find no other way to validate their existence because they have spent most of their lives indulging in racial hate. Moreover, because that standard was profitable for them initially, they have allowed themselves to get lost in bliss of ignorance (1 Cor. 10:12-13). The ancient snake bit them, the poison tainted their souls, and the poison is still in their veins.

This branding of the minds according to the exaggerated pride of man promotes these types of nonsense in men's hearts. The following is a great example of erroneous direction. On the one hand, the mark of the beast convinces the White supremacist groups that the pigmentation of their skin is a validation to enter

Heaven. These same groups, however, believe that Satan is evil, and they condemn him for allowing his beauty to pervert his heart. They often quote Ezekiel 28:17 in their sermons: *"Thine heart was lifted up because of thy beauty, thou hast corrupted thy wisdom by reason of thy brightness."* And still they go about clinging to their outer appearance as a badge of validation before God and man. Esau was deceived, and they simply cannot see it. Many of these White supremacist groups walk around with a giant cross calling themselves Christian conservative, and some practice Christian identity, which teaches that to be a real Christian, you have to be of the "pure white race" and pray for an all white world. However, they have failed to understand that if the former light bearer is to be cast into the lake of fire for his disobedience irrespective of his beauty, how can having white skin be justifiable before God? Many of those groups are part of the conspiracy theorist movement; they oppose the government and claim that they are against the mark of the beast, while simultaneously pledging allegiance to the beast's system with the Hitler's salute and racially motivated doctrines.

The Gentiles who live according to the precepts of God as mentioned in Acts 15:14-19 and Isaiah 14:1 will be united with Jacob, which are the Black people taken from Africa and brought to America (Deut. 28:68). However, God's judgment on Esau's kind began a long time ago. This epidemic of opioids, addiction to alcohol, and the violence of the biker gangs that are happening in these neighborhoods are no accident. All the evils that Esau meant for Jacob, such as the liquor stores and gun stores in the ghettos, keep crossing over back into their own communities. Wake up Esau!

The judgment (Grace) of Jesus Christ for the world at Calvary is for all people. Although in the past the Bible said, *"Jacob I have loved but Esau have I hated,"* the new covenant says: *"This is my beloved Son in whom I AM well pleased, listen to Him."*

Annotation: Now, let me be clear on my last point. Slavery is not from the white man. It originated from the ogre known as Lucifer, and the Father allowed it for a while as a tool in our realm. The Mosaic Law was supposed to govern its application. The tool was used on many occasions in the Bible, but in Egypt, God used it as a "basic training" tool to rid the Israelites of false doctrines and prepared them to receive His law (Psalms 105: [23-25]). God also wanted the Israelites to learn how it feels to be under bondage so they would learn compassion through exposition (Exodus 22:24; Deut. 24:17-22). It was never a green light to hate one another or to create a perpetual cycle of existence based on hate and greed.

Conclusion: The devil is not our friend; he is the enemy of our souls. He is the enemy of the Native American, the Israelites, and the Edomites. He is the enemy of all ethnic groups, and he has created a division within mankind by saturating our minds with a spirit of fear. The fear of understanding, fear of communication, and fear to admit our flaws; we are so worried about losing "cool points" from the wizard, which is Satan, that we cannot see our inner strength as a nation.

The reason President Trump could speak of civil war as an acceptable output for his ambition is because the forces of darkness influenced him, and the devil does not care if America actually imploded and burned itself to the ground. And although only the kingdom of Christ is eternal and America will not last forever, why precipitate the unknown timeline? Whether we like him or not, we ought to pray for him, pray for the wisdom of God, and pray that the love of Jesus Christ overtake him. We have that power.

To the LORD God Almighty is the glory forever and ever, for His grace extends to all people: to the rich and the poor, great, small, old, and

young; from the one who grabbed the heel, to the hunter of hunters, and to all the other nations under Heaven.

CHAPTER FIVE

JOHN 14:6

The Crossover

In Biblical times, people used to be honored and rewarded because of their talents. Their heroic or noble exploits would give them recognition among their peers, and their names would even carry across the sea to their enemies. Some chief examples are David when he killed Goliath the giant, and Samson, who killed a lion with his bare hands. King Solomon exercised great wisdom concerning the case of the two mothers and the toddler when he tried to figure out which was the real mother, and many other similar cases may be found in the Bible.

However, even outside of the Holy Scriptures, the principle was still the same. To receive honor, an act of honor was required. This is why our history books are full of stories of people like Genghis Khan, Joan of Arc, and Robert Smalls. Robert Smalls was a slave from Beaufort, South Carolina who was sent by his "master" to fight against the Union with a small crew, Smalls managed to liberate himself, his crew, and their families during the Civil War, he later served fives terms in the U.S House of Represntatives. Abilities and competence were generally rewarded, regardless of complexion, sex, or ethnicity. This kind of value system was extended to all, and notwithstanding the corrupt nature of man, friend or foe, rich and poor, holy and unclean. This principle was still prevalent in many nations.

One can argue about the many ways these rules have been violated, and I know that heathen nations used to publicly sacrifice their children. Nor have I forgotten the treatment received by the Buffalo Soldiers in Bisbee, Arizona in 1919. Black Americans have been part of the U.S. Army legacy since 1770, when more than 5000 Black men - both slaves and free - fought for America's independence from the British army in Boston, Massachusetts (source: army.mil./africanamericans/timeline.html). Following President Lincoln's Emancipation Proclamation on January 1, 1963, an estimated 186,000 joined the military to serve with great pride, and 38,000 of them died in battle in the American Civil War. They did all of that under the promise of freedom and equality by the U.S. government, and because they loved their country (source: buffalosoldier.net "Buffalo Soldiers & Indian Wars" and 9th Cavalry Regiment (1866-1944 and Blackpast.org). Despite all their sacrifices, they were continually treated as second-class citizens during that time period. Many of them were even wounded by white mobs, which included policemen, on July 3, 1919 in Bisbee, Arizona, for wanting to celebrate the Independence Day Parade (source: zinnedproject.org "Teaching people's History"). What happened in those days was ugly from every angle, and no one can dispute that. Black Americans and Native Americans were pinned against each other to fight for a liberty most never got the privilege to experience. However, in the middle of all the injustice the Buffalo Soldiers endured in those days, 18 of them were awarded America's highest military decoration - the Medal of Honor - for their remarkable courage in battle (source: The Smithsonian - nmaahc.si.edu/proud-legacy-buffalo-soldiers), and 16 Medals of Honor were awarded to Native Americans during the same time period (source: history.army.mil/topic/natam/natam-moh.html). The point that I am making here is that we used to have higher standards of value. The civilized world, even in those times of darkness, still had a spark of integrity and justice left in them. This spark is dying more and more each day.

Although the prophecies concerning Jesus Christ had to be fulfilled for our sake, in Matthew 27:11-26, we see the prevalence of a similar code of conduct displayed by the Roman governor who judged Him. In Matthew Chapter 27, the Bible tells us that all the chief priests and elders of the Jews took counsel to have Jesus killed. They brought Jesus to Pontius Pilate who was the Roman governor for that region, and they pleaded with Pilate to see Jesus crucified without cause. Pontius Pilate could not find any reason for their accusation, and in verse 18 of Matthew 27, the Bible says that Pilate knew that those priests and elders were just envious of Christ. Following the counsel of Pontius Pilate's wife (verse 19), the governor washed his hands before the multitude and said, *"I am innocent of the blood of this just man: see ye to it"* (Matt. 27:24).

Moreover, in Acts 16:16-39, the Roman magistrate becomes fearful in receiving the news of the citizenship of Paul and Silas. In Genesis 41:1-45, Pharaoh rewards Joseph for the wisdom, which God bestowed on him. Let us not forget the stories of Hananiah (Shadrach), Mishael (Meshach), Azariah (Abednego) and the prophet Daniel (Daniel 3:3-30 and Daniel 6:12-28).

All of these stories have the same common themes: integrity and justice. No one is perfect, and mankind has been flawed since the fall, but we used to have a higher morale. Today, however, our society's system of function is based solely on the hubris of man; this way of operating is the foundation of the mark of the beast. Satan has been conditioning us to willfully accept the official mark, which will be officiated by our governments in the near future.

In former days, kings used to offer their daughters in marriage to the worthy cavaliers to form long lasting alliances that brought peace and prosperity to their nations (Judges 4:17).

Back then, the meanest and most unjust king had more honor and integrity than the majority of our ministers and elected representatives today. The lack of empathy, which guides our societies today, is the mark of the beast. It creates a basis of division on the projected values and not the fundamental values. It has produced a crossover from empathy to apathy.

I once viewed a news report about a man who had witnessed a car accident. The report said that the driver of the first car had lost control and ended up in a nearby lake. The man who had witnessed the accident pulled over, came out of his car and began filming the demise accident of the first man was on Facebook live. While he was filming, he continued asking his audience not to forget to hit the "like" button; one man died, the other went to jail, and Satan took a victory lap.

On July 24, 2017, a similar incident happened in California on Instagram. This time, two young women were involved, and the outcome was the same. One woman got killed, the other went to prison; the survivor, the one who filmed the death, was only eighteen, and the victim was only fourteen.

These are clear displays of the spirit of the beast and the spirit of Babylon in action. This reduces the senses, promotes value where there is none, and promotes value on social likeness over the life of a fellow man and woman. The beast wants to be worshiped, and his mark is the acceptance of the finite over the Universal. He wants to make you trade the tree of life – Jesus - for the tree of knowledge (evolution, eugenics, pseudoscience, technology, social media, fraternities, street gangs, political affiliations, skin pigmentation, hate-fueled awakening, hate of self, greed, LGBTQ (P)(B), or the old classic "like my daddy use to say").

That list could go on for a few more chapters, but I am really only here to plant a seed. God will give the increase.

Lamentably, however, these ideologies have also become prevalent in the church today, creating ism and schism among church members over semantics.

The worship of the beast and the taking of his mark is the disposition of our hearts and minds, and it leads to eternal perdition; only those who keep their hearts and minds clear of his influence will be able to overrule its influence (Rev. 14:6-13).

Furthermore, I'm sure that all the hype about this computer chip that is supposed to monitor our every move is true, but we are not dealing with an amateur. This devil has been at his task for millennia. In add-on, I am afraid that Satan has already saturated the hearts and minds of so many, that even when that mandatory monitoring law becomes official, most people will still be more concerned about who gets the last roll of toilet paper.

We are in dire need of a revival; not a religious one, but a genuine heart to God and love for one another revival.

Jesus, The Lion of Judah, is prepared and willing to pour more of His Spirit on us for this revival. Let us be sanctified and ready to receive His fresh anointing.

CHAPTER SIX

The Remedy for the Mark

Back when our Lord and Savior walked the earth as the Son of Man, He predicted the return of the days of Noah for our generation and the effect that the mark of the beast would have (Matt. 24:12-22; Luke 18:1-8).

Jesus understood our pain well. He knew the perplexing challenges we would face, even before He gave us the book of Revelation and the remedy for the system of the beast. That remedy is written throughout the Bible, but our Lord consolidated it all for us in Matthew Chapters 5 to 7; it is known as "The Sermon on the Mount." As JEHOVAH SABAOTH, Jesus gave us our marching orders in those three chapters. He began The Sermon on the Mount with The Beatitudes:

"Blessed are the poor in spirit: for theirs is the kingdom of heaven. Blessed are they that mourn: for they shall be comforted. Blessed are the meek: for they shall inherit the earth. Blessed are they which do hunger and thirst after righteousness: for they shall be filled. Blessed are the merciful: for they shall obtain mercy. Blessed are the pure in heart: for they shall see God. Blessed are the peacemakers: for they shall be called the children of God. Blessed are ye,

when men shall revile you, and persecute you and shall say all manner of evil against you falsely, for my sake. Rejoice, and be exceeding glad: for great is your reward in heaven: for so persecuted they the prophets which were before you" (Matt. 5:3-12).

The message in this passage is very clear; we will be persecuted but we are blessed to receive such anguish in the honor of Jesus. We should rejoice and be extremely glad to know that we carry the tradition of the prophet; see also Apoc. 6:9-11.

This passage also makes it clear that these principles should be the primary application of the Ecclesiastic body of Christ, for in them reside the eternal blessings of God.

Similar to a combat general giving a heartening speech to his army before sending them into battle, Jesus takes the time to list each principle individually for us in the paragraphs of the Sermon on the Mount. He is open and concise on what to expect before, during, and after the battle. He would not sugar coat or downplay the situation at hand to His troops because He wanted to be transparent, and He wanted us to be prepared spiritually, mentally, and emotionally for the challenges of this world.

He was in fact presenting us with the Standard Operating Procedures for this journey and simultaneously equipping us with some heavy artillery.

The heavy artillery is to help condition our minds from receiving the supreme mark, which signifies allegiance and worship of the beast and pledging allegiance to its One World System. Jesus makes it clear that we will be persecuted for calling evil by its name and for following unapologetically after Him. This is a call for predisposition of the hearts and minds, and it takes consistency of faith in Jesus Christ to not only get there but to remain there until the end as well.

I know that it can be very burdensome to be around a bunch of people and still feel alone and to feel like you don't belong in any group in this world, including even your own. You may feel like it would be easier to go along and get along or just follow the evil ways of this world. But you know that this world just does not make any sense anymore, so remain firm in your commitment to serve Christ and glorify the Father through the Holy Spirit, regardless of men's opinion.

Jesus ended His sermon on the mount with the parable of the wise and foolish builders. I used the version of Luke below because the inquisition at the beginning makes it more specific to us who are saved, and because we are the ones with the authority to close and open Heaven.

*"Why do you call me, 'Lord, Lord' and do not what I say? As for everyone who comes to me and **hears my words and puts them into practice, I will show you what they are like. They are like a man building a house, who dug down deep and laid the foundation on rock. When the flood came, the torrent struck that house but could not shake it, because it was well built.** But the one who hears my words and does not put them into practice is like a man who built a house on the ground without foundation. The moment the torrent struck that house, it collapsed and its destruction was complete"* (Luke 6:46-49 NIV).

Let us look at some of the Beatitude qualities that a disciple, or worshiper of Christ, should have as stated in the passage of Matthew Chapters 5-7.

I do not believe that our Father would just condemn people who were born and died in misery or poverty without a just cause. For the purpose of this message, all viewpoints are related to the spiritual implication and application of the "Sermon on the Mount."

In my opinion, the poor in spirit are those who acknowledge their flaws and cry out to God for mercy. They do not hide their iniquities but confess it before Christ. Although they cannot justify themselves, they claim to be the justification of Christ. These are people wanting to be holy and acceptable before God but understand that only through Jesus Christ can they ever be holy and acceptable to God (Luke 18:9-14; 1 John 1:8-10; Philippians 1:6).

The mourners are blessed for rejecting the comfort and conveniences that the beast's system offers. Instead, they choose to suffer for their love for Christ (James 4:7-10). Sometimes the Christian may backslide (turn away from God) so far because of the love of mammon that we may not even feel worthy to return to our first love, but the Lord compels us to find our way back if we fall off (Rev. 2:5, Luke 10:38-[42]). Even if it involves some serious supplication and intercession before God just like David did, it is better to plead our case before God than to conform to this world (Psalm 136:6-8), and the Holy Ghost is the One that guides us back when we get lost. Therefore, we need Him in our life at all times, even when we fumble.

The next blessing is for the meek: *"Blessed are the meek: for they shall inherit the earth."*

Okay, let's slow down. First, we will look at the meek under the system of the beast, followed by some of my observations about the church. Then I will share some of my personal experiences about my journey to becoming meek. Hopefully, it will help some of you relate and get rid of that chip on your shoulder. Furthermore, I know that some individuals have had it much worse than I. My hope is that my testimony will empower people.

- Facts Check -

In our present time, being meek is frowned upon. By any means necessary, the young and the chronologically gifted, which are the older people, but some older folks get offended to be called old, so I use that term instead, but they are targeted first. There was once a time when the elderlies were honored and revered for their wisdom, but now the clout of the beast promotes insult and abuse towards them. He wants them out of the picture because they are assuming too much space in his new world. Nowadays, many of the nursing homes, which are meant to help them, are run just like morgues. On his Georgia Guidestones, located in Elberton, Georgia, USA, the beast proclaims his ten commandments proudly; he claims that he will reduce the world's population to 500 million. The truth is, his every breath breeds deceit (Rev. 6:5-8, 8:6-13, 9:[13]-[18]), but The Father has everything under His control; and yes, that admits the good, the bad, and the ugly. Nothing can escape Him.

There's been a disconnect between the older and the younger generations for quite some time now. The children don't honor their mothers and fathers anymore, and many mothers and fathers are too stressed and overwhelmed with life to spend quality time with their offspring. Consequently and sadly, in some cases, many of the children just cannot find any subsequent reason to honor their parents.

Dysfunctional spirits are influencing the making of dysfunctional families that go on perpetrating dysfunctional behaviors in our societies, and they enact a circular existence of reciprocated hatred by saying, "I was hurt, so I must hurt someone in return." The victims of yesterday have become today's monsters. As someone once said, "No one owns the pattern or franchise on pain and suffering." So as hard as it is, we should put forth an effort to move on past the hurt.

Now, we can clearly see how that type of disposition helped propel the success of shows like Jerry Springer, MAD TV, and SNL, among others, where mockery of our fellow men is the standard. The beast builds them up, then takes them down. He can do that because we are so quick to enjoy watching someone else suffer.

I know from personal experience that it can be very tough to forget the past, but this kind of behavior only glorifies the devil. We must learn to forgive and forget so that we can rise above the madness.

Our children used to be looked at as the future. The consensus across the board was the same; protect them and educate them, so they can help sustain our environment in the future. Now the system of the beast says, crucify them unto my servant Baal.

The beast's system gives women freedom of abortion in exchange for them sacrificing their unwanted baby to him; this world no longer promotes abstinence or celibacy because those things are frowned upon. Being a virgin as a teenager is a source of mockery among peers, and condoms are even distributed by high school nurses.

The system of the beast claims that these unborn babies know nothing and feel nothing so why bother. However, the Bible tells us that "the life is in the blood" (Leviticus 17:10-14), and we understand that wherever there is a pulse, there is blood being pumped. This is an act of pure wickedness and Moloch worship. I cannot speak for those women who became pregnant because of being raped, but I do know that the majority of these abortions do not apply to their situation.

With so many couples unable to conceive, why do we not invest more money towards adoption clinics?

Furthermore, the abortion period in America used to be between four to six weeks, which is around the same time the baby's pulse can be detected. Nowadays, in many states, the latest date for abortion is 20 to 25 weeks. The beast has pretty much made it more convenient to all parties involved to partake in Moloch worship. The more developed the consciousness of the unborn child is, the more sadistic is the child's sacrifice. And the more satisfied is the beast. Through these rituals, countless demonic portals have been opened in the spirit realm, ushering in increasingly truculent spirits to exert dominance over our realm and to fill the ranks of the army of darkness.

These demons have gotten so comfortable that now some elected officials in the state of Virginia are attempting to push Born-Alive abortion laws to be the norms. This means that a woman can give birth to a child (due to a failed late abortion), then give the baby away to be offered as a sacrifice to Satan as a fully born child. This clearly shows the attempt by the enemy to bring back the days of old, thereby bringing curses upon the land (Lev. 20:1-5; Jeremiah 19:4-7; Rev. 19:17-18). This level of wickedness can only lead to the seepage of more heinous spirits from the bottomless pit and to more heartlessness in our kingdom.

However, it does not stop there. Under the umbrella of science, the beast has been casting spells on involuntary constituents. Over the years, there have been many articles about whistleblowers from the biotechnological company called Senomyx. They claim that many of those aborted fetuses were actually getting processed and intercalated into our food as additives and flavors; also known as HEK 293 or Human Embryonic kidney cells. Those powdered babies' fetal parts were allegedly being injected into our food, drinks, cosmetics and vaccines, most of which is owned by major brands companies, such as Pepsi and Coca-Cola.

Side note: If you are just being made aware of these latter facts, do not freak out. Jesus has already provided us with power over those spells (Job 26:13; Isaiah 54:14-[17]; Acts 2:38-39; Psalm 91:9-13; Mark 16:16-18; Luke 10:19). If you have Jesus as the ruler of your life, you are covered. I would just recommend that you pray before you eat and pray the Blood of Jesus over your household every day. The Blood of Jesus Christ has never lost its power and is more than enough to keep us sanctified. Pray for your loved ones and neighbors as well.

Now, at the same time, under the system of the beast, in the Christian Nation, forty six of the fifty states allow underage marriage for children as young as 12 years old. Most of these states only require that the parents sign a form of consent, and here goes a tool for pedophilia. Two of these states, California and Mississippi, do not even bother with the parental consent form. Reform of these types of policies should be our elected official's number one priority, but I guess the people in power in our country are either too busy worrying about their re-election, or making side deals with Big Pharma to fight for the rights of their most delicate constituents. On the other hand, perhaps they do not care because they have an allegiance to the beast.

The wickedness of this world is reverting to the times of Noah; prophecies will be fulfilled; destruction is surely coming, but the revival will be first.

- My Observations -

We (the church) have lost our credentials for a while now. People do not see the light of Christ shining through us as they used to, and many people do not trust the words of our testimony anymore. This is because too many churches have taken Jesus out of our services and replaced Him with religion and worldly practices.

For example, on March 12, 2015, CBS News reported that a church in Panama City Beach, Florida held nude paint parties and sleepovers featuring the "sexiest ladies on the beach." Their tax-exempt license was later revoked by the state of Florida, but the damage to our image was done.

Most recently I stumbled on a documentary on YouTube named *Jehovah Witness Pedophiles*. In the documentary, many former members came forward to denounce the custom of the church clergy regarding the hiring of registered pedophiles as ministers and the sexual abuses that run rampant in their church. According to the documentary, it has been happening for decades now, and the people in charge of the head office for this faith are well aware of it but refuse to take action.

On that same YouTube channel, there is another video about a pastor being audited by the IRS. The whole video portrays a ridiculous man trying to justify an eccentric lifestyle. The last time I checked, that video had over 8 million views; that's 8 million souls being served a lie about the true meaning of the church.

I do not know this man and do not mean to offend him by using the word ridiculous, but these types of behaviors are getting old and frustrating. We are supposed to be the frontline of defense, but innumerable stories of similar churches with reprehensible behaviors continue to surface. These kinds of defiled ministries are a direct reflection of the demonic; they are directly related to the **synagogue** of Satan, which Jesus spoke of in Revelation 2:9 and 3:9. Their infiltration into the Church of God was destined for only one purpose: to discredit the validity of our testimony by inducing appalling behaviors, and their handprint can be seen all over our churches today; even many of our pastoral robes resemble the one worn by the Primate of Italy.

The members of the Kazharian Kabbalah run everything, and they have been after the innocents (Mark 9:42) for quite some time now. From pedo-hood to Washington, they've been working on releasing spirits that are more hideous over the land. In their Noahide laws, they even proclaim child sexual abuse and sacrifice as a justifiable evil against the heathen nations in reference to our children. They claim it is acceptable to do those things to little boys as young as 9-years-old and girls as young as 3-years-old because they are the only pure race and all other races are to be used as they see fit under the Judaic Law. These demons' origin only goes back 2,000 years. These perpetrators of darkness were converted into the Judaic faith, but now they hold the title of God's chosen nations. In the meantime, they still practice the Passover sacrifice in denial of the One True King – Yahushuah Hamashiach – while being active participants in Satan's masquerades.

Okay, I have to stop here and make another note: The statements above are not directed to any person born in Israel who worships the King of kings and Lord of lords as their Lord and Savior. I believe that if you are a true believer of Jesus Christ and are born in the land of Israel, you are my covenant brother and sister, and I love you. However, I know without a doubt that the original Jews were black-skinned. The acquisition of the land of Israel from the Palestinian government began in 1880 and ended (for the most part) in 1948 when the present State of Israel became official. Our history was rewritten because Satan— knowing that the original Israelites were under the curse of Deuteronomy 28— wanted to suppress our identity while simultaneously placing his overlords in a position of power. He did that because he knew that the world would be sympathetic to the struggle of "God's chosen people," but the promise made to Abraham is not concerning land, skin pigmentations, or the nation per se, the promise **is the Son of God** (Gen. 22:15-[18]; Gal. 3:16; Col 2:14-17). Furthermore, I am not here to contend about land, for the Creator knows who His children are. He will gather us all in due time and establish His chosen nation forever once and for all. Ultimately, whether you agree with this fact or not, if you are a doer of the Word, I shall see you at the Marriage Supper of the Lamb.

Most people are conceited or too ashamed to face the fact that we are living in filth, and this gunk is getting stickier every day. Some are simply naïve about the seriousness of this spiritual war and the depth in which we are into it. That's mainly because the Church has gotten too comfortable with this realm. We entertain everything advertised on TV and just bring anything into our homes.

Allowing objects like Ouija boards in your home may open demonic portals that may lead to demonic attacks. Even watching certain films, like horror movies, especially the ones where they speak in cryptic language can usher in satanic forces in your life. Once they are in your house, they monitor you to find any defect in your walk with Christ to take advantage of it.

I once heard a pastor make a powerful observation about the kinds of things we should watch as Christians. He averred, "If you would not invite the people you are watching on TV into your home, then you are probably watching the wrong thing; and you should just stop." This observation was sent to me from Heaven during the time of porn addiction in my life. It helped me resist and rebuke that demon. Maybe it can help someone else.

One of Satan's most enticing tools is music. Many even believe that he was one of the major maestros in Heaven before his rebellion (Ezekiel. 28:13), but even if he wasn't, we know for a fact that he is behind the malevolent influence behind music today. He works in secrecy and likes to disguise his works. Some songs are obviously evil to the ears by the way they make you feel inside, but many of the other songs we sing along to every day have the same hidden inclination.

For instance, I used to listen to a lot of old school soul music. It usually sounds positive, but after rededicating my life to the Lord, it became clear to me that most of these songs were just about having sex, how filthy the sex was going to be, and how hard the artist was going to ravish their lover. These old school songs are truly full of beautiful melodies, and the lyrics are definitely much cleaner than today's artists—but I still had to cut them out because they would arouse my flesh sexually. These days, I listen to only gospel and certain instrumentals. I do that to keep my mind clear of evil desires. Additionally, even some of the swimsuit posters that I used to have in my house, I had to take out. It seems I could not walk by the picture of the swimsuit models on my wall without stopping to fantasize about their consistency.

For a more detailed understanding of evil music, Look up *Satanism in the Music Industry EXPOSED! Stairway to Heaven Backwards* on YouTube.

One of the duties of the observers in the astral world is to observe our public and private march so they may mount dossiers against us or for us. The angels of Light hope for a good report, but the army of darkness observes any types of foul behaviors so they can capitalize on it at the right time.

Think of it as a seed. Satan wants to imitate God, so just like the Father works from the inside out starting with Jesus, a Seed that He cultivated into the true Vine (Gal. 3:16; John 15:2-6), Satan also operates like a gardener. The devil sows the seeds of obscurity, which he hopes to reap later (James 1:13-15, 4:7-8) because he is the gardener of death.

Satan uses the power of suggestions to put a thought in our judgments, then he waters it down until it grows and takes root, and we begin to believe that it is the truth. He wants to convince us that we are weak so he can patronize us. Remember these facts: **God always declares** to us His desires for our lives, and it is always geared towards our growth and development; but **Satan is a debater**, and he always suggests lies, errors, and evil thoughts. Only when we abide in Christ can we discern those lies and rebuke these thoughts. Without Jesus Christ, we cannot withstand him, and we will fall (Matt. 12:43-45; 1 Thess. 5:17-22; Deut. 11:18-21; Proverbs 3:3-8).

If you are saved, the blood of Christ covers you, and these satanic forces will not be able to overpower you, but they can still trouble your thoughts and affect your emotions if you let it.

When we use Satan's paraphernalia, such as drugs, watching porn, or anything that promotes sinful behaviors, we grant him license to come into our lives, disturb us or use us. To add insult to injury, he turns around and asks for payments, and these payments are always about committing more sins against God. He knows, from his personal experience, that the further away from God he can take us, the harder it will be to find our way back. These long periods of disconnect from Jesus can take years to recover while blessings go by, breakthroughs go by, and many Believers become discontent because of the lack of growth in their lives.

For the present time, Jesus is always happy to receive any backslider's back, but it will not be so forever. Although the backslider's offenses will be forgiven, the consequences of our actions remain. Just like when Adam listened to the hellion's counsel in the garden and was cursed for his action, Satan wants to bring curses upon us through misdirection and disobedience to God. To refute those attacks, we must walk in the Spirit of Christ daily and remain covered by His blood at all times (Rom. 8).

If the enemy cannot derail you off the righteous path, he will still try to slow you down or disturb you. Alcohol and drugs are his best tools for wasting our time. If he still cannot get to you, then he will go after your spouse or your children. Once those spirits are in your home, they will not come out unless you rebuke them and cast them out through prayers. In order for these prayers to be effective, you must use your weapon, and the Bible is our weapon.

I recommend that you also repent daily. Even unintentional sins may hinder our prayers. You should also memorize at least one verse a day; we will need it when the beast takes away our weapon.

Again, we need to be very vigilant in this last hour because the false prophets of the enemy are everywhere; from mega-churches to the average assembly, they've been sneaking into our departments for decades. They are sometimes hard to spot, but you will know them by their fruits. The only way you can discern them is through the Spirit of God. For the Spirit to fulfill His purpose, we must be in good standing with the Lord *"living self-control, upright and Godly lives in this present age"* (1 John 4:1-6; Titus 2:11-13).

In my time in the church, I met many good people, but I also met a few shady characters that were possessed by those evil spirits mentioned earlier (refer to Rom. 1:26-32); and on several occasions, I was the one possessed.

Over time, I realized that some of these figures were actually double agents because they did not seem to have the desire to change their sinful behaviors. On the surface, they acted holy, sanctified, and often had wonderful words of praise. As I approached some of them, and paid more attention, I realized they would really encourage sinful behaviors in the church. The Holy Spirit even showed me how some of them would come and speak hexes and curses towards church members as we were praying in the sanctuary on Saturday morning. You can normally tell them apart by their aura or spiritual energy. When they walked by, it just felt evil and dark around them, and they spoke in tongues unheard of before. It sounded like "Katikati, hook hate kill the kiti." When they spoke in tongues, these words felt more like incantations than prayers to me.

One of those witches once approached me and gave me a hug right after prayer service. I instantly felt like something had got on me, and the joy I just experienced being in the prayer service had turned to troubled thoughts. I began praying immediately to rebuke that spirit and commanded it back to its owner, and the peace of God came back to me. I became very particular about hugging strangers afterwards.

These spirits are able to do so in our congregations because of the lack of unanimous sanctification found in the church today (Mark 1:23-27; Eccl. 4:9-12).

Many of us go about with idols in our hearts. Evil spirits can perceive these things, and they will come and test us. Sometimes the evil spirits enter the church through double-minded Christians who are living in sin like church members shacking up together and sleeping in the same bed outside of God's marriage covenant. Or going to the club on Saturday night getting drunk, then showing up to church the next day acting all exuberant and holy. I know because I have also been that guy, but we must do better as members of God's army.

I once tried to denounce those Katikati witches, but the head of the church scolded me. After that situation, I kept quiet and to myself on the subject. On some other occasion, I confronted a warlock who was disguised as a prophet. He was sitting in the house of God pretending to be a man of God while secretly working against the pastor and his ministry by teaching the church members doctrines that went against the pastor's belief. One of those doctrines was predestination; he taught the assembly that no matter what we do, those bound for Heaven will see it, and those bound for Hell will end in Hell. Therefore, he believed that living a sanctified life only determined the amount of reward we will get in the afterlife because God had already made up His mind about who will be saved. That teaching is false because although God is Omniscient, He has set up the dynamics of the battle between good and evil so that His desire towards men may be fulfilled. His desire is that none - that believe in Jesus - should perish (John 3:16-21 and Matt. 15:22-28). We have the free will to serve or deny God; the choice is ours to make. He created us with free will; therefore, we have to put our faith to work towards our own salvation because faith without work is dead (James 2:14-26). Which means, if we do not apply our faith through righteous deeds, our faith (light) will then die because "righteous deeds" is an integral component of our faith and without faith, we cannot please God (Heb. 11:5-6; see also 1 Peter 4:17-19; 2 Peter 3:9 and Rev. 3:5-6). After the people in the church rebuked me for confronting this false teaching, I nearly lost my faith.

In fairness to those two overseers, at first, my walk with Christ was very shaky. I was still drinking and facing legions of familiar minds that would not see me free, so I felt disqualified to lobby on these issues anyway (Matt. 7:1-6). I know that I am justified in confronting witches and sorcerers in the Assembly of God. When it came to the legality of spiritual war, I was not properly equipped for battle, nor was I in charge of leading the flocks.

I was like a football player who came to the game with no uniform and no helmet and said, "Put me in, coach!"

On this journey, we need to be well equipped for battle; otherwise, we risk serious injury and even death (Eph. 6:10-18). If you are experiencing similar encounters in your church, make sure that you are walking in sanctification before you speak, and only protest if the Holy Spirit leads you to. Don't be temperamental, but as the Bible says, "Be as wise as a snake and gentle as a dove."

In conclusion, all this foolishness must end, for God is not the author of confusion. He will not support ekklesia, the Church, if the Church does not abide in Him.

- My Testimony -

I was born in 1979 on the little Island of Guadeloupe in the Lesser Antilles. Both of my parents were from Haiti, but I only knew my dad back then because my mom abandoned me at birth. When I was a kid, my father was never there. He was in the import/export business and travelled a lot. He would come by to see me, tell me how much he missed me, stay a few weeks, and then disappear for months. When he left, I stayed with one of his friends until he got home. I barely knew my dad.

At the age of seven, my father passed away, and I ended up in foster care. I was already pretty outspoken for my age, but at the foster home, I got introduced to porno and horror films because they were being played on the TV right before my eyes. Most of the guardians there did not really care about what we did or what we were exposed to. We were just a paycheck to them. The foster home soon turned into a depressing place.

While I was there, I once beat up a child who was trying to bully me. He was a couple years older than me, and he felt so embarrassed afterwards that he went and complained to his uncle about the matter. The 37-year-old man came the next day, cornered me, and beat me up like a runaway slave. When I informed the guardians about the incident, they bandaged my wounds, then I was sent on my way. They just told me to stop making a fuss about it; my guess is that the funding was more important to them than my well-being. That night, I could barely sleep. I pissed blood and cried out, but no one came. The whole thing was thrown into oblivion, and it felt like hell.

During my first year there, I was adopted twice. On both occasions, my indispensable rage and seditious behavior led to my expatriation back to Hades. One day, I got so tired of the place that I ran away, but someone noticed me wandering late at night in a vacant lot and called the authorities. I was once again repatriated to the inferno that they call the foster home. I was sexually assaulted there on a number of occasions by an older lady who worked there, and I did not even bother to mention it. Time seemed to have slowed down around me; but every day, I proceeded through the motions of life, but I felt no real existence.

Before my 8th birthday, my aunt came one day and decided to take custody of me. Although she cursed a lot, I loved her. She was a very strong and passionate woman, and I started to feel hopeful. Once the paperwork was finalized, she brought me home and introduced me to her family. She presented me with a kind side of mankind I had never noticed before, but it did not last.

At first glance, her husband seemed like a nice person. He was full of foul words, but nothing too disturbing for my ears. Nevertheless, I soon discovered that he was a drunk and a gambler. He would spend all day at the tracks betting on horses, lose, then come home and beat on me. Every time I complained to my aunt, he had a fabricated excuse. My guess is she needed a man around. Besides, they had a kid together, so it wasn't like she was going to leave him. This was the best place I had been so far, so I tried to tough it out.

By the time I turned ten-years-old, I was arrested twice, I was smoking pot, drinking liquor, and it wasn't long until I missed school and sold drugs. With the money I earned from drug sales, I could buy brand-name clothing. People seemed to like me more when I wore these items, and they showed me more respect. I was stringing up with thugs, dope dealers, prostitutes, and the pimps. They showed me more love than I was getting at home, so I considered them my family. After a while, I gave up going back home altogether. I had friends with money and was making enough money of my own, and had more than enough places to lay my head. I just couldn't take any more from the drunk. With my newfound family, there were a few near death experiences and a couple of hospitalizations as a result of street fights. My newfound family always seemed to have a lot of love and sympathy to go around, so I did not care about the near death experiences or getting hospitalized; it was all just a thrill. At the time, it felt liberating to walk hand-in-hand with the darkness and to "do as thou wilt." It was customary to examine a dead body on the side of the streets or to see people having sex on the staircase in those days. By then, it all just felt like a normal thing.

By the time I became twelve, I was having sex. There was nothing to it. It consisted of no love or emotion; it was only pleasure, another act of self-validation or a way to pass the time. I was so disconnected to reality that if a girl started getting too close or mentioned the word girlfriend, I would break up with her because that type of love was unfamiliar to me. It felt too scary.

In between sex partners, I watched porn. There were no strings attached there. Needless to say, I was friendly with some of the cocottes (slang for prostitutes where I am from), and I just kept it on the down low so that my "classic friends" would not judge me. The boundary line between right and wrong started to get more blurry, so I started drinking some more. That same year, I was hospitalized for alcohol poisoning, admitted to the emergency room, and the doctor had to pump my stomach out to save my life. It was only 10 a.m. at the time.

Before my 14th birthday, three of my friends and I went to rob a gambling joint. I'd never gone this far before, but the $5,000 prospect was too tempting. We entered the premises, the cashier pushed the panic button, and we ran away. My friends were arrested, and I got away. My "friends" told the officers about my whereabouts, and we were all soon reunited at the local police precinct. They were all over eighteen, so they went to jail, but since I was only 14-years-old, I was sent to Saint John Bosco Juvenile Center, a rehabilitation program, and that's where the saga continued.

As vagabonds, whenever we ventured out of the walls of the center, we were mocked for being poor and unwanted by our peers. Because of that, we formed our own little community of rejects within the walls and only ventured out in posses. We had three different workshops at the juvenile center: woodwork, welding, and painting. I signed up for the paint shop. The people in charge fed us, lectured us about making changes to our lives, and taught us about Mother Mary and her son Jesus. If there was a fight during the day, they intervened. Sometimes it would escalate to serious injuries, and the cops had to be called. Then the day ended, and they went home.

On the weekend, there were one, sometimes only two guardians watching over dozens of kids spread out among four buildings. We pretty much ran the place. There were drug deals for everything, but the two best sellers were marijuana, Playboy magazines, and videos. Although I was hundreds of miles away from my hometown, I was capable of adapting to this setup because this was familiar territory.

The kingpins were the oldest kids. Some had been there for years while others kept getting recycled in the program. They had connections with the gangs from that part of town and received help from the outside; the rest of us either put in work for them or were just customers. I was big for my age and very temperamental, so I became an enforcer.

Some of our biggest marijuana customers were members of the faculty. It felt wrong, but as a 14-year-old child, I literally had to go and flex my muscles at grown men and women over payroll. I never actually caused harm to any of these grown men and women, but it still felt wrong for me as a child to yell at grown-ups in order to collect money for the drugs we had sold them. There was no bargaining, and I had to survive. Besides, the whole system was corrupt. Some of these grown-ups entrusted with mentoring us would even tell us where to "hit-a-lick" for a percentage of the loot.

On the weekend, I remember the older kids calling out "movie night" in the hallway. All of us would come out to enjoy the preview; the selections varied between gore, gorier, half nudes and fully nudes. My life from childhood to adolescence was a transcendent version of "Lord of the Flies." Then the crack era came, and everything went to a new level.

People lost their minds because of crack cocaine. One of my friends raped his own sister; the details are too gory to mention, so I will spare the thought. Another beat his mother up until she was unconscious, then he tossed her from their balcony to her death. A third tried to slit my throat in order to steal my necklace. There were no more alliances between neighborhoods once crack came into play; it was all about survival of the fittest. I saw some of the so-called players become male prostitutes to feed their crack addictions. One minute they were walking around with a woman under each arm; the next minute they were walking around the boulevards in booty shorts, bending over and waving at passersby. Pregnant women were walking around half naked offering blowjobs for a rock. There were no more rules; to remain on top, you had to be willing to be the most sadistic person on the block or join his crew. I myself started going completely off the rail. I saw so much hate that I had no remorse left in me; I had no empathy or sympathy for no one. I expected that on any given day, I may have to kill one of my "friends" or that my life would be carried away by one of them.

This madness went on until I was almost eighteen, then I just felt like I had enough. I could not continue along that path. Too many people were dead or serving long sentences, and for what? I started looking for a change, and that's when I heard Him calling my name. I didn't know it then; I thought it was just my conscience talking to me, but now I know with certainty that it was Christ all along speaking to me.

That same year, I met my mother for the first time and moved to America. I had previously returned to my aunt's house, and she helped me look for her, and we found her. We each bought a ticket to go to the "Promised Land." With the assistance of some of her friends, we found her phone number, and she said she'd meet with us.

The first time I saw my mother, I was so excited. I reached out to embrace her, but she stopped me, looked at me and said, "You're such a tall boy, aren't you? You should join the NBA, so you can buy your mama a Big House!" I was heartbroken, but with a big smile I said, "Sure mama, anything you want." Needless to say, our relationship was worlds apart for a long time; however, over the years, we developed a stronger connection. In spite of our differences, one good thing she did as we lived together was convince me to be baptized. When she passed away two years ago, I sat with my hands on my face and cried for the loss of the mother I barely knew; it was as though I had lost another part of myself.

I wish I could say that since I have been saved it has been a smooth transition from the darkness to the light, but I have many scars. I had too many fumbles and backslid a few times back to sin, more times than I care to remember at this time. I am afraid that the truth is this is an ongoing process. The truth is, I was baptized impulsively, and I did not understand what being saved implied. Moreover, my mother's church was full of double-minded people, and I found myself surrounded with amateur sinners pretending to be saved, so I just picked up where I had left off.

For example, I saw one of the daughters of the elders negotiate the cost of a prostitution deal called the "top and bottom." While sitting right in front of the church with her clients, she offered her mouth and vagina to men for a fee, and this happened immediately after the Sabbath service. At 18 years of age, witnessing these types of behaviors made me feel like the church was just a big fat joke. I could hardly distinguish the contrast between the church and the world. After about a year, I chose to leave the church. It took me 20 years before I decided to go back to God's house. The crud that I have experienced and witnessed with my eyes has haunted me for years. I wish I could travel back in time and fight harder to preserve my innocence, but I cannot. What was seen cannot be unseen, and what was done cannot be undone. I must push forward and denounce this wicked world, or as someone once said, "Tell the truth and shame the devil."

Later in my late twenties, I joined the military and enjoyed a new journey for some time. I was not the best soldier in my unit, but I was still quite noticeable. I served for eight years as a combat engineer, deployed two times, then I decided I wanted to be a civilian again because I noticed that, as a TV show called *The Wire* used to say, "The game is rigged" from all angles.

Since I departed the military in 2016, I have recognized the Hand of God in my life. He protected me and guided me to this point of time. From the sewage of life, He cleaned me and molded me for Himself. He has replaced my thuggish robe with a holy robe and placed my feet on solid ground. I now know at present and recognize the voice of the Son of God who rescued me long ago. I also understand now—concerning assemblies actually preaching the gospel of Jesus Christ—the church is not perfect. The church is a hospital full of sick people trying to get right or stay right with God. I overreacted by leaving the church when I was 18 years old. I should have dug in and held the line or maybe even looked for a more sanctified church. Things could have gone very bad during my 20 years hiatus from God. I could have died in my iniquity and gone to Hell. It is only by the grace of God I can stand today to share these words with you.

Since I have regressed to the civilian sector, I have rededicated my life to Christ and have been walking with Him since. And yes, all the observations that I have made earlier about the church took place after I rededicated my life to Christ, including the part about me going from the club to the church. All those things are in the past; I am now a new creature in Christ Jesus. I do not hold a degree in ministry, but I am currently studying towards one. As of this moment, I am simply known as brother Michael, and that is fine by me.

Since then, the Holy Ghost has been speaking to me and sharing the thought of our Lord and Savior with me concerning many matters. I was confused at first and wondered:

"Why me, sayeth the man? Because I do as I wish, sayeth the Lord."

So here I am, writing about things I feel unqualified for, but I'm duty bound and convinced in my spirit of these revelations. I trust that this book found you well and whole, and that these words may be uplifting to you as you continue to read on. God's blessings to you.

CHAPTER SEVEN

Back to the Topic

According to Webster's dictionary, the word meek means:

"Having or showing a quiet and gentle nature: not wanting to fight or argue with people."

The world called it being a pushover. In spiritual warfare, this does not mean that we are pushovers; it means that we willingly choose to walk away from the Pyrrhic system of the beast. It means that we are mighty in Jesus' name, victorious in taking down strongholds by the power of the Blood of the Lamb of God, and that the devil acknowledges the anointing of Christ upon us and knows our names personally (Acts 19:13-[15]).

To be a meek man in the eyes of the Lord means to be free from the macho mentality of this world where muscle cars, big biceps and having a woman with a big butt is supposedly what makes you a man. All those things are finite, and they do not hold any value. All these things are just superficial things that will perish with time, and they do not represent the essence of man. The true essence of man can only be found in the Creator because we were made in His likeness and in His image (John 6:63). Self-respect, compassion, Christ-like chivalry (John 8:1-[11]), courage, honesty, and wisdom, those are qualities of a real man. Even the wealthiest man understands that eventually he will get old and die, and only the legacy you leave behind matters. Once more, only the work of righteousness will follow us. I know from personal experience that it can be hard to find the motivation to be upright sometimes, especially when all you ever knew was misery and hatred. However, this is why Jesus came to Earth. He came to give us abundant life, eternal life, and set a foundation for us to follow (Isaiah 53:3-5).

Can you imagine what it felt like being there in the presence of the Son of God? Walking among men, cloaked with humility and showing love and compassion, even to those who crucified Him? Well, if we endure until the end, we will all get to see Him face-to-face one day and experience that joy for ourselves. We must pray to the Father for strength daily so that He can teach us how to reciprocate the type of love our Maker extended towards the world some 2,000 years ago. This is the only way.

Now the "crafty snake" knows that not everyone will fall for the machismo bait, so just in case this exaggerated form of masculinity does not get you, it's on with the scholarly spirit. This spirit often gives birth to pompous personalities where one can speak, but no one would hear because no one can understand the fancy words he speaks, or people simply choose to reject the arrogant tone projected by the one speaking. The conceited spirit that usually walks with these pompous ones creates narcissism syndrome. Instead of trying to be more relatable to his peers, the narcissist man says, "You can't understand me because you are inferior." Then he goes and creates himself a vanity circle, and calls it "The Brotherhood."

From his self-propped high chair, the now high priest then begins to preach to his chosen ones. Another secret society is born; a cult founded out of pride based on the system of the beast. They all have the same rituals, but there is a little variation here and there. At the end, they all demand that you take an oath and drink from the "witch's cup."

Brothers, this is not the way of the Lord. These oaths are all part of the witch's ritual, and they signify pledging allegiance to the beast and taking his mark. They will not validate you before the KING (Mark 4:11-12). In addition, the machismo and pompous charismas are pinned against each other in the mainstream media, but they are of the same spirit, and they both glorify Satan, the ogre.

Now, let me be clear on something. To be an athlete or intellect is not evil in and of itself. To use these gifts to belittle your fellow men and/or to glorify oneself is the same as worshiping the beast and taking his mark or pledging allegiance to the beast's system.

- To My Sisters -

To be a meek woman in the eyes of the Lord is to turn down the beast's principle of objectification. Beauty is truly only skin deep. You age and then you die. Preserve your inner virtue, sisters.

I realize that women are no longer valued for their inherent beauty, and sisters are just objectified and exploited under the "sex sales" motto of this generation. All the same, you have the power to rebuke that sentiment by refusing to settle for this standard.

Too many women choose to fall for this "booty shaking and breast implant standard of validation" because they feel left out. They need to be reassured to feel validated (Gen. 3:16), but women should stop surrendering their God-given properties for the admiration of any man giving them compliments.

As a man, let me tell you, the only reason men have been getting away with objectifying and treating women like a piece of meat is because they let us. Truth be told, without the silicone and the miniskirts, we will still chase you because you are "flesh of my flesh," so maintain your virtues. The right man will come to you in due time. Stop settling for finite validations that will never fill the void you feel inside. This only leads to a deplorable existence; you must know who you are for yourselves, and only in Christ Jesus can you find your self worth. Otherwise, a dog dressed like a man will come and treat you like a female dog, and he will make you forget that you were made in the likeness of The Most High God. Neither should you let him mistake you for a bitch by dressing or behaving like one.

Furthermore, many sisters who are intoxicated by hate have been infiltrating the "Me Too" movement. When this movement first started in 2006, it was about rallying victims of sexual abuse so that their voices could be heard and they could find justice since the men elected to serve justice would often not do their part and reportedly: "Out of every 1,000 sexual assaults, 975 perpetrators will walk free" (source: rainn.org/statistics/criminal-justice-system). I say, let the women fight, give them a sword and a shield, let them "toe the line," and stand for righteousness. Lately, however, this movement resembles another tool created to destroy the remnants of the family structure. The protests I have seen in recent years have focused on promoting messages such as: "Women are the Future" and "Simply because I dress like a whore does not make me a whore." The last quotation is an oxymoron. The only reason a woman would feel comfortable dressing like a whore is because she is a whore. No respectable woman would ever walk around with clothes exposing her private parts. The spirit of whoredom that influences that type of logic may sometimes lay dormant for years while it secretly grows, but if it is not suppressed, it will eventually begin to influence sexual decadence in the host.

I saw this a lot growing up. I saw teenage girls following groups of women who also promoted slutty clothes as a norm. These girls were just trying to fit in, but before long, they would begin stripping their clothes off at private parties. And many of these girls then went on to stripping in strip clubs once they became old enough to legally dance in the club. And some even went on past the strip clubs into prostitution.

Anyone intoxicated by hate will always broadcast the wrong message because the wrong spirit influenced them. Hate only begets more hate. The devil is behind the behaviors of these evil men that abuse women, which led to the commencement of that movement. I stand in support of any victims of sexual assault. However, we should not forget who is the real enemy. It is a salutary thing for women who have been victims of sexual abuse to tell their story and shame the devil, regardless of the status of the perpetrator. In the Biblical epoch, these kinds of men were put to death (Deut. 22:23-27).

While I support the women's movement in dealing with their oppressors, it has taken a negative twist.

Just like with The Women's Rights Movement that started in 1848, The Great Depression of 1900, and The Civil Rights Movement in 1954, the beast is at it again. His favorite chess moves have always been problem>reaction>solution. These moves equate to Satan manipulating the population by introducing a problem, which causes a desired reaction; then he uses his own means to solve that problem. But the problem is never truly solved; it is just redefined to give us a false sense of resolvement. This is why the world keeps going in a circle chasing after its own tail, and we can never seem to find permanent solace.

Just like he behaved in the Garden of Eden with Adam and Eve, he has created a system of confusion and oppression between men and women, and now when he pulls the strings, it creates uproar and division between mates.

Let me expand about the Women's Rights Movement. This drive has been ongoing since 1848; it started with women demanding more equality and the right to vote.

According to the history of creation, I personally believe that women were created equal in essence to begin with, but Eve was created to play a supporting role. Men and women were both created to glorify God with their essence and existence, but men are supposed to lead (Galatians 3:23-28; Eph. 5:22-28; 1 Peter 3:1-7). This is the order established by God concerning the role of each personality. Due to the oppressive nature of men, women in the 19th century began to demand for their existence to be equally acknowledged. Acknowledgement that is in effect their own because it was already consecrated to them by God at creation (Gen. 1:27). Even though women have a supportive role to play, they should not be treated as second-class citizens, the Bible clearly states that husbands should love their wives as Christ loved the church (Eph. 5:25). The whole conflict could have been solved through Biblical principles, similarly to the case of slavery, the men of that period refused to listen to the voice of reason. Women of various ethnic backgrounds joined their voices to demand their heavenly imputed value.

During that process, no one took the time to inquire of Heaven above for a solution, and what was a justifiable request at first, turned into a battle of the sexes. This led the women standing on one side pushing for every impulse desire that entered their hearts because of their long-suppressed frustrations. At the other end, men cheerfully suppressed their voices because they felt that their virility was contested. This dispute later led women to exchange their femininities and nourishing qualities for a career, which made them feel equal and validated (Deut. 22:5). This further contributed to generations of children being raised by the Tell-lie-vision and the growth of dysfunctional family structures. With both parents now working full time jobs, this also contributed to a rise in the divorce rate due to an ever-present disconnection between the sexes.

What's more? Women wanted to be competitive athletes and started jacking themselves up with steroids to prove they could be stronger than men, while simultaneously losing more of their womanhood in the process.

What's more? God made both man and woman with testosterone and estrogen, but man has testosterone for their main hormone, and woman has estrogen as their main hormone. The testosterone in man's DNA is to help us fulfill our role as hunter-gatherer (provider). The estrogen is to help our women with their nurturing and protective roles. Once the DNA alteration began to take place through steroid injections, a conflict that should have been solved by going back to our Biblical foundations became a science project, which led to behaviors that are even more dysfunctional. Before we knew it, the dyke's movement was born, followed by lesbians and gay pride parades, and now 82 different gender identities are slowly becoming the new norm.

The demon knows that God's blessings are for the family structure according to God's design. This is why he constantly influences conflicts, which cause great discord between men and women. He then provides a tainted solution that leads us farther away from God. Each time we reach a resolution concerning one of his orchestrated problems, he creates another one more hideous for us to solve.

I will not attempt to defend the wealthy, but concerning my community, the like of chivalry that we have been experiencing since the 19th century was premeditated. The beast has bred a generation of "players and pimps boys" who were brought up without proper guidance. Let me first lay some foundation, then I shall connect it all back together to show why the Black community, specifically Black men, are so unstable and just don't seem able to get a good footing in life in general.

Following the Emancipation Proclamation, this demonic-fueled political system decided to go after Jacob, also known as Israel, from different angles by using new systems of oppression. Israel is everyone that carries the original gene (seed) on their chromosome going back to Abraham, who was the first Hebrew. These include mostly Black Americans, Caribbeans, Afro-Latinos and Africans; but also many other ethnics groups as well, such as Latinos, Native American, and White people with the actual Hebrew chromosome. The people ruling the land of Israel right now were inserted by the anti-Christ to create confusion and civil unrest. To understand the Israeli-Palestine conflict read: *The General's Son* and *Injustice* by Miko Peled. Miko Peled is an Israeli-American activist and the grandson of Dr. Avraham Katsnelson. Miko Peled's grandfather helped establish the current State of Israel and is also a signatory of the Israeli Declaration of Independence. The insertion of the misled and corrupt Israeli state in our history is why Jesus referred to them as the synagogue of Satan in Revelation 2:9 and 3:9. With that being said, I am not advocating for any type of hate against anyone; I am just stating the facts. God has a registry of all those belonging to the bloodline of Jacob. He will deal with this matter in due time accordingly.

One of the systems of oppression used by Lucifer in America to oppress Jacob after the Emancipation Proclamation included Jim Crow laws used to advocate segregation of laws, rules, and customs between Blacks and Whites; or better yet, between the minority classes and the ruling classes of those days. Jim Crow laws were legal in America until the mid-1960s, but many states in the U.S. today still secretly operate under that umbrella. Jim Crow meant there were (is) 2 different rules of laws to govern the White and other communities. The ruling class in those days happened to be the White folks, but it could have been anybody. This is why I don't hate White people because the Bible tells me that God warned our ancestors of this conditional prophecy concerning the prosperity of the original Jews in Deuteronomy 28. In this passage of the Bible, God laid out the blessings for obedience and the curse that would befall us if we went astray from His ordinances. We went astray, and the curses of Deuteronomy 28:15-68 have been heavy upon us throughout the century as a result of our disobedience. Notwithstanding, the Lord spread out the curses so that they would not all fall upon us in one generation. Otherwise, the world would not have a Savior, "for salvation is of the Jews" or a remnant of the Sons of Israel left upon the Earth (John 4:22; Gal. 3:16; John 14:6; Rev. 7:1-8).

Some of the key verses in Deuteronomy 28 in regards to the last paragraph are: 23 (this represents shackles and chains), 26 (Blacks slaves getting eaten by dogs, crocodiles and vultures), 29 (the desperate attempt by Blacks slaves to gain freedom), 30 (our women getting raped in front of us in the plantations), 32 (the children of Blacks slaves being taken from them), and 37 ("nigga" is the only byword recognized among all the nations of the earth).

One other way we can tell that the actual Jews of the Bible are mostly the Black folks that were taken from Africa and spread all over the world is the fact that they were taken from a place called Negroland. "Negroland " was in West Africa, and it was where, first the Europeans followed by the Americans, went to get Black people and brought them to the New World to be slaves. The main communities in that area in those days were called "Jews of the Bilad al-Sudan." These West African Jewish communities were connected to known Jewish communities from the Middle East, North Africa, Spain, and Portugal. "Various historical records attest to their presence at one time in the Ghana, Mali, and Songhai empires, then called the Bilad as-Sudan" (source: *Jews of the Bilad al-Sudan* Jerold Angelus (Ed.), Duct Publishing, 16 Aug 2011). The name Negroland is the translation of "Bilad al-Sudan," which means, "Land of the Blacks" in Arabic. The term "Negroland " was established by Geographer Herman Moll for the European settlers in 1729 in order to differentiate what belonged to England, Holland, Denmark and other colonizers in those days. The decrees in Deuteronomy 28:29 and 68 state, *"No man shall save thee,"* and *"No man shall buy you,"* which mean that Jesus is the only one with the authority, power, and will to restore Israel. The strength of man will not prevail against these curses. Black, Brown, Afro-Latinos, and all other ethnic groups carrying the Hebrew gene on their chromosome will continue to be undermined, patronized, and persecuted until the time of Revelation 7:1-8.

However, this does not mean that we should continue to be ignorant of our true identity or of the understanding of the continuous persecution of anyone who has even just a hint of melanin in their skin. The curse is not black! God did not curse people with black skin and made them three fifth of a man. Black people are under the curse of Deuteronomy 28 because we are the ones who killed His son and broke the covenant that God made with our forefathers. Notwithstanding, in Deuteronomy 30:1-10 the Lord states:

*"1. And it shall come to pass, when all these things are come upon thee, the blessing and the curse, which I have set before thee, and thou shalt call them to mind among all the nations, whither the LORD thy God hath driven thee, 2. And shalt return unto the LORD thy God, and shalt obey his voice according to all that I command thee this day, thou and thy children, with all thine heart, and with all thy soul; 3. That then the LORD thy God will turn thy captivity, and have compassion upon thee, and will return and gather thee from all the nations, whither the LORD thy God hath scattered thee. 4. If any of thine be driven out unto the outmost parts of heaven, from thence will the LORD thy God gather thee, and from thence will he fetch thee: 5. And the LORD thy God will bring thee into the land which thy fathers possessed, and thou shalt possess it; and he will do thee good, and multiply thee above thy fathers. 6. And the LORD thy God will circumcise thine heart, and the heart of thy seed, to love the LORD thy God with all thine heart, and with all thy soul, that thou mayest live. 7. And the LORD thy God will put all these curses upon thine enemies, and on them that hate thee, which persecuted thee. 8. And thou shalt return and obey the voice of the LORD, and do all his commandments which I command thee this day. 9. And the LORD thy God will make thee plenteous in every work of thine hand, in the fruit of thy body, and in the fruit of thy cattle, and in the fruit of thy land, for good: for the LORD will again rejoice over thee for good, as he rejoiced over thy fathers: 10. If thou shalt hearken unto the voice of the LORD thy God, to keep his commandments and his statutes which are written in this book of the law, **and if thou turn unto the LORD thy God with all thine heart, and with all thy soul**"* (Deuteronomy 30:1-10 KJV).

The prophecy in the Bible passage above is the reason why more and more minority groups—mostly Blacks—have begun to identify themselves as the actual Jews of the Bible within the last century. These minority groups made up mostly of Black people also began to fulfill the prophecy of Isaiah 44:5 when they started changing their names back to Hebrew names and surnames:

"1. Yet now hear, O Jacob my servant; and Israel, whom I have chosen: 2. Thus saith the LORD that made thee, and formed thee from the womb, which will help thee; Fear not, O Jacob, my servant; and thou, Jesurun, whom I have chosen. 3. For I will pour water upon him that is thirsty, and floods upon the dry ground: I will pour my spirit upon thy seed, and my blessing upon thine offspring: 4. And they shall spring up as among the grass, as willows by the water courses. **5. One shall say, I am the LORD'S; and another shall call himself by the name of Jacob; and another shall subscribe with his hand unto the LORD, and surname himself by the name of Israel"** (Isaiah 44:1-5 KJV; read also Isaiah 43-44).

For a more detailed breakdown of who is the true Israel, I recommend reading: *From Babylon to Timbuktu* by Rudolph R. Windsor; *Into Egypt Again With Ships* by Elisha J. Israel; *Hidden in Plain Sight* by Yoshiyahu & Huldah David; and *The Bible is Black History* by Dr. Theron D. Williams.

Under the new covenant paid for by Jesus at Calvary, "There is neither Jew nor Greek" (Gal. 3:28), but there are a couple of distinctions to be made. First, the woman in Revelation 12:1-6 who fled into the wilderness after giving birth to the man child—Jesus—who was to rule all nations with an iron rod represents the true Israelites of the Bible—not the Church of Christ! The woman (Israel) lived in the wilderness for 1,260 years after the ascension of Jesus Christ, where she was fed until the time for the curses in Deuteronomy 28:15-68 to run their course. Second, the persecution of the Church of Christ is what we are experiencing right now all over the world.

Christians in countries like China, Pakistan and Nigeria are persecuted publicly, and many are killed everyday. Since 2012, in Mexico, many of the religious leaders who dared to criticize the drug cartels or the Mexican government were kidnapped, tortured, and killed (source: USA Today, *23 Church leaders have been killed*). If the church was truly supposed to be raptured before the last tribulation spoken of in Matthew 24:21-31, then where is the rapture for all those people getting killed for their faith everyday? In America, we've been blessed thus far, but we can see the writing on the wall; the Christian's faith is slowly getting suppressed. The "Equality Acts," which is currently being developed by President Joe Biden's administration, have content clauses that aim to suppress the Christian faith, such as making it illegal for a minister to denounce same sex marriage (source: U.S. News.com-Equality Acts).

Okay, the foundation has been laid; let's go back to our sisters. Lucifer unleashed his arsenal against the woman (Israel) who gave birth to the Savior of the world to persecute her (Rev. 12:1-6). From the legislative to the executives' branches all over the world, to the institution of Jim Crow laws and the Willie Lynch principles here in America, these effects are still prevalent in our neighborhoods until this day. And only through the power of the Holy Ghost and a disposition of our hearts and minds towards Christ can we overrule its effects.

Taking off around the 1970s, this monster created chaos in the poor communities by promoting gang cultures, drug use, gun violence, and any other similar narratives, this led to a rise in criminal activities and the destruction of self-respect in our communities. This caused mass incarceration of our fathers and brothers. That same beast saturated the mainstreams with the images of men in fur coats and gator shoes, gold chains and gold teeth, walking around with perms and jerry curls in their hair, with pants sagging showing their ass. The purpose of these saturations was to project bogus role models. This caused generations of black men to be raised under this substituted influence.

Many of the brothers during that period stood in the gap to help make a positive difference, but the darkness was overwhelming. Just like our big brother Adam, we as men have failed as a whole to protect you from the serpent. It is because of that, this ogre managed to get to you and our children. For that, I present to you our sincere apology.

To declare that, "Just because I dress like a whore, does not make me a whore," is an oxymoron. When it comes to spiritual warfare, you cannot play with Satan's stuff or dress with clothes from his wardrobe selections and expect to receive honor from this world. Wearing clothes from the devil's closet invites evil spirits to allure you, and it awakens men sexually. These clothes do not serve any other purpose. You cannot say that you went to the store to buy sexy clothes hoping that it will dissuade men's attention. You buy them with the hope to be noticed by a charming prince, but instead, the jackals come out to play. The sediment of sexual assault and sexually abusive relationships often substitute the woman's yearning for affirmation. This serpent has capitalized on the fruit of his mischievousness at the garden, and women should resist these evil spirits and not play into his traps. In addition, you should exhibit caution for your little ones because if those seductive spirits cannot reach you, then they will go after the ones you love. The weak ones in the pack are usually the children; therefore, teach your daughters to behave with dignity, consideration, moderation, and stop entertaining these celebrities.

Women should stop dressing like whores and stop following these celebrities. They are not role models. They are just vessels being used by Satan's goddess spirits. They are possessed with the spirit of the "Queen of the Coast," which is just another name for "devils," and that's how they call the spirit of Jezebel in Africa, and their job is to magnetize you and to seduce men. Jezebel, Lucifer's daughter, to be idols of sexual arousing, has anointed them. Their jobs are to make women feel empowered and promote the practice of sexual liberty with or without a man, but God created man and woman to be mates. Anything external of that norm is an abomination and a curse before the Lord. I do not know if they are even aware of this fact, but as God's children, you should not follow along after them. Although we are in the world, we are not of the world (Ex. 20:1-7; 1 John 2:15-17).

Conclusively, many women say there are no real men left, and that is a depressing reality in too many of our communities. At the same time, these women are looking for a good man to provide for them in the "players and pimps boys bin" aka the club. Women have to stop looking for a significant other according to the beast's projection, and raise their sons to be the type of man they would want for themselves—the type of man who will improve our community (Matt. 7:12) and not contribute to the problem. We need more people in political office and less on the streets. Where does it say that strong black men can only succeed at sports and hip-hop?

Likewise, the men complain about the deficiency of good female counterparts, but too many of us have given our sex a bad rep, and most of us do not even know what a good woman is. We want a mother figure that looks like Nicki Minaj to cater to our needs. Furthermore, this player and pimp mentality must stop. The fact that we did not have a father growing up should be our motivation to be there for our children and not an excuse to leave. By being the bigger man today, we will stop the perpetual cycle that we have been tricked into. Stop following these puppet celebrities! They are not our representatives. They are part of the beast's system, and living their type of lifestyles will require your souls. I do not know if they are even aware of that fact, but as followers of Jesus Christ, we cannot live like them (Deut. 4:15-19; Acts 7:42-[43]).

All those misconceptions are from the devil. He is a principal illusionist, and he has many millennia of experience. However, it does not mean that we have to embrace those misconceptions or live by them. Our Comforter is here to guide us into all truth, so we ought to let Him guide us.

- To Protect and Serve -

As stated before, there is more darkness than light in the world right now. It's always easy to blame the offending party, but the truth is, Satan has been working on the law enforcement officials for a long time as well. They were slave hunters before they were cops. They shoot first because they fear. They fear because they were trained to fear, and they were trained to fear because perfect fear cast out love (1 John 4:18).

Many police officers are corrupt, but I also believe that God has children everywhere (Rom. 11:1-5). Moreover, this is a sad position for a righteous individual to be in: wanting to do the right thing and to make the world a better place, but having to do it under the system of the beast. There are no winners under this system because it has all been pre-conditioned to collapse in order to usher in the desperate need for a savior. The anti-Christ is clearly getting ready to make his grand entrance. Nevertheless, I will remain optimistic as in the days of Judges, until the King tells me otherwise.

A few years ago, I saw a story about a mental health physician in Florida who was shot in the leg by a police officer while lying on his back with both hands up.

As the story goes, the mental health physician was just trying to reassure one of his escaping mental patients. He was persuading the patient to return with him to the psychiatric hospital to continue his treatment. However, someone in that area called the police and said that they were two black men suspiciously sitting on the curb. The police showed up and instructed the doctor to lay flat on his back with his hands in the air. The man complied and explained that the young gentleman was a mental patient of his. Everything was going well until the cop decided to fire three shots at the man while he was lying on his back, and one bullet hit the man in the leg. I felt irate. I wanted to see this cop's head in a basket, removed by the guillotine. I wanted to go out on the street and march to protest against such an odious crime, and if need be, even burn the community.

As the story unraveled, the mental health physician is shown being treated in a hospital with the police officer that shot him by his side. The victim asked the officer, "Why did you shoot? I was compliant and my hands were up in the air." The cop looked at him with a distant stare in his eyes and said, "I don't know. I just don't know why I shot you." This made me feel even angrier, but my wrath was no longer towards the officer; it was redirected towards a world that is so crazy because fear rules the heart of those who vowed to protect us. That day, I said to myself, "This foul beast is annoying and has become a nuisance to my soul, Lord." Then I cried out, "Yahushuah Ha-Mashiach, we need you Lord! We need you now!"

The reality of systemic racism in America is true, and I cannot deny it because I have been a victim of it myself. If I was not saved, only God knows where I would be. In the system of the beast, the reality is that even those who strive to make a difference in the application of law and policy are repressed. The sellouts are bought off, and those who cannot be bought are shot in the head in broad daylight while riding in their motorcade.

If something starts to work too well in the community, legislation quickly gets changed to smother it, and any new policies that aim at improving the land and promote righteousness are stalled until forgotten.

Let's use the example of the President's Council on Youth Fitness for instance. It was established by President Eisenhower in 1956, and later renamed the President's Council on Physical Fitness by President Kennedy in order to reach out to all American's citizens. Under this program, President Kennedy demanded that all U.S. citizens participate in regular physical activities, as well as that all military personnel be physically fit. There was just no place for the fatties in President Kennedy's army. This promoted a healthy and most capable military force for the U.S., and the American's citizens alike, both physically and mentally. This made us a stronger nation to contend with. That program has been sustained by various administrations since then, but its effect is no longer visible. Big Pharma and the spirit of consumerism have made sure of that. And obesity, which causes all sorts of illnesses, has become a national issue.

Likewise, if we had kept the principle of Deuteronomy 20:7 and 24:5 in place, or at least built our military standards based on them, many of our military brothers and sisters who have committed suicide would still be with us today, and less members of our military would be divorcees. Every provision mankind ever had need for, whether it be spiritual or natural, is in the Bible; all we have to do is take the time to look for it. In Deuteronomy 20:7, God tells us that a newlywed soldier should not be sent to battle (deployment) and leave his wife behind, "*lest he die in the battle, and another man take her.*" God also stated in Deut. 24:5

that the newlywed soldier should stay at home with his wife for one year in order for them to consume their marriage in peace. That's because even though chariot's wars were a necessary evil in those days, the Lord valued marriage as a sacred institution well above the need for blood (Gen. 9:5; Lev. 17:11; Hebrew 9:22; Gen. 2:24; Matt. 19:3-9). Nowadays, military contracts, crude oil deals, minerals, and "dead presidents" are valued above the well being of the constituents.

Finally, everyone is talking about the ever-increasing crime rate in Chicago, but no one wants to talk about the mysterious crates of machine guns and ammunition being dumped in the ghettos at night. Who are the mysterious delivery drivers who keep fuelling the appetite for destruction in that part of America? Whoever they are, they're on Lucifer's payroll for sure. It seems to me that the same hand that militarized law enforcement militarized the streets. It's all just a game to these monsters.

I am not a cop, and I don't know what I would do if I was walking in your shoes, but as a preacher once said, "Regardless of where or who you work for, remember that the one we all have to answer to is God. He is the first line Supervisor of all mankind. When you walk on the job each day, He is who you should picture yourselves clocking in for."

The same Satanic hand orchestrated all of those aforementioned conflicts; the problem>reaction>solution move is intended to create so much frustration within the populaces, that people get desperate for whatever form of relief comes next. Then the devil comes and offers a solution to his own trap to make men feel good in exchange for their allegiance. This move is getting old, and we can no longer afford to be ignorant to Satan's devices.

Ergo, although I recognize the values of activism - because our Lord loves to take what was meant for evil and use it for good - let us not forget that the goal is Heaven.

- Dead Men on Parole -

Whether we are rich, poor, black, brown, or white, we are all meek. All the money in the world cannot buy us eternal happiness; skin pigmentation will not validate us, and no flesh will be glorified before the Lord. Only through Jesus Christ can we be glorified (1 Cor. 1:27-31; Phil. 3:4-9). Moreover, God is looking for true worshipers to worship Him in Spirit and in truth, and as His children. He wants us to walk in a quiet and gentle nature as well so that we can bring honor and justice to His name through the diligence of our faith. Moreover, even unbelievers are expected to be unpretentious in their lives because no one can truly control their destiny.

Some people may still say they're not meek and feel like the statements above do not apply to them because of a certain gift, beauty, or inner strength; but compared to whom do they measure this logic? Certainly not God, so let us do justice to God for a moment.

We are an ingrate and disloyal creation (Roman 3:9-24), and the only reason we are still here is that God spared us (2 Peter 3:9). So, let it be known to all men:

Long ago, in the eternal realm, the judgment of the earth was held; The Trinity and His counsel gathered on top of the Holy Mountain of God, and the tribunal of the earth began. Similar to the days of Noah, the whole land was found to be guilty. The sentence of that verdict was a re-creation, following the complete annihilation of the earth. The archangels dispatched the holy angels, and as the sentence was about to be executed, the Father lifted His index finger and said, "POSTPONE THAT JUDGMENT."

The Heavens stood still as the Father explained to His holy angels His final plan of salvation for the sons of man. The angels were perplexed, but they understood that the wisdom of God is flawless. The archangels regarding the earth gave new directives. Following this marvelous revelation to the armies of Heaven, the four angels dispatched to the four corners of the earth in Revelation 7:1 were then instructed to hold back the four winds of the earth until all the Elects were sealed as commanded by the sovereign God (Matt. 13:24-30, 24:31; Rev. 7:1-17).

To put it plainly, we are all dead men on parole. Whether or not we choose to acknowledge it is irrelevant; the fact remains the same. The Bailsman of the earth will return shortly to collect on His bond, and He will start with His bondsmen, the church.

This is why we must be meek before the Lord (Rom. 12:1-3). To be honest, without Christ as our Savior, we are merely "animated dust particles." 120 years at the most is what the Lord permits, then the body must return to the dust from where it came. The Spirit of God returns to Him, and the souls go to sleep until judgment day. Eugenics may allow for a few more years, but the final judgment cannot be avoided.

We have already been given an extension with the cost of which was the life of the KING at Calvary. We must use this time wisely. We have been commissioned to carry our cross while operating wisely and with gentleness (Matt. 10:16; Matt 16:24-26). We are bidden to be humble even with our anointing, just like Jesus was obedient to the Father. Despite His authority as the Son of God, He did not follow His own will but fulfilled only the will of the Father who sent Him. This will distinguish us in the final test: obedience to the Father who speaks to us through the Son, who lives within us as the Holy Spirit (see Proverbs 3:31-35; Proverbs 29:22-27; Luke 12:35-40; John 6:35).

CHAPTER EIGHT

Food for the Soul

"Blessed are they which do hunger and thirst after righteousness: for they shall be filled" (Matt. 5:6).

Have you ever felt tired and overwhelmed by this world, sensing that this world's injustice and immorality is simply unbearable? If your answer is yes, do not worry. It is during these periods that your soul thirsts, and you hunger for justice and just feel a deep desire for Heaven. You are not alone. Jesus promises one day to satisfy this thirst and hunger (Apoc. 21:3-7).

- Civil Unrest -

Given the recent turmoil in America, this verse also means that burning the entire city over justifiable frustrations will not quench this famine. It is a constructive thing for the people of the land, from every ethnic background, to come together under the desire for justice and peace. I am in no way excusing the action of fear-driven or demon possessed, trigger-happy cops. However, I must stick to the revelation given from the Text. The only true utopia is in the eternal realm, the new heaven, and the new earth. The only true peace is in Christ Jesus. I truly hope that God will use all those protests to lead us to something positive.

While all this pandemonium has been unfolding, the puppeteers were working behind the curtain all along. The first thing that the Lord had brought to my attention was the re-launching of their SpaceX Dragon spacecraft on May 30, 2020 from Launch Complex 39A from Cape Canaveral, Florida. The first time NASA launched the spacecraft was about 8 years ago on October 8, 2012.

If you study biblical numerology or simply look for the biblical meaning of numbers 8, 20, 12, 30, and 39 online, you will know that those numbers are not accidental. The number 8 represents new beginnings and denotes a new order of creation. 20 means holiness and redemption, 12 signifies government of God but also government by election. 30 represents the beginning of ministry. The number 39 (which is 3 times 13) relates to punishment carried out upon oneself or administered by others. This reinforces my belief that witches and warlocks run NASA's space program. This leads me to believe, as mentioned earlier in this book, that these demon worshipers are preparing the stage for the beast.

What I mean by that is: Heaven is God's domain, and the devil's authority as the prince of the power of the air was devastated at Calvary. We know that the second beast will be working signs of wonders and will be able to make fire come down from Heaven to deceive men (Rev. 13:13-18). To secretly create such a grand illusion requires much work, and what a better time than now? NASA even recently proclaimed that an asteroid named "god of chaos" is now heading to Earth for 2068. I don't know what this new lie is about, but it sounds more like a strong man or a principality breaking through one of CERN's satanic portals from the bottomless pit into our realm than an asteroid to me. CERN is "The European Organization for Nuclear Research." They have over 680 institutes spread out around the world where they are conducting various research on how to create new elements such as "the god particle." At their headquarters in Geneva, Switzerland, they've been conducting experiments by smashing particles together at nearly the speed of light in a tunnel 17 miles long, about 574 feet underground with the hope to create the said particle. This is what their webpage tells us. However, the symbol in their logo is clearly the number "666" interlocked together, and the main monument at their headquarters is a statue of Shiva, the Hindu god of destruction (source: The Wall Street Journal/CERN's symbols). These symbols lead many people, including myself, to believe that the CERN organization is doing much more than scientific studies, such as potentially attempting to open doorways between the physical realm and the spiritual realm using science mixed with dark magic. The sole purpose for such doorways or portals would be to usher in demonic spirits here to Earth. Sadly, they are probably hoping for some sort of rewards from these demons, but demons have no care and no love for mankind, that's why they are called "demons." Not to worry, if the Almighty God allows them to succeed, it will surely be for His purpose and because He has a plan in place (see Gen. 50:20; Rev. 6:1-11; Rev. 9:1-21 and Rom. 8:28-31).

I don't know if the MK Ultra Mind Control Program really exists, but it's strangely convenient for recurring tragedies, such as road rage and mass shootings, to escalate in the midst of a pandemic. At a time when the country's patience is weak and frustration is very high, it is a perfect formula for a state of agitation, which then leads to recklessness, followed by a formal policed world. The forced vaccination of the people is then put in place. Later, the one world system is justified for the sake of "the greater good." The devil is really looking forward to cashing out on his long time investments of hate, division, and paranoias, but I remain optimistic and hopeful in our God's mercy. I believe that

Jesus allowed all those recent events so that we can be conscious of the time; think of it as a wake-up call. Although the devil will eventually have his Pyrrhic victory, the final judgment will come, and it will be the end for all of them walking the path of darkness. We have nothing to fear but God Himself.

The second matter that was brought to my attention is the LGBTQ community joining the Black Lives Matters protests, and now the Civil Rights Act is being proclaimed as justification for their practices. This led me to dig more into the creation of the Black Lives Matter (BLM) movement, then I found out that two of the founders and leaders of that movement are queers.

It may seem counterintuitive for a black man to talk that way, but BLM can't lead us out of Egypt into the promised land. It is simply not possible for the spirit of sexual decay to provide tangible relief toward the children of God. If any genuine good comes out of this movement, it is because of God's zeal for His chosen people (Rom. 8:28). In my view, the devil is just trying to intercept our repatriation to the holy city in Jerusalem with this organization. This is a prime example of the devil disguising himself as an angel of light, but I know who my God is (Luke 19:20-24; Cor. 11:14-15; Gen. 50:20-21).

The devil did something similar in the past to the Moab nations of Nepal and India. He provided them with a messiah, Siddhartha Gautama, to hinder the reception of the gospel of Christ for generations to come into that part of the world. This happened in the 6th century BC with a character known as Buddha. This is one of the reasons why the Holy Spirit had to delay Paul's entry to the Moab provinces of Asia and Mysia (Acts 16:6-10). The Lord was breaking the fallow ground for apostle Paul before sending him in that region to preach the gospel due to the many false gods, traditions, and teachings that were—and are still—prevalent in this part of the world. This is yet another reminder of the importance of walking in the Holy Spirit so that we do not get hurt by taking on the right task at the wrong time, or the wrong task altogether (see also Matt. 12:28-29).

In the story of Buddha, it is said that he became god through enlightenment after sitting under the Bodhi tree in meditation and finally achieved full consciousness. That is why he is referred to as the "awakened one." Before getting to that point, however, he was born the son of emperor Suddhodana in Lumbini, Nepal. He was raised in the royal palace sheltered from the reality of the world outside the palace's walls. It is said that when he became of age, he decided to venture outside to see the world and became greatly troubled after seeing poverty, death, and miseries. This led him to leave his family in an effort to resolve the problems he had witnessed after venturing outside his father's kingdom. After contemplating the injustice and inequality of the land for a while, he decided to fast for 40 days, and it is during that time that he developed the principle of "nothingness," and found his "dharma." This revelation came after he observed the water flow off a stream nearby during his fasting. That was where he realized the water just followed its course to its designated point. The nothingness principle simply dictates that if we just follow the flow of life and cease to seek material things, then we have nothing to worry about. The universe will provide the need if we get rid of the want. He then went forward to renounce his name, family, and wealth to live among the common folks. They in turn nourished him, clothed him, and even gave him a temple to practice and teach his faith. He was eventually beheld as the Buddha and later became known as the great awakened one.

The problem with this story is that Buddha never truly gave up his name. Regardless of his disposition, the son of emperor Suddhodana was still the son of royalty. What I mean by that is, in that part of the world, whatever people of privilege say is law. The poor and the less fortunate do not have a voice. The nobility recognizes you only if you have a dollar sign or some sort of prestige attached to your family name. The average and the poor people of the land are quick to prostrate themselves in front of the rich inhabitants in the hope of a blessing in return. The same may be said here in America, but we just have many more opportunities here. Our lips do not have to embrace any keister unless we choose to. Thus indeed, the people in Buddha's time had no choice but to honor him. The thought of the emperor's son dying of hunger, hyperthermia, or any other cause during his stay in their city was simply not an option. In those days, it was not uncommon for entire villages to be destroyed at the behest of an unhappy leader. Who of sound mind would question the king's son and dare not give him shelter or alms? This monarchy is what the devil used to cloud the mind of the people of the land of Nepal and the surrounding Buddhist country. This false doctrine of nothingness, which supposedly leads to enlightenment, has cost millions of peoples their souls since then. Some even went as far as setting themselves on fire because of this belief.

If a servant or slave of king Suddhodana had left the safety of the palace to go around and attempt the same thing, there would have never been a Buddha. This servant would have been killed because another would have taken his place and dressed in his clothes to attempt to enter the palace and have a better life for himself to supply for his family. In my opinion, Siddhartha Gautama, also known as Buddha, should have used his wealth and power to help bring reliefs in the region, such as a water irrigation systems to help support the farmlands so that the people would have more substance in order for them to support themselves.

He should have shared his wealth with the needy instead of having the needy feed him; this would have brought more prosperity for all the people of the province.

Buddha's observation of the water stream, which led to the "nothingness" principle, is flawed. Water does not just go to its predestined point; water follows the path set by the Creator. It follows God's injunction. Scientists call it the "hydrologic cycle" or "water cycle." These cycles are condensation, precipitation, infiltration, runoff, and evaporation. It's a long process, but the short version is: Condensation forms clouds, resulting in precipitation, which leads to rain. This rain falls to the surface of the earth and infiltrates the soil or flows to the ocean (through rivers, lakes, and water streams) as runoff. That same water later on evaporates (with the help of the sun) returning moisture to the atmosphere to replenish the formed clouds. This is the cycle of nature concerning water, and it is comparable to the cycle of life. The clouds represent Heaven, the ocean, the established order (government of the land), while the surface water, the inhabitants of the land, condensation, precipitation and evaporation would be the spirit realm. See, an Indisputable Force connects all things, and His name is Jesus (Isa. 55:8-11; John 1:1-3; Ps. 119:89-91). The concept of nothingness has no value. It is just the brainchild of a confused young prince. Although he meant well, he was just another pawn in the enemy's hand. Buddha has no power, and he cannot save anyone, not even himself. Likewise, no queer will be able to bring genuine peace to the Black community. Besides, the main financial contributor for the Black Lives Matter Organization, George Soros, is from the synagogue of Satan (Rev. 3:9).

The Civil Rights Act that was supposed to guarantee equality for the Hebrews is now the justification for some sort of alliance between sexual perversions and the oppression of slavery. Now to be clear, this law in of itself cannot set Israel free (Deut. 28:68), but the whole concept of equating sexual preferences with 400 plus years of oppression is a travesty. This is the type of parody the hidden hand likes to create. Satan knows that the only way out of our dilemmas is Jesus Christ, so he keeps shifting the play to keep us in a trance. He knows that all the ungodly fuss will only benefit him, so he'll just keep adding fuel to the fire. Until America, "The Christian Nation," includes the King of kings and Lord of lords in the battle, this charade will continue.

I know how some of you feel. I sometimes wish life would be that simple so that we could simply rise up and make everything right, and through our sheer strength, we could solve all of our problems. This would make the decision-making process simpler. However, Heaven rules over the earth, and we are on borrowed time. The prophecy of the end of time will come whether we accept it or not. The Creator is the only one who can reset the current atmosphere and extend the hour. It is my prayer that the Father would give us another hundred years, but nevertheless, not my will, but thy will be done Father, in Jesus' name, Amen & Amen.

Now, let's say God obliged the prayer above; here lies a dilemma. If we get the hundred-year extension, what will be our demeanor, and will our attitudes change? For if we do not honor God for His mercy, and we forsake to honor His name moving forward, the case of mankind will be worse than before.

In closing, as painful as it is to see a man get choked to death on live television, I cannot allow my skin pigmentation to lead my thoughts because this will only feel my heart with hate. I must do the work of the Father who sent me, who raised me up when I was dead and delivered me from a legion of demons. For if, it was not for Him, I would not have made it this far. Praise be to the Son of God, born Son of man, who came in the flesh, died for me, then rose again on the third day, who has promised me life eternal.

Deviating one way or the other from the truth will leave room for Satan to attempt and discredit the message given to me by the Holy Spirit.

May "the peace of God, which passeth all understanding, keep your hearts and minds through Christ Jesus," and "The grace of our Lord Jesus Christ be with you all. Amen" (Philippians 4:7, 23).

- Suitable Steps -

"Blessed are the merciful: for they shall obtain mercy" (Matt. 5:7).

This verse speaks for itself, so I will only point out a few points on the relation between the instruction and The Instructor.

In Exodus 33:18-19, Moses asks the LORD to show him His glory, and the LORD answered:

"I will make all my goodness pass before thee, and I will proclaim the name of the LORD before thee; and will be gracious to whom I will be gracious, and will show mercy on whom I will show mercy."

In the next chapter, verses 5 to 7, the LORD comes down and proclaims:

"The LORD, The LORD God, merciful and gracious, long suffering, and abundant in goodness and truth, Keeping mercy for thousands, forgiving iniquity and transgression and sin, and that will by no means clear the guilty; visiting the iniquity of the fathers upon the children, and upon the children's children, unto the third and the fourth generation."

This may sound sappy to some of you, but when I first read this story, I was walking with a young and naïve faith. As I was reading it, I was expecting the glory of the LORD to be manifested like a scene from an action movie. I was expecting a magnificent demonstration of power and thunder, like the kind of exhibition you see in these Marvel movies. I guess being a new-age baby, I was preconditioned to look for a superficial show of force; however, our God does not work that way. He is beyond the understanding of man. His revelation is converse, and His nature is pure. I believe what Moses witnessed was still the most magnificent unveil the eye of a man has seen, but the records only speak of what was proclaimed; and what was proclaimed is God's attributes.

The glory of The Lord is His attributes, His nature, and His temperament if you will. He is merciful and gracious, long suffering, and abundant in goodness and truth. Who He is as the Creator, manifested through His action, is His glory. No magic trick there, just the essence of The Living God manifested to a mortal.

Furthermore, in Deuteronomy 23:14, the LORD commanded Israel to keep their camp holy because He is in their midst. As a Holy God, He demands that His subjects be holy. He also warned them He would turn away from them if He saw unclean things in the camp.

In addition, in 1 Peter 1:13-16, brother Peter reminds us that God wants us to be holy in all that we do, and that we ought not to conform to our past and our evil desires because it is written, *"Be holy because I am holy."*

The attribute of mercy is an essential part of a good relationship with the Quintessential. This means that if we are in Christ, and He is in us, we should of course have a merciful heart. This response is simply a suitable step of fellowship with God. Therefore, the promise of blessings for the merciful is in direct correlation to the command of being holy, as our Father in Heaven is Holy.

The reward of obtaining mercy in return, is for being good and obedient children and walking in the likeness of our Father. Furthermore, as Christians, it ought not be a burden to love God because we want to be good sons and daughters of the Most High.

It's like when you were a kid, and your dad said, "If you clean your bedroom, I'll take you out for ice cream." Although you may have cleaned the room because of the incentive, deep inside, you really just wanted to spend time with your dad. The taste of the ice cream is long gone, but the time spent in fellowship with each other remains. Fellowship with the Father shall be eternally more memorable.

- A Servant After My Own Heart -

"Blessed are the pure of heart, for they shall see God" (Matt. 5:8).

In 1 Samuel 13:14, the prophet Samuel referred to future King David as a man after God's own heart. Since we have all sinned and fallen short of the glory of God, they must be certain attributes that led to David earning such a noble title. Now we know when we read about David the king of Israel, he was far from perfect, but God still established his throne as a perpetual rulership (Ezekiel 34:23-24, 37:24-25). The definition of the term *"a man after my own heart"* is:

"Someone admired by another because of perceived similarities," or "someone I can agree with."

David is given such honor by God, but not because he was perfect. God, who looks inwardly, saw honorable qualities in King David that made him acceptable to Him. When David misbehaved, however, God did not withhold His disappointment or judgment against him (2 Sam. 11:26-27; 2 Sam. 12:1-12). The same can be said about Moses who is labeled a friend of God (Exodus 33:11; Deut. 34:10-12; Deut. 32:51-52).

Like David, Moses also had many flaws, but God bestowed great honor to his name. The like of which no other man, until the Son of man, had received in Israel. These two men were pure of heart in the eyes of God, so He recognized them and honored them accordingly. In addition, they both "saw," or experienced the attributes of God on a more intimate and personal level. Seeing what great honor was bestowed on these two men, one can't help but ask: *how do I get a pure heart of my own?* Reading about the life of Christ is fulfilling enough, but I know the pressure of trying to fit in Jesus' shoes can bear, so I will use the examples of David, Moses, and Job instead.

Throughout the book of Psalms, we can see David's qualities on display. His reverence can be found in Psalms 62:1-12, his obedience in 40:1-10, a repentant heart crying out in 25:11-20, and his faith in the LORD is an anamnesis in Psalm 23. King David is also recognized as a man who longed and pursued justice and mercy for God's people (1 Samuel 24, 26:7-25; 2 Sam. 4, 9:1-13, 21:1-14).

David operated in righteousness towards his people, even with those who would persecute him. His sole desire during his life was to bring honor to God. Although he fumbled many times on the way, he remained confident and persistent in his quest to walk in God's precepts.

King David is awarded the "Golden Age" era during his rulership because he determined that we are merely subjects of a higher conflict in which God holds all the cards, and we can only be made whole again through Him (Psalm 8:4-8; Psalm 84; see also Job 36:22 to Chapter 42 and Jude).

Just like David, Moses displayed discretion at the mount towards Israel. Despite their stiff neck, he interceded their preservation (Exodus 32:7-14), and Moses' disposition was extremely unselfish. I don't know if I could have done the same thing if I were in his place—refusing an offer from God Himself to make me one great nation. It was quite a proposition, but the heart of Moses was more concerned with the reputation of the Almighty and the security of the people. He pleaded with God for the people so that God would not go down and kill them all for committing idol worship, then Moses went down and chastised them himself for dancing around a golden calf naked.

According to the Text, this display of compassion by Moses towards the children of Israel changed the mind of God on the matter, and the nation of Israel was spared on that day. Only those who had participated in the idol worship were slain.

When the captains over thousands and hundreds returned from battle with the Medianites women in Numbers 31:13-24, Moses quickly moved into action. He remembered the plague that befell upon Israel concerning similar behaviors (Num. 25:1-2) and began the cleansing of the camp.

Moses was often faced with the challenge of preserving the life of the children of Israel. He even had to plead for his own sister's life at one point (Numbers 12:1-15). God gave him the authority to be as a god for the people (Ex. 4:16; 7:1-2), but despite his high title, he remained humble before the LORD (Num. 16:1-5). Moses, to the best of his ability, kept his heart pure and free of pride. However, despite his humility, he also made some mistakes.

Moses was forbidden to enter Canaan because he stroked the rock twice with the staff of the Lord the second time instead of speaking to it as ordered by God (Num. 20:1-12). Moses was commanded to do that in order to provide water for the children of Israel, but his frustration with Israel caused him to lose his temper. The rock here represents the Rock of Ages - Jesus Christ, striking the rock twice the second time symbolized that Christ would be crucified twice for the sins of men. What he did was out of frustration of dealing with the stiff-necked nation of Israel, but it was a dreadful act that required judgment.

God made Moses as a god, and God's words cannot return to Him void. In effect, what Moses did as a "god man" when he stroked the rock twice could not be overlooked, but God still showed mercy and allowed Moses to see the land He promised them from a distance. Our Father knows that we are weak, and the level of authority He put upon our brother Moses bore much weight. To whom much is given, much is necessary.

In the case of brother Job, he believed his good deeds and offerings were the foundation of righteousness, and he thought he knew God. His test was authorized by God to produce humility and dependence upon God and God only (Isaiah 64:6; Psalm 103:10-22; Job 11:4-6; Job 42:1-6). Job and his friends did not understand that in those days, God declared righteousness upon men according to His mercy because all our good deeds are as a spoiled rag before the Lord. Nevertheless, Job was pure of heart because he was living under the law at the time, and he was obedient to the law of sanctification and offered burnt offerings to God continually (Job 1:1-5). Nonetheless, the law was mainly an educational tool; our justification comes from—and through—Jesus Christ alone. By the time God was done ministering to Job and his friends, they were again acceptable in the sight of the LORD (Job 42:1-9).

When Satan came to inquire of Job, God chose to oblige because the whole earth was technically guilty of sin. However, the Father is always a step ahead (Gen. 50:19-20; Ex. 22:9; Job 42:10-17).

Quick Note: Satan cannot be compared to God because they are not equal. There is just no comparison between them. One of God's steps equals a thousand of

Satan's steps. It is only because God allows it that Satan is still able to move freely.

Throughout all the generations until Jesus, the Blameless One, came to fulfill God's standard, men were handpicked as righteous by God, according to His estimate of each era. However, this system of measurement is no more. For those of us who are saved today, God no longer sees us. He sees His Son living in us. The blood of Jesus has purified us and sanctified us, so now we are as Adam was in the garden before the fall, covered in God – Christ – glory.

Okay, now Zophar, Job's friend, was right to say, "God exacted of thee less than thine iniquity deserveth" (Job 11:4-[6]), but he was unknowingly speaking about all of mankind, including himself. Zophar did not fully understand God, and no man defines God's standard; only God can reveal the true intent of His actions towards us. Zophar condemned himself by speaking such vain words against Job. He was speaking out of self-proclaimed righteousness, just like a true Pharisee.

Here we can also see another example of God's temperament, for He is not a respecter of person but a rewarder of faith (Acts 10:25-35; Luke 18:9-14). God allowed such a harsh test to overtake Job because He was looking forward to giving brother Job double for his trouble according to His Law. Additionally, God wanted to bless Job so his story would enlighten and empower us for generations, confirming the principle that God blesses us to be a blessing unto others (Job 42:7-10; 1 Sam. 1:1-28).

From the examples of these three men, we can therefore conclude being pure of heart means being transparent in our infirmities before God. It means that we acknowledge our iniquities, our nature, and place all our hopes upon Him. Additionally, it does not mean we will not see adversities, but Jesus promises that we shall see the Hand of God working for us throughout the storm (Isa. 54:17; Ps. 34:7, 17-22; John 6:40).

In the end, we shall all see Him face-to-face (1 John 3:2-3; 1 Cor. 13:12). The pure heart may fall, but they shall not remain down for long (Prov. 24:16-20) because Jesus will restore them all. In this life and the next, the Lord is with us.

When judgment befell upon David for sleeping with Bathsheba, he pleaded with God through Psalm 51 in verse 5. He acknowledged his inherent iniquity in verses 6 and 7, confessed the lust of his heart and asked God to clean him. In verses 8 and 9, David declared that his joy is in the LORD and pleaded with God for their relationship to be restored. In verses 10 and 11, he asked to be purified and renewed with a right spirit. He also petitioned that God would not cast him away from His presence or remove the Holy Spirit from him. In verses 12 to 19, David proclaimed his commitment to serve God and to continue giving Him praises. The Father had not yet answered him, but David knew and professed there was no one else he would turn to but God. Compared to King Saul's unrepentant and gratuitous behavior, the whole attitude of King David is an example of what a pure-hearted man or woman should be. This is why the Son of Man was taken from his lineage.

Likewise, God knows that we are feeble creatures shaped in iniquity, and our inward parts are full of malice. Nevertheless, He expects our best effort. He wants us to be faithful, honest, do what is right before Him, and recognize that only Jesus Christ can purify and restore us. Only through Him can we accomplish something worthy. Having this outlook in our walk with Jesus Christ makes us pure of heart.

This level of faithfulness, despite all of his adversities, is what God foresaw in David when He anointed him as king. Furthermore, this level of commitment from David, Moses, and Job is what God demands from us. Their transparency set these men apart before the LORD because they acknowledged their flaws before God openly (Matt. 6:5-8), and they remained obedient to Him.

The Father is looking for men and women in this last hour who are in the likeness of King David, Moses, and Job who will emulate Christ.

- Hold the Line -

"Blessed are the peacemakers: for they shall be called the children of God" (Matt. 5:9).

One of the greatest things I have seen in my generation is the twinning of mixed ethnicities. I have not had this experience personally, but I see nothing wrong with mixed Christian couples. The only thing that really counts under the new covenant is our communion with Christ.

I think it is a wonderful thing because in a world full of hatred and division, I applaud people who challenge the belief system of the beast vis-à-vis racism and walk against the odds. I also applaud people like Brother Brandt Jean who forgave and hugged Officer Amber Guyger after she murdered his brother. Sister Sharletta Evans forgave, advised, and even adopted a young man named Raymond Johnson who is responsible for killing her three-year-old son. I have also taken notice of Abdul-Munim Sombat Jitmoud who also hugged and forgave Trey Alexander Relford who participated in his son's murder in Lexington, Kentucky in 2017. Also, Barbara Mangi in Illinois who forgave and even wrote letters to minister goodness to the man who took the life of her daughter. Lastly, Azim Khamisa who lost his son in North Park, California in 1995 and later teamed up with Ples Felix (the shooter's grandfather) to promote the Tariq Khamisa Foundation – an organization dedicated to "stopping children from killing children." My heart goes out to all others who have displayed the principle of forgiveness towards their culprit.

All of the people I mentioned above have made the news over the years regarding their response to a family tragedy and the loss of a loved one. I don't know them personally or their religious beliefs, but I do know their reaction to such horrific experiences is in the tradition of walking with King David, the king of Israel. Even greater than David, those individuals are displaying the kind of love the Father extended to mankind at the Cross.

It is a formidable thing to desire peace for your malefactor and extend an olive branch to them after they have caused you harm.

In addition, I cannot say that I have been in their shoes or could easily express the same sentiment towards such horrors. However, when I feel frustrated with someone, remembering their testimonies gives me motivation to turn the other cheek. This inspires me to reach out to those who have harmed me and sow the seeds of understanding, forgiveness, and peace. By doing such things in the sight of the Lord, we testify that His Spirit lives in us, and our core values are not based on the beast's system. Jesus tells us that by doing so, we are blessed and shall be called the children of God.

Being a peacekeeper doesn't have to be so extreme. I just used their examples to paint a striking picture of their test; some of us just have to be better neighbors, stop gossiping about each other, and learn to walk away from arguments.

Speaking of which, I remember when I was still a fresh Christian and still channeling a lot of anger into my heart. One day, I was dressed in formal attire with a clean shave and dress shoes at the shopping center when some random guy ran into me. I turned around, and before I could even say a word, the thuggish gentleman started hollering profanities and said, "You're not about that life, man. Trust me." I chuckled a little bit under my breath and thought to myself: if only he knew of the evil I have partaken in. I wanted to tell him, "Don't let these clothes fool you," then show him I could be crazy too. But there was Someone holding me back; so instead, I walked away feeling embarrassed.

Later that day, as I was meditating on the incident, Jesus spoke to me through the Spirit and said, "What happened today was sanctioned by me. I wanted to show you that you have changed so that you may see My work through you." He said, "I wanted to show you how far I brought you so that you can be encouraged and your faith strengthened. Do you know what this vessel meant when he said you are not about that life?"

To which I replied, "He meant that I was not able to knock him out even if I wanted to."

Jesus said, "No! What he meant was that because of his lifestyle, he had more demons available to him than you. The devil was enticing you through him to ascertain if you would open yourself to be possessed as he was, but you are My child now. There are no alliances between Light and darkness, for they work against each other. You are an agent of peace now, and you do not behave as you used to any longer, nor should you try to be a puppet for demons."

This struck me and opened my eyes to the kind of involvement that someone with demonic ownership can bring to you. Everyone's test in life is different, but the intended result is the same: we must not conform to this world; we must renew our mind and learn to be more like Christ each day (Luke 10:25-37; Matt. 22:36-40; John 14:6; 1 Peter 1:15-16; John 13:34-35).

In our realm, we suffer too many customs and traditions, which originated from nothing and lead to nothing. Most of them are based on despotisms and men's thirst for blood and violence. Too many people are living and dying for the crew, from the police force to the street gangs. It's also all about the crew from the Vatican to the White House and the orchestrated conflicts worldwide. It is the same spirit at work, conditioning the mind of men and preparing them to willingly receive the official mark of the beast. However, we must not forget that the Bible tells us that although we are in the world, we are not of the world. The customs of men should not guide the children of The True Living God, especially now that iniquity is more abundant in the world.

Even the customs of Jehovah concerning how He dealt with men in the Old Testament have unfolded throughout the generations. The way He dealt with us in the past was merely foundational. He did that until The True Living God, Jesus Christ, came in the flesh and fulfilled the Law and the Prophets (Exodus 21:23-25; Lev. 24:19-21; Deut. 19:18-21 / Matt. 5:17, 38-48; Matt. 27:50-54, 28:110; Hebrews 4:15-16). Jesus has restored what the first Adam lost in the garden, and He broke the yoke of condemnation that Adam's disobedience brought to Earth. Before Adam, God had not pronounced any condemnations towards men, nor had there been a tree of the Knowledge of Good and Evil (Rom. 5:12-21; 1 Cor. 15:45).

Although Jesus restored what was lost in the garden, which was a relationship with the Father and eternal life, this does not mean that the curses of Genesis 3:14-19 have been lifted. As we can see, the serpent still crawls on its belly, women still go through sorrows at conception, and their desire is still directed to their husband who rules over them.

The woman's curse concerning her desires has to do with her always needing to be reassured and comforted compared to before the fall when she was initially prepared as a suitable helper (Gen. 2:18). Her hubby is given authority to rule over her because the serpent managed to captivate and seduce her into temptation. To be fair to Eve, Adam should not have left her wandering around, as he was the one sanctioned to guard the garden to begin with; however, we reap what we sow in life (1 Tim. 2:9-15).

Moreover, Adam's curse also still remains. This is why men have to work hard to make ends meet. Even the rich man has to break a sweat every now and then and needs a good accountant to keep up with tax laws to retain his wealth. Some may fly under the radar all their lives, but we all have to face the Creator one of these days (Proverbs 19:28-29).

Since we are still under the curse of the fall, what purpose is there for men and women to constantly bicker? We have a purpose to fulfill, and we are in the last hour.

Husbands (men), you will not stop your woman from speaking; she is merely seeking to be validated. It is part of the curse, so make the most out of it and stop complaining. As one man said before, "Women... we can't live with them, and we can't live without them." You ought to rejoice to have someone who loves you for who you are, dirty underwear and all. You should give praise to God for creating such a wonderful match for us. Moreover, if you are so blessed to have a wife who is like Sarah from the Bible who continually called Abraham lord (1 Peter 3:1-6), you should cherish her even more (1 Peter 3:7-8).

Wives (women), really? You do not need a man anymore? You can do it all by yourself? So, what are the dildos for? Why the sperm banks? Who are these sperm suppliers? You must pray before getting married and ask God for a good God-fearing husband. As for you who are already married, ask for divine intervention. God will not ignore a true request that is based on His sacred institution. Stop falling for these players and thugs. Life and having children are not a game, and marriage is not easy. Do not be ignorant of Satan's devices. He likes to inflate bad situations to make them seem bigger than they really are. Do not let him play you like a fool. We have received the cards that our ancestors drew, but love and mercy have overcome this bad hand at the Cross. It is for us to make the best of it now.

When God created us, He told us to be fruitful and multiply. He gave us sex as a means to execute that command, but all the perversions that follow after the fall came from the kingdom of darkness. Some of these perversions came from the twisted hearts of men, and others directly from the fallen angels. The amount of pressure we put upon ourselves in trying to follow these porn-stars is unnecessary. Sexuality under God's rules is blessed and wonderful. I will even go as far to thank the Lord for the conjugal blessing!

The commission to be fruitful and multiply does not involve fellacio or anal sex. Foreplay and sensuality are welcome (Song. 7), and the Lord gave us sex as a form of enjoyment and proliferation, not defilement (Gen. 38:6-[9-10]). The ancient Babylonians are those who popularized these extravagant sexual practices. It was all part of their Beelzebul (or lord of the flies and dung) ritual, and the world refuses to let them go. They love them so much that the meaning of the aforementioned Song of Solomon has been reorganized to justify sexual immorality. In Biblical times, the main sorrow of a married woman was not being able to conceive, and the main sorrow of the married man was not being able to provide for his loved ones. Most, if not all, arguments and division between men and women come from the distractions of this world and the false objectives of the master illusionist and his psycho-sexual-fueled society. Sexual sadist-fuelled porn, such as "ghetto gaggers" and "Max-hardcore", has gotten extremely popular over the years as a result of these demonic indoctrinations.

Here comes another rabbit trail. On my time on Earth, I have literally witnessed a "Christian woman" threatening to leave her husband for not being able to buy her a $1,000 Michael Kors purse. She swore on Heaven and Earth she had to have it because it was the new style, and all of her girlfriends had one. Unfortunately, her husband worked a dead-end job; therefore, he had to prioritize their spending. However, the "Christian woman" would not come to reason. Eventually, the husband succeeded in getting her the handbag, and the argument declined. Let's translate this whole argument into the tongues of angels for further consideration.

First, Michael Kors is an openly gay married man and a multimillionaire. He is living in sin, and he has no need for that measly $1,000. Furthermore, I reckon Heaven's record of that incident is that a "Christian woman" threatened to leave her husband because he did not have $1,000 to give to a gay couple so that she could walk around with a cheap purse and glorify a homosexual-based fashion design company.

I understand that this may sound far-fetched to some of you, but believe me; it is the rapidity with which the enemy can make us forsake the Universal for the finite. It is just stupid, and we must learn to let the Spirit of God regulate our minds.

Moreover, I have also witnessed many men who would neglect their obligations as a father and husband to go hang out with the boys. They also enjoy spending exuberant money on the superficial, some even more than women. This «circus of desire» often leads both parties involved to go looking for love in all the wrong places. After the one-night stand, STDs generally follow. Then it's the divorce court. Round and round we go with the circular existence, and for what? All this does not change the words spoken by God after the fall; it only makes our time here more difficult.

Now, I am not judging people for wearing brand-named articles. To be honest, I have a few regalia of my own, and I would not be surprised if some of my articles are made by companies that are held by homosexuals as well. I used the incident above to paint a picture of the frigidity of relationships and the sad reality of Christianity today. As long as the garment is conservative and does not send the wrong message (i.e., drug promotion, sex, or something publicizing the kingdom of Satan), you are fine. The fabrics have no power of their own. The symbols they are projecting are what we should be careful about. The gold, silver, and the raiment from Egypt had no power of their own, and God gave those items to Israel as a blessing (Ex. 3:19-22). However, the hearts of the people were so twisted that they gave the objects authority over their souls and defiled themselves (Ex. 32:1-6, 25). All I am saying is we should not be so quick to trade the substantial for the perishable. Our priority should not be to keep up with this world but to live Godly lives in all things, especially in marriages (Matt. 22:23-30). However, if you feel concerned about buying clothes from general stores, just pray on them and rebuke any spirit that may be attached to them before you purchase them out of the store (1 Cor. 8:4-[7]).

Here is the formula for a successful relationship:

"Wives, submit yourselves unto your own husbands, as unto the Lord. For the husband is the head of the wife, even as Christ is the head of the church: and he is the savior of the body. Therefore as the

church is subject unto Christ, so let the wives be to their own husbands in every thing. Husbands, love your wives, even as Christ also loved the church, and gave himself for it; That he might sanctify and cleanse it with the washing of water by the word, That he might present it to himself a glorious church, not having spot, or wrinkle, or any such thing; but that it should be holy and without blemish. So ought men to love their wives as their own bodies. He that loveth his wife loveth himself" (Eph. 5:22-28).

Peace is defined as, "A state of tranquility, freedom from civil disturbance, and a state of security or order within a community provided for by law or custom. It is the freedom from disquieting or oppressive thoughts or emotions; harmony in personal relations, a state of mutual concord, a pact to end hostilities between those who have been in enmity, and it offers the possibility of a negotiation."

Be at peace today. Be free from the unnecessary burden of this realm today, and be a peacemaker for the Lord. In Jesus' name, Amen & Amen.

- Beauty for Ashes -

To conclude the Beatitudes, our Lord and Savior proclaimed three more promises (Matt. 5:10-12).

"Blessed are they which are persecuted for righteousness' sake: for theirs is the kingdom of heaven."

*"Blessed are ye, when men shall revile you, and persecute you, and shall say all manner of evil against you **falsely**, for my sake."*

"Rejoice, and be exceeding glad: for great is your reward in heaven: for so persecuted the prophets which were before you."

These last three promises are directly tied into what we ought to expect from the world if we are walking according to His commandments. Jesus makes it clear that we will receive opposition for our faith, for His name's sake. But He guarantees that we will inherit the kingdom of Heaven. He also wants us to know that we are not alone in this tribulation. All the prophets before us were persecuted for their faith. For these reasons, He commands us to rejoice and to be exceedingly glad because we are heirs of Heaven and walk in the tradition of the prophets before us (Hebrews 12:22-24).

As many pastors have already said, you ought to be extremely cautious with preachers who teach only prosperity and success in this world (Matt. 4:8-11). That which makes our faith stronger is the struggle of the journey and the trial of life. Not running through any challenges in life would make us soft and spoiled (James 1:2-4). This would make us self-entitled brats in need of private jets.

Now more than ever, we need strength because everything is looking bleak, and the whole world is on fire. What do we do when the churches are closed, and we are living in a pandemic-fueled existence? Who else will support us through this live exercise population control? The schools are falling behind in their curriculum, the meat markets are empty, the local populaces are being forced out in the streets, and the illuminati police are kidnapping American citizens in broad daylight. Whether or not we choose to acknowledge it, the last persecution has begun.

Even if the current state of the world subsides as it did after the Spanish flu pandemic of 1918, it will never go back to the way it used to be because we are in the last quarter now. The overlords will not lose the footing they have recently gained, and new laws are coming to make our life even more mobilized.

Only the Creator has the power to stop the sun in the midst of Heaven (Joshua 10:12-14), to turn back times (Isa. 38:1-8; 2 Kings 20:111), and restore us (Isaiah 61:1-3). If we humble ourselves and earnestly seek Him, He will hear from Heaven and answer our prayers. This is the prosperity Jesus promised us. For all of our troubles, we receive beauty for our ashes. This beauty is translated into many blessings, such as resiliency, compassion, wisdom, a unified faith, and even a unified America – if we so choose. In the eternal realm, we shall shine like the brightness of the firmament and the stars forever and ever (Daniel 12:3). As Christians, we owe Christ a fight every day. Even when we feel down and depressed, we must give God our devotion each morning before we start our day. Read a few Psalms in your devotion each day; it will revive your faith because we walk by faith not by sight or feeling. We don't give up on the battlefield because of the sand storm; we clean our weapon, dust off our gear, and get back on patrol. Even when we don't feel like it, we must fight. Jesus gave us His all at Calvary; therefore, we have to give our best each day. This fight is a spiritual fight, so we fight with prayer, fasting, and we need to feed our spirit the Word of God daily in order to be proficient in spiritual warfare. It's just the way it is. Even when we cannot feel Him, we press on and remain faithful to the Holy Scriptures. In addition, God is not a genie in a lamp. We ought to learn to apply our faith and speak to our problems with a sense of healing and restoration to the land. He has given us that power.

CHAPTER NINE

JOHN 14:6

We Must Conserve Our Beauty

Now let us take another spoon of the medicine:

"You are the salt of the earth. But if the salt loses its saltiness, how can it be made salty again? It is no longer good for anything, except to be thrown out and trampled underfoot" (Matt. 5:13 NIV).

Most Believers read this verse and automatically attribute it to church members committing sins, such as drinking, doing drugs, fornicating or watching porn; all of those are valid affinity to the Text. Practicing any of the sins above constitutes a violation of both the old and new covenants. If any of us ever fall victim to these temptations, we must repent and ask God for forgiveness before we can move on.

The eschatology of this warning is directly connected to the Spirit of God living within us. The Holy Spirit is our guide, and we are commanded not to quench or grief the Spirit (1 Thess. 5:12-23 and Ephesians 4:23-32). We grieve the Spirit when we commit sins against God's principles. This is where the conviction or guilty feeling comes from when we fumble. These sins are not limited to the open-and-shut cases mentioned above; they also include the sins of Proverbs 6:16-19.

We feel guilty when we sin because the Spirit of God - which searches the deep things of God - testifies of Him. The Spirit of God testifies of the Father's attributes or character concerning the way He feels about us sinning, and the attributes of the Lord are written in Exodus 33:6-7. The reason we feel guilty is because in verse 7 of Exodus 33, the Bible says that God "will by no means clear the guilty;" therefore, it is necessary for God to make us feel guilty. Otherwise, we would not know that we are in the wrong and would just continue on the wrong path. The Father knows all things (Psalm 90:8), and when we sin, our iniquities separate us from Him (Isaiah 59:1-8). The feeling we experience when we fumble is the Holy Spirit formulating to us what it means to be separated from God. When we sin, we are estranged from Him. It is meant to warn us of the reality of eternal damnation and alienation from the Lord. Although the Father loves us, and we are living in the age of grace, or the acceptable year of the Lord, the Father's standards never changed. We have to be careful not to get complacent or overzealous in our walk with Christ so that we do not lose our saltiness or anointing (Isa. 54:17; Ps. 7:8-17; 1 John 1:9). The Bible tells us of many instances where God did in fact remove His anointing from man. We will use King Saul again as an example.

In verse 23 of 1 Samuel 15, the prophet Samuel says:

"For rebellion is as the sin of witchcraft, and stubbornness is as iniquity and idolatry. Because thou hast rejected the word of the LORD, he hath also rejected thee from being king."

This was the second time God dealt with King Saul concerning his attitudes because Saul was still unrepentant. Initially, God declared him to be unfit to be king, and Saul should have humbled himself and genuinely repented (Gen. 4:6-7;

Isa. 1:18). Instead, he continued walking in error while making excuses (1 Samuel 15:14-23).

God is a very reasonable Father, and He is always looking for a juncture to interact with us. If we don't have a pure heart, we are only fooling ourselves and bringing condemnation upon our own heads. God had to be so stern with King Saul because the DNA of the Messiah had to be from a righteous man. Saul brought shame to God's plan of salvation for mankind when he didn't maintain his integrity or repent as the king of Israel. As a consequence of that, in the next chapter (1 Samuel 16), the prophet Samuel is commanded to stop mourning for Saul and anoint David as the new king of Israel. The LORD finally removed His Spirit from Saul, and an evil spirit took His place.

Likewise, the Bible tells us that in 2 Thessalonians 2:7-10, the Spirit of God will finally be taken from the earth, and when the Holy Spirit is taken away, we can expect to see anarchy as an official norm. This must take place in order for the anti-Christ to appear because the Holy Spirit is the One restraining him for now, and He is the reason why we still have a leg in this fight.

When the Holy Spirit is removed, lawlessness will be unrestrained. For the Holy Spirit has been working against the forces of darkness directly of His own accord, but also through us who are doers of the Word. We will keep our portion of Christ until the end, but the portion working in the world at large must eventually return to Heaven in order for the end of all things to come. All those who have been chosen and are still here will have to endure the final test—the systematic persecution of the saints—but Jesus will support our faith to the end (Matt. 28:20).

The way this rapture concept has been taught in the churches is wrong; there will not be multiple gatherings by the holy angels. Those who are taken first will be taken through the process of death, and this process has already begun (Isaiah 57:1-2). They are taken away so they won't endure the last tribulation because they have fulfilled their calling. Consequently, we ought to be glad and rejoice when we hear of the man or woman of God passing away in this last hour because we know it's God's plan for them, and their deeds follow them. Those of us still here must fulfill our purpose before it is too late (Rev. 3:1-6; Rev. 6:9-11 and Rev. 7) and our names are blotted out of the Book of Life (Ex. 32:31-33). The warning in Revelation 3 is to let us know that just like with King Saul, God can still remove His Spirit from the disobedient man or woman, cowards, fornicators, and all who persist in practicing sin in the last hour and give them over to a spirit of strong delusion. We ought not to test His patience. He is not one who can be fooled, nor will He tolerate complacency and foolishness forever.

God is not a respecter of person. It is because of our faith in His Son, obedience to His Word, and the courage to walk in the Spirit, that He will honor us (Acts 10:25-35; Roman 2:11-16; Luke 9:26).

Withal, in Luke 17:26 and Matt. 24:36-44, Jesus uses the reference:

> *"As it was in the days of Noah, so shall it be also in the days of the*
>
> *Son of Man."*

Jesus does not use that term lightly, and there is no such thing as multiple rapture encounters, as many believe. For some believe the church (elects) will be taken in batches, some pre-tribulation, and some throughout the tribulation, but in Matthew 24:29-31, Jesus makes it clear that His second coming will be immediately after the tribulation of those days. Just like in the days of Noah, those who are sealed by the Spirit of God and still here when the last tribulation is officiated will be taken through the "flood of persecution" (see Rev. 6:9-11). At the allocated time, Christ will send His angels to gather all of His Elects at once (Matt. 24:21-27; 1 Cor. 15:51-58; Rev. 20:4-6). First the dead, followed by the remnant.

Just as the Father has given us children for an heritage (Ps. 127:3), the Lord is building an heritage for Himself out of the Believers because He desires for the offsprings of the sons of man to enjoy the new earth He will create after the last judgment (Rev. 21:1-8; Deut. 32:8-9; Isa. 19:22-25). The Father wants us to come and enjoy the glory of Jesus along with Him in paradise (Rev. 21:22-27). He has a quota in mind for His inheritance, and He dares to reach it because He can.

Once the Father has met His quota, the door of Grace will be closed (Gen. 7:15-22; Matt. 24:32-36; Proverbs 1:20-33; John 7:32-36), and only those who walk in the Spirit of Christ and those anointed with the power of God can complete their test (1 Chronicles 28:9-10; Isaiah 4:3-6; Jer. 29:13; Isaiah 65:1-16).

We have no means of knowing who will make the final cut, so we must not waste time being busybodies. We ought to strive to fulfill our purpose and our callings instead. There are still so many people who have not yet received an understanding of what the Love of God truly means, and their provisions were given unto us who are saved to be shared with them (John 10:1-16; Romans 10:11-17; Acts 2:17-21). Ultimately, just like brother Noah, we also have to reach out to those who are perishing and warn them of the judgment to come. If we grieve the portion of the Spirit given to us into frustration, as per Revelation 3:5, our name will be blotted out of the Book of Life. Eternal death will be the consequence.

Now I know there are various interpretations of what the messages to the seven churches in Revelation represent. Notwithstanding, we must not forget that we are the church and our body is the temple of the Holy Spirit. During our journey here, many of us have already gone through the various phases described to the seven churches.

If any of the warnings applies to your personal life, follow the prescribed measure in the Text.

The one thing that Jesus keeps repeating in those passages is, "I know your work." However, God desires worship, for He made us for this purpose. Through worship, we draw near to Him, get whole again, and our shame and nakedness get overwhelmed by His glory (Ps. 103). Through worship, we activate the power of the Blood. The yoke of the enemy is broken, and we get refreshed and sanctified. Through worship, the name of God is lifted up, and men are drawn to Him. So worship, our "first love," is our primary need in life (Luke 10:38-[42]; Acts 16:16-34; John 12:31-32).

- Once Saved Always Saved! -

[1]

Let us now turn our attention to controversial topics that can cause complacence.

First, we must know what the word means; according to Webster's dictionary, a complacent person is, "Someone marked by self-satisfaction, especially when accompanied by unawareness of actual dangers or deficiencies."

There is a teaching within the body of Christ that has Christians believing that once they receive Christ, they should not suffer any more burdens. They also teach that no matter what they do in this life, they will enter Heaven. Many believe their cross will somehow carry itself. It is the alter ego of the prosperity gospel, and it is based on the belief of predestination. This teaching is counterproductive and can induce backsliding, laziness, and Balaamrism. It is referred to as "once saved, always saved." This teaching is extremely palatable to the new-age churches, but I am afraid this microwave meal is lacking in macronutrients.

In Matthew 25:1-13, Jesus gives us the parable of the ten virgins. This parable shadows the example of the days of Noah, and the example of the two servants given by Christ in Matthew 24:36-51. To elaborate, the foolish servants in the ten virgins' parable lived recklessly. They kept no oil for their lamps and weren't consistent with good works. They were drunkards and backsliders and felt justified in their religiousness. When the Bridegroom, who is Christ, came to receive them unto Him, they were not ready and were therefore cast asunder. All ten virgins in the story were made aware of the Bridegroom's coming, and of the need for them to be ready for His return, but only five wise ones took the matter seriously. The foolish ones had backslid into gluttony and drunkenness because they were blind to the danger at hand and felt that Christ's return was taking too long.

These five foolish virgins represent the kind of Christians who are under the spell of religion. Many of them believe they can do as they wilt and still get themselves ready for our Bridegroom at the last minute. That is impossible.

On the opposite end, the five wise vessels kept the oil for their lamps and did many good deeds in the Lord's name. The meat that was given to them to share with the saints, they each shared according to their calling (Matt. 24:45). They wore the beauty for ashes the Lord had given them with faithfulness to the end. Although time got rough, they carried on the tradition of the prophets and preserved their virtues even against all odds.

Conclusively, these are the types of Christians God is looking for: the ones who walk with Christ daily and preserve their virtues by remaining sanctified and free of the beast's controls. The ones who remained focused on the task, took notice of the signs of the end, and continued teaching the truth of the Gospel of Jesus Christ with wisdom but without compromise (John 4:23-24).

The foolish Christians in the parable were doomed and could not see their way through the darkness because their lamps were empty. They were desperately trying to negotiate for oil, but it was too late, and nobody could help them.

Only the five wise Christians could make it to the King. They were able to push through the night because the Holy Spirit shone the Light to the narrow path. They were found acceptable in the King's sight and were gathered unto Him for eternity. They were saved by the testimony and application of their faith in Jesus Christ (Rev. 12:11). They were welcomed into Heaven because they had kept their oil—the anointing—given to them for their lamps and fulfilled their calling. In the parables, the foolish virgins even required some oil from the wise ones, but the wise ones could not share because what was given was just enough for their own journey.

We ought to embrace our scars in this last hour because the beauty for ashes is the wisdom, endurance, and discernment that we have or will acquire through our trials and errors. And I am in no way trying to generalize everyone's burdens, but the time for pity-parties has passed. This world is a wicked and cold world, and it's only going to get worse. Therefore, embrace your scars, glorify God for sustaining you this far, and let the beauty of the Lord shine through you instead.

In conclusion, the moral of the story is we must apply ourselves in this journey of life, and no one should be placing their faith in another man or woman. When we hear the midnight cry and behold the sign of the King of kings manifested in

Heaven (Matt. 24:29-51), we should be like the five wise virgins. For when that day comes, there will be no more time left, for it will be the day of the gathering. The dead in Christ will rise first, followed by the living (1 Thess. 4:15-17). Those foolish Christians will not be part of the first resurrection; however, their part will be in the second resurrection (Rev. 20:4-6). We have to keep the oil for our lamps so that we can make the journey through the darkness and not feel ashamed at the sign of our Salvation.

The pastors' faith cannot save us, neither is mama's faith or daddy's faith. We have to put our own faith to work toward our salvation. We each have our own cross to bear and a calling to fulfill, and the idea that anyone can pull a fast one on God at the last minute is a trick in itself, a trick of the devil. Praying for one another, standing in agreement in prayers, and if needed, the laying of hands, are all honorable Christian expressions. In the end, we each have to give a personal account for our own lives to the Creator.

Jesus prayed to the Father for us to receive a perpetual Comforter, who is supposed to be with us from now through eternity (John 14:16; Eph. 1:13-14). Nevertheless, similar to the days of Solomon, we have to fulfill our end of the bargain, or the contract will be voided (2 Chr. 7:12-22). The anointing and gifts of the Spirit given unto us are to be used for the purpose of the kingdom within the allocated time, and this goes for both the *dorea* and the *doma*—the anointing that stays, and the one that is borrowed. Jesus fulfilled the promise he made to us, and now we have to do our share.

[2]

In the parable of the ten minas (or pounds) in Luke 19:11-27, Jesus gives us another warning with a new variable, and He reiterates that God is fair and impartial in judgment.

To recap, a Nobleman goes on a long voyage, and before He leaves, He gives His servants three months worth of salary to invest in trading. When the Nobleman in the parable returned after His long voyage, He called the servants to get an account of His investments. The first servant is told, *"Well done, good and faithful servant,"* for investing faithfully. Then he was given command over ten cities. The second is told, *"Well done,"* and he was given charge over five cities for his faith. The heritage of the last, the lazy one, was taken away from him and given to the good and faithful one—the one with charge over the ten cities.

The lazy servant in the parable was rebuked for his laziness. In Luke's account of the parable, the lazy servant was not condemned to utter destruction with the enemies of the Nobleman in verse 27, but His judgment was still noticeable enough that the angels who were standing by made the remark, *"Lord, he hath ten pounds"* (verse 25). Jesus then concludes with the declaration,

> *"For I say unto you, That unto every one which hath shall be given; and from him that hath not, even that he hath shall be taken away from him."*

I would like to call the variable in that story, "The lazy servant variable." Unlike the complacent person who is satisfied with the way things are and does not notice the danger until it's too late, a lazy person knows there is danger but chooses to play possum (Luke 19:20-[22] 23). This variable lets us know not everyone will be a ruler in the new creation. For the lazy souls shall not inherit a great reward from the Lord, and I believe it is the meaning of the lazy servant's minas getting taken from him and given to another (Luke 16:10-12).

I believe in the new heaven and on the new earth, we will all be free, but only those who are found worthy to lead will be put in that position. Although that lazy servant may still receive one of the Five's Crown of Salvation for not losing his or her virtue, he or she will not receive any command in paradise. Some of us will be placed in charge of ten cities; some will rule over five, and some will simply be servants to another. Each one will receive according to their devotions to the kingdom of God in this lifetime (Mark 9:33-41; Daniel 12:3; Rev. 21:23-27; Rev. 22:1-5; 2 Tim. 4:7-8).

It is also an insight into God's temperament concerning His Elects, which explains that God is not an enabler and will reward each one of us only on the basis of how we use His investment (Haggai 2:1-9, 23; Num. 25:11-13). In this version of the parable, the ending is fairly good for all parties involved, and none of the servants are cast into Hell. Only those who reject Jesus Christ as their King are sent to the gallows (Luke 19:27). Still, who is to say that this will be the outcome of every lazy servant (Matt. 25:30)?

I used the version of the Apostle Luke above because I think that as Christians, we can often underestimate the Power of Christ, which lives within us (Mark 4:13-32; 2 Cor. 3:4-18). Furthermore, I like the way the late Bishop Nate Holcomb used to translate the book of Romans 12:3-10. He used to say, "We were all given the same measure of faith but different anointing for various offices, and so what we are actually lacking is confidence in God's ability to fulfill His promises. Our confidence in Christ is what we need to develop." This lack of confidence is often caused by our inability to let go and allow God to complete His work in us. At the end, the expectation of the Nobleman is the same; He wants us to use His anointing wisely (1 Cor. 1:18-31).

In Matthew's recap of the same parable (Matt. 25:14-30), we are given a different breakdown concerning the ten minas. First, we are told that the anointing (talents) is given to *every man according to his several ability* (Matt. 25:15). According to Matthew, one servant received 5 talents, the other 2, and the last one 1. This signifies we were each given the measure of faith and a specific anointing based on the Holy Spirit's assessment of each individual (Rom. 12:3-10).

Second, in Matthew's version, the lazy servant ends up getting cast out with the heathen. Therefore, I believe that the wisest thing one can do, based on these two possible outcomes to laziness, is to avoid being that lazy servant.

In my opinion, the lazy servant represents those Christians who just go to church, place a few dollars in the offerings basket, and go about their life feeling satisfied because they are afraid to take a stand. These are the ones who hear the call to ministry, but they are too comfortable in their religious practice to take the leap of faith. These are the ones who hear the call of the Holy Spirit towards a special task, but they sit and wait for the pastor to give them the thumbs up, as if pastors don't already have enough to do. These Christians like to sit around and judge everything that went wrong in the service; however, when the pastors ask for volunteers, they have a list of excuses already rehearsed in their head. They are like a twelve-year-old child who still walks in baby diapers (Heb. 5:8-14).

One of the ways you can tell that you are being called into a specific ministry is:

If the first thing you want to do when you awaken in the morning is preach, sing praises, or give praise unto the Lord through prayers, this is your calling or motivational gift. The initial expression that you experience each morning is the testimony of your spirit man confessing to you what he has witnessed throughout the night in the astral realm (Eph. 2:4[6]-10). Better yet, think of it as your spirit repeating to you what the King of kings has declared about you in the heavenly.

The second sign is bearing on those called to preach. God may wake you up around 2 a.m. to minister to you the desires of His heart concerning His people.

These messages are not for you to keep to yourself. You are to write them down and deliver them to the intended parties (Habakkuk 2:2). Utilize the social media platform if you have to, but get the Word out, and all of this must be done in the Spirit. Without Him, you are risking the temptation of adding or taking away from the message. Remember, incomplete obedience can be a cause for dismissal; remember King Saul.

Concerning singing praises unto the LORD, some people may not understand the power that this gift holds; but it is in fact a potent influence against the forces of darkness (See 1 Sam. 16:14-[23]). Our songs of worship are usually inspired by the Holy Scriptures or by our personal experience with the Lord. Demons flee at the name of Jesus (John 6:63). Furthermore, they cannot stand a joyful soul because it is a disturbance to them. Alternatively, that endowment is also shown to be pleasing to the LORD as well. In 2 Kings 3:4-20, a pure and beautiful melody lifted towards the Creator steered Him into action towards Israel. In the latter verses, the Text tells us that following their praise offering (Hebrews 13:15), the Hand of the LORD came down on the prophet Elisha, and the victory was awarded to Israel once more. This happened despite King Jehoram's evil practices (2 Kings 3:1-3). Just like in those days, things are not looking promising right now, but God has repeatedly proven to us that He is more than able to move in our favor. The Father has everything under control; we can trust Him wholeheartedly, so we must give Him praise at all times regardless of the season (Isaiah 10:27; Ps. 107, Ps. 91 and Ps. 150).

Regarding prayers, we all ought to pray without ceasing, with all supplication, and give thanks in everything. This is the will of God in Christ Jesus concerning us. The reason that we ought to pray without ceasing is that prayer is the "God particle" of Christianity. Without prayer, we can often find ourselves confused as to what the will of God is over our lives, and the future in general. Think of prayer as a council meeting where people come together to discuss the issues in our community. Or perhaps even as a huddle during a game timeout when the coach is informing his players about what they did wrong, what they should do better, and he encourages them by saying that they are still in the game and can still win. Without those timeouts, and or half-times, the players on the field may find themselves disoriented, running with the ball in hand towards their own end zone ready to score a two points safety for the opposite team. Additionally, through this application of our faith, the gift of speaking in tongues can be obtained – according to the Holy Spirit's assessment.

Being a Christian in God's army is similar to being in the natural military in many aspects. For instance, when it comes to military promotions, some of us get handpicked because of perceived abilities from our superiors. Others receive promotion through perseverance and application of our (faith) skills. Moreover, Jesus has already made it clear that if we ask anything in His name without doubting, it will be done. Likewise, He has made it clear that we shall,

"Ask and it shall be given you; seek, and ye shall find; knock, and it shall be opened unto you" (Matt. 7:7).

Therefore, prayer and Christianity are homogeneous. Also, there are those among us that have a heart predisposed for intercession, a heart full of love, and compassion. We need your warrior's gift right now more than ever before.

As a soldier in God's army, there may be times when He will wake some of us up in the middle of the night and impress on us to pray - to stand in the gap for the kingdom. These calls usually come around 12:00 AM to 04:00 AM, which is the time witches and warlocks are most active. This may feel inconvenient at times if you have to go to work in the morning, but remember that the Father is our Sustainer. He will never put more on us than we can bear.

Concerning prayer, the Bible also tells us that if the wickedness of the Ecclesiastic vessel is so bad, the vessel is to be delivered to Satan for the destruction of the flesh, but the spirit of that person may be saved (1 Cor. 5:1-5). This has to do with the fact that sins bring sickness to the body, and we have been given power over the spirits of sickness through the prayer of faith (James 5:14-15). If someone is hopelessly bound to sin, we ought not be their enablers. Furthermore, we are not saved because of our work. We are saved by grace, but faith without work is dead (James 2:14-26).

The battle between Light and darkness is a full-scale military operation. We do not get to choose when the enemy gets to attack, so we must be ready to fight back in season and out of season.

According to Deuteronomy 28, the term "his citizens" in the Text is usually associated with the **actual Jews** because they in fact rejected Him as King and were cursed. However, we all have sinned and fallen short of the glory of God, so the term can essentially be applied to all people on Earth who reject Christ as their Savior.

We can choose to be the good and faithful servant, the one who is giving authority over the five cities, or the lazy one who is rebuked. The choice is ours, but if we cannot exercise proper rulership or stewardship with the little that we have now on Earth, how can we expect to be put in charge of anything mighty in the eternal kingdom? This last statement also involves our money and how we share our blessings with our church and those less fortunate (Rev. 21:24). The Lord even goes as far as authorizing us to be shrewd or to hustle if we have to. God would prefer we finish the race completely out of breath, with a few litigations, than for us to just sit by the sideways beaten (Luke 16:1-13; Rev. 3:5).

The Nobleman in the parable is Jesus. He went to prepare a place for us, and He is coming back soon to establish His kingdom once and for all. He left each one of us three months' pay and the task to invest into the "Great Commission" until He comes back. The Great Commission is the task that Jesus gave us to teach all nations and to baptize them in the name of the Father, the Son, and the Holy Spirit (Matt. 28:18-20). Although the time of His return is unknown, the signs of the time are clear indications that the end is near. Let us not procrastinate any more on our part.

[3]

The last groups of Elects I will cover are leaders who are compromised. They are false prophets who are deliberately misleading the flocks, but not all false prophets started as such. I used the term Balaamrism earlier in the text to describe those anointed with great gifts, such as prophet Balaam, who lost their way along the route. This last warning is for anyone who started the journey faithfully as a minister, but somewhere along the way decided that profit was the "greater god." As the saying goes, "Heavy is the head that wears the crown," and by the mercy of our Lord and Savior, your names may not get blotted out from the Book of Life. However, you will not escape the consequences of your actions.

As the other saying goes, "We are all called to ministry" (2 Tim 1:8-9; Rom. 8:28).

He who holds the keys of Hell and death also regulates their admission's roster. I believe the meaning of Matt. 5:20-26 is a warning to that effect.

At the Great White Throne of Judgment, many who were cast down to Hell and death for their insubordination on Earth will be recovered and saved (Rev. 1:18; Rev. 20:12-15; Matt. 19:28-30; James 3:1; 2 Peter 2:1-22; Rev. 19:10; Numbers 16). The dominion of Hell and death are under the Father's command, and they are used as the Lord's prison. Just like a man who violates his probation has to pay double, there are spiritual debts as well. The number of cases Jesus has to veto each day is innumerable; if only we could see how much work our Advocate in Heaven has to put in for us. It would make us more humble (Luke 22:31-34; Mark 16:6-7; John 21:7-17).

Furthermore, overzealousness is a gateway sin, which is why I must keep reiterating the importance of following the guidance of the Holy Spirit. For He is our Guide until the end of times, and when we obey Him, we will be at peace to know that Christ is in control. This leads me to my next topic:

- Unnecessary Zeal -

There was a man who lived long ago. The man was a renowned heathen and feared not God, men, beast or principalities. The man had great power, and he was greatly feared over the land. He did as he pleased, and no man dared to withstand him. Since he had no fear of God, he did not honor Him. However, one day, the man got old then sickness followed. The man called on all the healers of the land and on all the pagan gods but to no avail. Desperate and scared to death in his last hour, he called on a God foreign to him, The One True God. The Father, in His infinite grace, showed him mercy and answered the man's prayer. The man died, but with his last breath, he proclaimed the name of the Lord over the land. His soul was then received in Paradise.

Upon reaching the Garden, he broke down and cried with great joy and gratitude before the King, and the man was overwhelmed with joy to have received such grace. Jesus welcomed him and gave him a place in His kingdom, but the man was not content. He felt so unworthy that he pleaded with God to give him a task in His army in order to repay Him. The King told him he could never repay Him; what God had given to him was of His own accord. "TAKE THE FAVOR AND GO REJOICE WITH YOUR BROTHERS," said the LORD to the man. Nevertheless, the man insisted. His pride was boastful even in the afterlife.

Annoyed by the man's demand, the King finally agreed to his demand. He assigned him to the angel's regiment, which supervised the gates of Hell. "Go with them," Jesus told the man. "They will train you for battle, then show you to your post. You shall guard the outskirt of Hell to help prevent the escape of demonic spirits." Happy to have met the Living God and to have received a charge, per his own demand, the man descended into the pit with the angels to fulfill his assignment.

While at his post, the man began to feel disturbed by the agony of the condemned. He felt more and more disturb to see his loved ones in this place and others that he himself had killed by the sword. The man persisted to fulfill his mission he had received per his own demand. At last, his soul cried out. He pleaded with the archangel to speak to the King, and the archangel obliged. When the man arrived before Jesus, he bowed down before the King with his face to the ground and implored Him to be decommissioned. Jesus, the omniscient, said to the man, "Fear not, for I knew beforehand that this would be the outcome. Now go. Rejoice with your brothers as I have commanded you before." The man stood up with gladness, thanked the King, and sung praises to His name for His great compassion.

As the man was walking back to Paradise with that same archangel by his side, he looked up and told the archangel, " I do not know how you can do this and not feel troubled by the terrible sight of Hell. I have lived a very harsh life, and I was a very wicked man. However, this felt like the longest year of my life. The archangel looked at him with compassion and said, "Well, for this very purpose, I was manifested by the will of the Father, and I am prepared to serve in this capacity. Moreover, the archangel said, "You my friend. You were only at your post for merely three days!"

The moral of this story is God has already determined the size of every cross, and He will never put more on us than we can bear. We must walk according to His will and avoid the showboat. The zeal that Jesus requires from us is a zeal that is led by the Holy Spirit (Ezek. 47:1-5; Jer. 33:3). If we are not operating in the right office, we will feel burdensome; three days will feel like a year, and at the end, we would have wasted our grace in vain.

The LORD God Almighty will not be mocked (Luke 12:45-48), and His judgments are fair and impartial. Just and unjust, we must all pay our dues according to our walk in this realm, our faith, and whom we have pledged allegiance to. Once saved, always saved, amen, but there are still consequences in between this kingdom and the next for our actions; this is a call for faithfulness (Rev. 17:14, Rev. 22:18-19). Since the Father believes in free will, afterwards, He will take precautions to protect us against any possible impulses in His new creation (Ezekiel 11:19-21; Isaiah 66:22-24). Since we know that nothing can escape Him, let us then press on with fear and reverence in our hearts and with love and commitment as our banners.

- My Fair Maiden -

I would like to take another quick rabbit trail here to elaborate on something.

There has been a division within some churches for quite some time about whether or not the Ecclesiastical Church is the Bride of Christ. The main argument has been that Paul, in Ephesians 1:20-23, referred to the church as the body of Christ. Some people wonder, *how can the church be the body of Christ and His bride at the same time?* Let me remind everybody that nothing is impossible for God, and the Bible is a spiritual book, so looking at the spiritual with our natural eyes is already misleading. We need the Holy Spirit of God, which searches the deep things of God, to understand the mystery of God.

Second, Genesis 2:21-25 tells us that the LORD God took one of Adam's ribs, made a woman, and brought her unto the man. Adam said,

"This is now bone of my bones, and flesh of my flesh: she shall be called Woman, because she was taken out of Man. Therefore shall a man leave his father and his mother, and shall cleave unto his wife: and they shall be one flesh. And they were both naked, the man and his wife, and were not ashamed."

If God can take a rib from a man and make a woman as his bride, why is there such a big discord about the body of Christ eventually becoming His bride?

Paul even elaborates that fact in Ephesians 5:28-33; verse 28 states,

"So ought men to love their wives as their own bodies. He that loveth his wife love himself." In addition, verses 31 and 32 says, "For this cause shall a man leave his father and mother, and shall be joined unto his wife, and they two shall be one flesh. **This is a great mystery: but I speak concerning Christ and the church.***"*

The second Adam has done a marvelous thing that no one can fully understand (1 Cor. 13:9-12). Paul was giving a pivotal piece of the mystery, in relation to his calling (Eph. 3:4-7), and the identity of the Bride of Christ (2 Cor. 11:2). Likewise, the prophet Isaiah declared in Isaiah 54:5:

"For thy Maker is thine husband; the LORD of hosts is his name; and thy Redeemer the Holy One of Israel: The God of the whole earth shall he be called."

Read also Hosea 2:16-23; Gal. 3:28; 1 Cor. 12:13-28 and 1 Thess. 4:16-17.

These semantic arguments are just silly and unnecessary; they create division and can be a cause for dismissal. If we do not know who we are in Jesus Christ, this allows another to define us—and the deceiver to deceive us.

Others claim that the Bride of Christ is specific only to Israel remnants. I am an Israelite, but Ephesians 3:6 refute that belief. Israel will be first (Rev. 14:1-5), and that great city is dedicated to the twelve tribes (Rev. 21:12-14). All those who are saved will be part of God's tabernacle (Rev. 21:2-3). According to those last two verses, the Bride of Christ is the New Jerusalem and also the tabernacle of God. Furthermore, in verses 22 to 27 in that same chapter of Revelation, the Text makes it clear. The New Jerusalem, The Bride of Christ, is prepared to receive the *"nations of them which are saved,"* with the Lord God Almighty, and the Lamb as its temple.

"And the gates of it shall not be shut at all by day: for there shall be no night there. And they shall bring the glory and honor of the nations into it."

See also John 14:1-3, Rev. 19:7-9, and Rev. 22:12-17.

The Bride is clearly the Holy Tabernacle of God where all people who walk in the Spirit and are saved will be welcomed. An eternal "Church City," if I may, with God and the Lamb of God as the Eternal Temple. Additionally, Jesus is the Eternal High Priest, and the patriarchs of Israel will be His clergy (Psalms 110:4;

Heb. 7:1-17; Ex. 19:6; 1 Peter 2:9; John 3:29; Rev. 3:9-12). Moreover, just as when we join a church here on Earth, when we come to this glorious day, we shall all be united to that church. We shall all be officially members of the everlasting ministry of God. It will be a religious-free ministry, pure and unaltered, coming straight from the Source of Life Himself. There will be no Baptist, Adventist, or whatever religion you may be. There will be only one doctrine: the eternal doctrine of God and the Lamb. Our spirits will become one with Him, and He will feed us eternal rhema.

Even here in this realm, if you've been to church for any length of time, you should have noticed that our souls get connected to the pastor's when we join a church. He begins to see our light, and you can often feel his frustrations. However, in Heaven, God will be our everlasting light, and in Him, there will be no frustration.

The name of the church will be "The New Jerusalem," in honor of God's chosen people: Moses, Joshua, David, Elijah, Ezekiel, Isaiah, Daniel, and many other patriarchs. However the Lion of the tribe of Judah will be the Crown Piece (Isaiah 46:13; Rev. 3:12; Jer. 31:31-40), and all the Saints will be welcomed there.

The religious practices that we have anchored ourselves with have replaced the hankering of our souls for true fellowship. The only important thing we should be concerned with, regarding The Bride, is for us to make it to the wedding of the Lamb in proper attire. This can only be done through the guidance of the Holy Spirit (Matt. 22:1-14).

Again, all quarrels between different churches are just semantics, and we should stop with the politics of religion. Churches should truly seek to please God in spirit and in truth.

Now, let us look at the word church. According to Zondervan's dictionary, "The English word 'church' is derived from the Greek 'kuriakos,' meaning 'belonging to the Lord.' It stands for another Greek word ekklesia, which denotes an assembly."

From this definition, we can conclude that if you have received Christ as your Lord and Savior, you belong to Him as a member of the body of Christ. When you get born again, you instantly receive a membership to the New Jerusalem. You then are washed in His Holy Blood and sealed with His Holy Spirit. This means Blacks, Whites, Latinos, and whomever else is walking in the will of the Father through the Spirit belong to the Lord.

Conclusively, we were giving the parable of the ten virgins, the ten minas, and the faithful steward as a warning of what may happen if we do not maintain our anointing. It is of utmost importance in this last hour that we do not be distracted by the beast's illusions or give heed to our sinful desires. We can clearly see that the signs of the end are in full display now.

"This I say then, Walk in the Spirit, and ye shall not fulfill the lust of the flesh. For the flesh lusteth against the Spirit, and the Spirit against the flesh: and these are contrary the one to the other: so that ye cannot do the things that ye would. But if ye be led of the Spirit, ye are not under the law" (Gal. 5:16-18).

The whole chapter of Galatians 5 is about how we are to walk in the Spirit of God and refrain from the works of the flesh. As Jesus said, we are the salt of the earth, and we must strive to retain the savor that Christ has instilled in us. If that savor is lost, the salt has no value, and it is only good to be trodden under the foot of men (Matt. 5:13). We must not allow the system of the fallen to distract us, nor shall we take the same chance as the foolish virgins or the lazy servant, nor dwell in Balaamrism (Rev. 22:10-19). God has given us free will to do as we chose, but the truth is when we refuse to listen to the Holy Spirit, we are directly rebuking the counsel of the Father. We are limiting our spiritual growth and development (John 16:7-15, Philippians 4:13). We are the Bride of Christ, His fair Maiden, and He has adorned us with spiritual beauty. Be not so concerned with where you will sit. Be joyful that you have been invited to the wedding, and make—and keep—yourself ready (Matt. 22:1-14).

- Furthermore -

"Ye are the light of the world. A city that is set on a hill cannot be hid" (Matt. 5:14).

This declaration of our King is comparable to a king in medieval time placing his ring in a trusted servant's hand before sending him on an important mission.

I use that comparison because the Bible tells us that Jesus is the Light (Isaiah 9:2; John 14:6), and as repetitive as it may sound, He has given each one of us a portion of Himself in the form of the Holy Spirit to shine the pathway to Heaven for others and ourselves. The significance of the king's ring being placed in the servant's trust in Biblical and medieval times was to denote the urgency and the validity of the message being delivered (Esther 8:1-[8]). This also meant the servant was trustworthy and reliable. Jesus has, in effect, bestowed a very great honor upon us.

In verse 15 of Matthew 5, Jesus uses the logic of men to amplify the importance of our calling:

"Neither do men light a candle, and put it under a bushel, but on a candlestick."

A bushel is a basket used for measuring various commodities. Jesus is simply saying that if we have enough sense to use the light from a candle, how much more sense should we have concerning the Light of God? He gave this light to us for the purpose of the Kingdom. He expects us to maintain His anointing, let our light shine, and allow GOD to increase our gifts as needed for the kingdom.

The way we allow God to execute His will towards us is by learning to be obedient to the voice of the Spirit who lives in us, to learn to trust in Him, and to let go and let God lead us.

Those things can only be accomplished through empowerment in the presence of God. When we fast or spend time with Him in prayer and meditate on His words, we do not give in to temptations.

For the light of God, who is Jesus Christ, to shine through us, we must not be ashamed of His Gospel, and we must not be afraid to let the world know who we are. In good times and bad times, the Light should always shine through our testimony and our good deeds (John 12:35-50, John 15:1-11; Col. 1:9-14; Ephesians 6:10-17; Galatians 5:16,26; James 2:14-26 and Mark 8:34-38).

CHAPTER TEN

JOHN 14:6

The Law vs. The Law of Grace

In the next paragraph, Jesus declared:

"Do not think that I am come to destroy the law, or the prophets: I am not come to destroy, but to fulfill. For verily I say unto you, Till heaven and earth pass, one jot or one tittle shall in no wise pass from the law, till all be fulfilled" (Matt. 5:17-18).

These two declarations encompass many things. First, Jesus tells us that the law was never destroyed, but He was sent to fulfill it. The law is still valid, but since no one could carry out the 613 commandments of the Mosaic Law, Jesus came and fulfilled them. The application of the law as a standard ceases by virtue of Christ's new covenant because the law and the prophets testify of Him, and He reigns over them both as the Son of God. Secondly, it would also mean that since the law is not destroyed or abolished, the apostles, prophets, and supervisors have the authority to use certain principles of the law, as long as it does not contradict the New Covenant. Therefore, there is no charge against leaders preaching about tithes and offerings in concurrence with the law (2 Tim. 3:16-17; Deut. 14:22-29; Mal. 3:8-12).

There were three types of tithes in the Old Testament: one for the Levites, or clergy (Lev. 27:30-33; Num. 18:8-32), and this was the first fruits of all the land; one for the Lord's feast intended to bring blessings on the land for the people (Deut. 12:4-12); and one for the poor (Lev. 19:9-10, 23:22). The argument I usually hear regarding tithing is, "Since Jesus is now the perpetual First fruit, do I give tithe of my gross pay or increase only? What is my increase?" As far as what is the increase of an individual, I will leave that to the overseers. However, the basic necessities or absolute minimum of life are food, water, shelter, and clothing. If we take away all the distractions of this realm, there would be more than enough to support the Gospel of Jesus Christ. PlayStation, the new iPhone, plasma TVs, and Michael Kors' purses are not priorities or even necessities. Most of these products are made in sweatshops in third world countries for a few pennies on the backs of poor people who are barely paid enough, many of whom are children and women detained against their will. We create burdens for ourselves in trying to follow this evil world, and it often leads to rebellious behavior. The Gospel of Jesus Christ is the only thing we can take with us into the afterlife. Even the New Covenant allows the clergy to receive monetary compensation for their services (1 Cor. 16:1-2; 2 Cor. 9:6-13; Luke 6:38 and Acts 20:35). This means we should also be considerate of their needs in our offerings. No man of God should be living in poverty. It is the will of the Father that all things are done in good order and fairness (Ps. 23:1; Phil. 4:6-7; Gal. 6:6-10).

This does not mean we should be blind to the spirit of greed that has overtaken some churches. The same Book that authorizes the tithe and offering also contains warnings for the gluttonous ministers (Acts 20:29-35; Numbers 18:13, 30-32; 2 Thess. 3:6-15). Hence, if there are any false prophets among us, we should not carry their unnecessary burdens; let them starve (Matt. 7:15-20; Gal. 5:19-26).

Furthermore, Matthew 5:17-18 is in direct conjunction with Matthew 11:27-30, which means after Jesus fulfilled the Law and took over the mantle of the prophets (Heb. 1:1-3), He then gave us a lighter load to carry.

The narration of the Bible from the Old Testament to the New Covenant can be compared to the parable of the twelve sons.

A Father had twelve sons and many adopted children. He was a very wealthy man. One day, he was determined to bring them all together under the same roof. He called his 12 sons and granted them a task. "Build me a deck in the backyard," he said, "so that you, my immediate sons, and my other children may all be able to relax under the same roof and escape the hot summer days. Here are the nails (The Ten Commandments), the wood beams (The Ark of The Covenant), the drills (The Prophets), and the hammers (The Judges)."

The Father gave specific instructions on how the deck was to be built; he even personally helped along the way by guiding them and giving them a helping Hand from time to time. However, the twelve sons were rebellious and complacent; they were stubborn and would not complete their Father's task. However, strangers walking by were filled with a divine zeal and stopped to help them. The first was a prostitute by the name of Rehab, and another went by the name of Ruth; she is said to have even carved her name on the center beam. The last one was a narcissist neighbor by the name of Nebuchadnezzar. They were all impressed by the Father's wisdom and were compelled to help. Nevertheless, the twelve sons would not finish the task. One day, when they least expected, the Father came and built the deck all by himself, called the twelve sons and his adopted children, and gave them a new task. He said, "See, I have done all the work myself. Go now and gather enough people to come here and enjoy this relaxing setup with us. I have done the heavy lifting; now all you have to do is extend my invitation to passersby."

This is truly all that Jesus is asking of us now: to go and teach the great message of salvation provided by Him without further philosophical ties or man-made yokes. He did not give us permission to scrap over the law, compete to see who can keep most of the law's requirements, or attempt to see who can still observe the original Sabbath. He simply ceases and desists the power of the law and redirects all things to Him (Malachi 1:6-14; Hosea 2:10-11; Amos 8:4-8; Lam. 2:5-9; Gal. 3; Col. 2:15-17). Since Jesus is the Word of God made flesh, God's foundational standards proclaimed in the Ten Commandments remain as the everlasting foundation of the Gospel of Jesus Christ (Matt. 22:36-40; John 5:39). Everything in the law, which is an expression of the everlasting temperament of God, is forevermore applicable with the rule of thumb, "Be holy as I AM is holy," with the original Commandment, love, as the glue (Matt. 22:37-38; John 13:34). Still, some men are not satisfied with the works of His Hand, and thus, they have added yokes for themselves and others to bear.

A prime example of a man-made yoke is the Sabbath, excluding the special feasts in the Old Testament. Originally, the weekly Sabbath was observed every seven days starting with the new moon of each month (Ezekiel 46:1-3; Psalm 104:19). The purpose of the Sabbath in the Ten Commandments is to let us know that we should not work without ceasing; we are not machines, and God created us to enjoy this earth within the boundaries of righteousness. The Sabbath signifies that we should have a day in the week set aside to rest from work, a day when we should come together and glorify God for His loving kindness. The observance of the Sabbath under the Mosaic Law in the Old Testament was based on the lunar calendar of the early Israelites. This calendar was not a man-made calendar; it was given to men by God Himself. They were to specifically use the moon to observe the seasons.

The beast's overlords replaced that principle with their solar calendar, which is based on the solar years, or the so-called "cycle of the earth around the sun." It is all part of the beast's attempt to have us worshipping him (Daniel 7:25-27; Deut. 17:1-5; Acts 7:42-43). Our omnipotent Savior took that burden away from us so that we do not have to be walking in trespasses in these last days (Col. 2:8-17). Because the truth is, if we were to observe the Biblical Sabbath in our present time, we would totally need to have a very flexible work schedule because the Lunar Sabbaths fall on different days each cycle. Additionally, according to Leviticus, Exodus, and Deuteronomy, there were also seven annual Sabbaths observed under the law.

It is a binding gesture for men to set apart a special day for the Lord each week to honor Him and to take a break from work. This was the initial intent of the Sabbath in the Ten Commandments (Ex. 20:8-11), and it's the least we can do. However, teaching others that they will burn in hell unless they honor the current seventh-day solar Sabbath which respects the sun is a farce.

This is the silliness of the anti-Christ spirit: the Christians who worship on Saturday, which actually stands for "Saturn-day," label the ones who worship on Sunday, "sun worshipers." Saturn-day, however, is named after Saturn, which is the Roman god of agriculture and harvest, and some even believe that the name Saturn is actually derived from the name "Satan." Meanwhile, the Christians who worship on Sunday often mock those who hold to the seventh-day belief and label them a cult. However, they are both observing the same solar cycle. What a spoof! The current seventh-day Sabbath is actually derived from the Rules of

Postponement written in 358 A.D. by Hillel the second. Later in 1582, these rules eventually led to the Gregorian almanac and our current weekly cycle.

No one that I know of today is keeping the original Sabbath. The Israelites long ago steered the Father to anger, and He eventually disowned His own ordinances (Hosea 2:11). He then redirected all things to the Son, who is the eternal promise (1 John 3:4-[8]; Gal. 4:1-[10-11]; Col. 2:15-17; Matt. 17:5; John 14:6). Ultimately, whichever day you choose to observe, Jesus got you covered (Rom. 13:1-2). In addition, according to Isaiah 66:22-23, God will remake everything new, and His Sabbaths and New Moon festivals will be honored as they were intended (see also Mark 2:23-28 and John 7:14-24).

Now, there are some who have removed the yoke of the law concerning the Sabbath but have added pagan celebrations like Halloween and Easter to the church based on Colossians 2:16. Halloween, as we all know, is the day of the dead. People believe it to be a day the dead walk freely in spirit among the living. Easter is just the American translation of Ishtar, who is a Babylonian goddess of war and sexual love; she is also known as the queen of heaven according to Jeremiah 7:17-19. I covered her identity in Chapter 4 under "resolution 217." The Bible makes it clear that our God is a jealous God and does not share His glory with other gods. Moreover, the only One who is Holy and can declare a day holy is God (Lev. 23:4). Although He has put a cease on the requirement of the law, there's just no way He would glorify any pagan deities (1 Sam. 5:1-7; Jeremiah 7:12-30).

Many overseers today worship this queen of heaven during Easter because they do not think that God is enough. They have said into their hearts, "Just in case God is not enough, let us make a little money on the side" (Acts 5:1-11); they have forgotten about the power of the Almighty (Acts 4:32, 5:32). They have spoken these words into their hearts because they know that many people only go to church on holidays; therefore, they expect a full church during Easter, Thanksgiving, Christmas, and New Year's Eve. What a great time to reach the masses and testify of Christ's love for them, but instead, many pastors just go along with the narrative of this world concerning these so-called holidays in order to fill the offering baskets. The harvest of funds is greater than the harvest of souls for the Lord to those types of pastors. The late pastor Stephen Darby - from Destined Ministry - has a message on Youtube labeled, "They're Killing Birds." I recommend you watch it when you get a chance.

This is not a light thing for the children of God to set an abomination in the house of God to pollute it.

The conflict comes from the misunderstanding of some of Paul's statements in the Bible concerning holidays; these statements can be found in Colossians 2:16-17 and Romans 14:5-6. Most churches believe those verses imply that all holidays are acceptable to the Lord, but contrary to popular belief, in those passages, Paul is **not** saying that it is okay to observe all holidays. What Paul is saying in the texts above is that we do not have to observe the Jewish holidays or keep observing the Jewish traditions because now we live in Christ, and for Christ alone (Rom. 14:7-18; Mark 2:27). Therefore, the burden of the Mosaic Law is no longer a yoke for us to carry because Jesus has taken that burden away from us and made our load lighter. This does not mean that everything goes or is acceptable before the Lord; what it means is that (although the curse of the fall stills stands) everything that was once declared impure is now restored to its previous value through Jesus' sacrifice (Gen. 1:31; Gen. 3:17; Lev. 11; Lev. 25:8-10; Acts 2:1-5, 10:9-16). This is why we are no longer called servants, but also friends; and not only friends, but also heirs to the kingdom of God, heirs to the new heaven, and heirs to the new earth to come through our Lord and Savior. The value of the pagan deities, however, remain the same: they've been anti-God since their rebellion in heaven, their time for repentance has pass, and there's just no room for them in the kingdom of Light (2 Peter 2:1, [4-9]; 2 Cor. 6:14-18; Acts 16:16-24).

The principle, "Be holy as I AM is holy," can never be abolished, for our Creator is the Eternal One, and He does not change. The temperament of GOD is part of His attributes, and He is a jealous and loving Father. This pagan celebration of the goddess of fertility just does not have any place in our Father's house.

Now, just because we are no longer under the yoke of the law, and we are heirs of The Most High does not mean that we can go around changing His standard.

One thing we have to keep in mind when reading the Scriptures is the timelines and the atmosphere of each season portrayed in the Bible.

During the time of brother Paul, the culture was driven by the idea of painting pictures with words, but not every painting is verbatim. Another thing to consider about Paul's time is the level of morality and justice they were still privileged to (Acts 16:36-39, 22:3). Clearly, every judicial trial was not fair (Matt. 27:22-25), but they still had esprit de corps for their fellow men. To declare "all things are permitted" in our current generation can be misleading because the state of our societies has been corroded. To properly apply Apostle Paul's principle "all things are permitted," we must first go back to our roots, essence, and core values. These can only be found in our Creator. What the apostle Paul was saying in these various passages is that the integral value of God's creation is now restored through Jesus (Gen. 1:31; Isa. 55:10-11; Acts 10:9, [15-16] and Luke 3:23-[38]), and the earth was made for us. Ergo, meaning "everything is permitted, but not everything is expedient," is the code most people live by, but we should ensure the "everything" that we live by is pleasing to God. This is the key difference between, "Do as that wilt," and "Thy will be done." It all goes back to the Holy Spirit (2 Kings 5:13-[26] 27).

There are too many examples of the wrath of God exacting vengeance against the immoralists throughout the Bible for us to claim that the apostle Paul has given us carte blanche to do as we will and to celebrate all deities. If this is the case, I have an idea. Satan is a deity, so let us set apart a day out of the year to celebrate Satan. We can call it: The Day of Stupidity. The argument that brother Paul was having, which led to him making so many of these remarks, was similar to the arguments that Jesus and John the Baptist were having with the Jews. The Jews wanted their customs and traditions to be the standard, but Christ **is** the standard (Mark 2:27). He rules over all things, and **likewise**—in a Christ-like matter—the earth was made for man to rule over. Therefore, eating and drinking (**conservatively**) are not offenses (Matt. 11:16-19, 15). The failure to observe a Mosaic holiday is not a sin (2 Chr. 31:2-3; Matt. 12:1-8; Rom. 14:5), but all things must be done according to God's will and within the full persuasion of one's mind. In other words, we ought to walk as Abel and not Cain. They were both fully persuaded in their offering, but only Abel's sacrifice was acceptable to the LORD because Abel brought "the firstlings of his flock" (Gen. 4:4), the best of what he had, but Cain brought a mediocre product as an offering to God (Gen. 4:3).

Some of the other arguments our brothers had to endure include marriage and divorce, life after death, and the traditions of the elders. God never approved the celebration of the pagan deity of fertility, nor can we find any part of the Gospel that validates this ritual. The only place in the Bible where the word Easter is found is in Acts 12:4 in the New Testament. It is tied to a Jewish politician by the name of King Herod, a persecutor of the early Church. Notwithstanding, it is also important that I mention the original King James Bible actually used the word Passover in that same passage. In some Biblical interpretations (like the NIV by Zondervan Publishing), the term Passover is still being used as well. How, when, and who decided to change the word Passover to Easter is not clear, but it is not an approved feast in neither the Old nor the New Testament.

Furthermore, many of us have set up a date to "honor the Son of Man" each year, just to turn it into the celebration of a wizard named Santa Claus. Lastly, I have even seen Halloween celebrations in my church in the past. The coming apostasy must be at hand (2 Tim. 3:1-17).

The desires of the Lord for His Church according to the Holy Spirit are:

Try Me sayeth the LORD, remove all of the abominations from your midst, and evict this whore of Babylon from the house of the LORD. Purify the vessels of the LORD, and you shall see My mighty hand in action once again.

- Why Grace? -

Now remember, all of the conflicts in the spiritual and natural realms started because of one disobedient, stubborn child named Lucifer. The purpose of the law in Heaven was to maintain order, and the purpose of the law for Earth was to teach us God's precepts and to bring conviction against our corrupted and sinful nature. Once a conviction was made against us for violating the law, judgment then followed accordingly. The book of Leviticus as a whole was given just for that purpose, and in Leviticus 20:7-8, we can see the summary.

Now, conviction is not the same as condemnation; conviction is simply a citation for the violation of God's precepts. The law used to be the Judicial and Executive Code for that violation, but the Holy Spirit now holds that post as the Comforter. Withal, the intent is still the same as back then, "Consecrate yourselves and be holy" because we are Jesus' earthly temple, and He dwells within us. Besides, as our Redeemer and our God, we should follow His precepts.

All the people who claimed, "God is not like that anymore," or "We don't live in the Old Testament anymore," have failed to understand the same God who said, *"Turn the other cheek,"* is the same one who said, *"An eye for an eye, and a tooth for a tooth."* The marching order may have changed, but God remains the same (Psalm 110:1; Rev. 14:9-10; Isaiah 66:23-24).

The Father has given all authority concerning the salvation of men over to the Son, and Jesus made it easier for us to obtain it (Matt. 11:26-30). Jesus has fulfilled the requirement of the law and took over the mantle of the prophets before Him as Son of God. All that was prophesied has not yet come to pass (see the parallel from Psalm 110:1 and Rev. 14:9-11).

The Father also testified as a witness to the authority of the Son three times in the New Testament. The first time was after Jesus was baptized, found in Matt. 11:16-17. The third time was before His crucifixion, pinpointed in John 12:28-29. The second time is the most specific because during that interaction, the Father makes it clear that all things are redirected to His Son, Jesus. The second time can be found in Matthew 17:1-5:

"And after six days Jesus taketh Peter, James, and John his brother, and bringeth them up into a high mountain apart, And was transfigured before them: and his face did shine as the sun, and his raiment was white as the light.

And, behold, there appeared unto them Moses and Elijah talking with him. Then answered Peter, and said unto Jesus, Lord, it is good for us to be here: if thou wilt, let us make here three tabernacles; one for thee, and one for Moses, and one for Elijah. While he yet spake, behold, a bright cloud overshadowed them: and behold a voice out of the cloud, which said, **This is my beloved Son, in whom I am well pleased; hear ye him**.*"*

These verses are the most specific because under the law, what Peter said would have been justified. Peter suggested they set up three "Tabernacles of Meeting." In the days of Moses, that tabernacle was where the people consorted with the LORD – Exodus 33:7-10. For Peter, the three of them being there in the presence of the Son of God transfigured before their eyes demanded a proper disposition. However, GOD refuted Peter's claim and informed him that Jesus was the completion of the law, and the prophets. Walking with Jesus is all we need now to please the Father. What Jesus did for us is comparable to the parable of the big brother and the bee.

In the story of the big brother and the bee, a family is traveling down a country road with their windows down. Suddenly, a honeybee enters the car. After conceding that it was stuck in a moving vehicle and unable to find its way out, the bee begins to buzz and fly around and about looking for an output for its frustrating fate. As the bee was approaching a little girl in the car that was allergic to bees, her big brother jumped between her and the insect to save her. He was stung in her place, but the fear of the bee sting had taken hold, and she could not stop weeping. Her big brother tried to reassure her, but to no avail. Disturbed by all the commotion, the parents turned their attention to them and asked what was the matter? The little girl first explained her dilemma, and afterward, her big brother informed their parents of his action. Following the depiction, the parents smiled at the little girl and said, "Baby girl, there is nothing else to fear. The bee is dead, and your big brother took its stinger out when he stood between you and the insect."

When a honeybee stings a mammal, it cannot pull its stinger back. It must leave it behind because when it stings its target, the stinger gets stuck in the target's skin. When the bee pulls away, parts of its digestive tract, muscles and nerves stay with the stinger. This abdominal rupture is what leads to the honeybee's death. There is just no way the insect can put itself back together, and it has no choice but to lay there until it dies (1 Cor. 15:55-58). There's also no longer a reason to fear its power, for its fate is inevitable. We only have to cling to our Big Brother's completed work now, and grace is the only valid compensation for our sins. Therefore, the Law of Grace commands us to walk in the love of Christ—the kind of love He demonstrated for us at Calvary. This is the type of love that would defend both the earthly vessel and the congressional church from the guiles of the enemy (James 2:1-13).

- Danger of the Law -

Now the next two verses that follow give us a warning about the danger of those very guiles. After affirming all things unto Him, Jesus then gives the remedy for the snare of religion that we have been saturated by. Matthew 5, verses 19 and 20 in the NIV state:

"Therefore anyone who set aside one of the least of these commands and teaches others accordingly will be called least in the kingdom of heaven, but whoever practices and teaches these commands will be great in the kingdom of heaven.
For I tell you that unless your righteousness surpasses that of the Pharisees and teachers of the law, you will certainly not enter the kingdom of heaven."

This passage makes it clear that anyone teaching salvation outside of the precepts Jesus has set-up is called least in the kingdom of Heaven. Therefore, Hiram Abiff, a dead man that was worshipped because King Solomon supposedly brought him back to life because he was deemed holy for his service to the king, nor any other entity cannot validate men outside of Jesus Christ. He makes it even more personal when He says that our righteousness must exceed the righteousness of the Pharisees and the teachers of the law, or we will not see Heaven. This means that the custom and standard of the Pharisees must **not** be our criterion for ministry, but Jesus, as the Love of GOD incarnated, must be the benchmark. Now, let us look at some of the characteristics that specifically defined the Pharisees and religious leaders of those days.

According to Zondervan's Compact Bible Dictionary:

"The Pharisees, who were the higher echelon of the religious groups at that time, believed that they were 'the separated ones, separatists,' and they were also known as the Chasidim, meaning 'love of God' or 'loyal to God.' They became a closely organized group, very loyal to the society and to each other, but separate from others, even their own people. They pledge themselves to obey all facets of the traditions to the minutest details and were sticklers for ceremonial purity. They made life difficult for themselves and others. They despised those whom they did not consider their equals and were haughty and arrogant because they believed they were the only interpreters of God and His Word."

Moreover, according to Zondervan:

"The Scribes were a class of learned men whose professional occupation was the systematic study of the law and its exposition. They were also known as 'lawyers' (Matt. 22:35), 'doctors of the law' (Luke 5:17), and 'rabbis' (Matt. 23:1-8). They devoted themselves to the preservation, transcription, and exposition of the law.

To safeguard the sanctity of the law, they gradually developed an extensive and complicated system of teaching, known as 'the tradition of the elders' (Matt. 15:2-6). They were not part of the priesthood."

Lastly, Zondervan also states that the Sadducees, the third religious Jewish group of that time, "accepted only the Law and rejected oral tradition. They denied the power of resurrection, immortality of the soul and the existence of the spirit world" (Mark 12:18; Luke 20:27; Acts 23:8). They were denounced by John the Baptist (Matt. 3:7-8) and Jesus (Matt. 16:6, 11, 12). They held positions in the high priesthood, and they opposed Christ (Matt. 21:12; Mark 11:15; Luke 19:47), and the apostolic church (Acts 5:17, 33).

In other words, they each believed that the law in and of itself was the purpose of the Judaism faith. In their desire to maintain that faith, they created their own order based on their own traditions and customs. Their concern became solely to safeguard and maintain the order that they had created. Additionally, each one of these organized religious groups believed they were the nucleus of the Judaism faith, and they each claimed that all their standards were based solely on the law. However, they were each in opposition to each other until Jesus came, and they found a reason to unite. They had become so saturated with the ceremonial aspect and application of the law that they neglected to grasp the true meaning of the Word of God.

They study the law to show themselves worthy and approved of men, but they did not understand or believe what they were all claiming as their validation (John 5:37-47). They were much like the cults of today. Just like in the days of the Son of Man's first visit, they will unite against us once we find our unanimity in the Lord.

These dispositions from these religious leaders caused both Jesus and John the Baptist to label them as vipers and a brood of vipers (Matt. 12:34, Matt. 3:7 and Matthew 23). Those terms "vipers and brood of vipers" are in reference to their true allegiance being to the kingdom of darkness. Due to their blood ties to their forefathers, Jesus even accused them of being tied to the killing of the prophets who lived long before them, and to the killing of the prophets, wise men, and scribes that would follow (Matt. 23:29-36). The reason Jesus charged them with those crimes was because these men were of the same spirit as the ones who committed the actual slaying, which is the spirit of the beast that has been operating in darkness throughout generations and persecuted the saints of God from righteous Abel to Zechariah, son of Barachias.

As stated earlier, the purpose of the "Tabernacle of Meeting" was for men to consort with the LORD. It was also a place where men could go and give praises to God, and it was meant to be a house of prayer (Isaiah 56:1-8, Psalm 93). Instead, they made it a den of thieves (Jer. 7:1-11), and they sought to destroy Jesus for reminding the world of the true purpose of the tabernacle or the church (Matt. 21:12-16). Likewise today, Satan, once again has managed to infiltrate the church and destroy the true intent and application of the Father for the "Tabernacle of Meeting," or "Tabernacle of the Congregation," with religion and religious hang-up because we have allowed him to do that. This lack of perception leads to the Father removing His power and His protecting fence from around us. When men decide to honor the LORD their own way and alter the rules and standards set by God, they make themselves worshippers of Baal—the idol god (Gen. 19:15-23, 30, 36-38; Num. 25:1-5; 2 Chr. 15:1-19).

Everyone wants to panic now, but the answer for our dilemmas is Jesus Christ, the Word of God made flesh. He is the Father's greatest weapon, and He now lives in us (Ps. 18:30-39, 119:89-96; Zech. 4:6; John 6:63; Matt. 21:21).

We are currently experiencing what the prophet Jeremiah has prophesied in Jeremiah Chapter 7. It may be a difficult thing to find a registered point of worship in this generation that has not been tainted with idol worship. Remember the body is the temple of God where the Holy Ghost resides; therefore, we ought to preserve our assigned temple (Josh. 24:15). Our faith should not be centered on any idols, and no honor should be given to the queen of heaven, Saint Nicholas, Saturn-day, or Sun worship. Jesus should be the sole foundation for our religion and faith. Pick a day; set it aside in honor of the KING of KINGS, and stop with the pettiness. Soon we'll be living as the apostles in the New Testament anyway, running and hiding away in various locations while still maintaining the faith. We must keep our eyes on Christ, and we must keep our hearts and minds clear of Baal worship.

The Father's Grace is more than enough, and the religion that the Father honors is one based on the love that only God can give. If he is not the sole foundation and supplier of that faith, that faith is in vain (James 1:19-[27]; Luke 10:25-37; Numbers 11:18-23).

In the story of the good Samaritan, Jesus is talking about "a certain man traveling from Jerusalem to Jericho," or perhaps a Jew from Jerusalem traveling to the "moon city" to trade some goods. He ends up falling victim to thieves who beat and rob him. A priest and a Levite both walk by and avoid him by walking on the other side, and they neglect to render help to their fellow man. However, a stranger from a less desirable part of the country passed by. Seeing him dying, he takes pity on him and treats him as though he were his own brother.

In today's terms, the story can be told as follows: A certain Christian man on his journey to the eternal kingdom took a detour down the path of temptation. On the way there, he is stopped, beaten, and robbed by the devil because of his sin.

By chance, a pastor was walking by and witnessed the man's dilemma. When he saw him, he passed by on the other side. Likewise, another Christian, an elder of the church, came by, looked at him, and passed by on the other side as well. Their self-proclaimed holiness would not allow them to see past the brother's spiritual debility to offer even a prayer. However, a less favorable member, an ex-drug addict turned usher, noticed the fate of the man, felt compassion towards him, approached him, and encouraged him with prayers and supplications towards God. The usher shared this man's pain and pleaded with God for mercy until the man was restored. The lesser one was in fact the greatest among them.

The purpose of the parable was to emphasize the value of mercy over religion, charity over tradition, grace over the law, and shine the light on the sin of antipathy toward our neighbors (1 Cor. 13).

This is not to say that we should be enablers, but we should not be like the Pharisees who claimed to be "the love of God," but due to their self-proclaimed holiness, they despised their own neighbors (Gal. 6:1-5).

According to Google, there are seven major groups and over 33,000 protestant denominations or religions in the world. I know they are not all misled and misleading. I believe there are still some Joshuas and some Esthers out there in the front line and on the sideline, watching and procrastinating. I cannot tell you who is the closest to the unaltered truth, but I can tell you it makes no sense that we would have so many denominations, divided by the customs of men, all believing or claiming to be the only interpreters of God and His Word. I wonder what would happen if they would decide to join their voice in one accord to denounce this world and glorify the One True God (1 John 4:1-[2-3] 6).

Some may say this is an impossible request now because the Book must be fulfilled; and since the great apostasy must take place, the same sentiment was felt back in 1918. The great apostasy is a period of time where the church will become openly divided over our foundational doctrines concerning living a chaste life for Christ, and the new world doctrines of an all-inclusive culture. The all-inclusive culture has to do with all lifestyles being approved as a normal thing, and it has already begun. That culture revolves mainly around sexual liberty concerning society's sexual orientation and perversion, and this is why former President Obama legalized homosexuality (see Luke 17:28-32; Gen. 19:1-[5]). The church getting divided will cause many to be put out of their home church and persecuted for withholding Jesus' standard about sexual behavior (John 16:2; see also "California Law SB 145"). This whole conflict about LBGTQ and their sexual liberty has to do with Satan wanting to bring back the mind state of Sodom and Gomorrah. The days of Noah are already upon us, so now Satan is working on "as it was in the days of Lot" (Luke 17:28-32; Gen. 19:1-[5]). The great tribulation Jesus warned us about in Matthew 24:4-31 will follow once the systems of the days of Lots are officially set in place. Before that time arrives, we will first have a revival. Boy, oh boy, what a great revival it will be when we are all with one Spirit in Jesus Christ. The pillars of Baal (or idols) that have been incorporated in our churches will be cut down, and we will just have "CHURCH" as the LORD intended (2 Chr. 15:8-19). Great powers will be released from Heaven, and we will see the glory of the Lord GOD in action as the apostles before us (Acts 5:12-16). Through the grace of God, we are still here because God's grace endures forever!

- Thy Should Not Murder -

In Matthew Chapters 5 through 7, Jesus laid out the foundation to His ministry and established Himself as the centerpiece. He gives the remedy against the mark of the beast and breaks down the true intent of the church in this world. He goes on to enumerate each key point of His gospel. In verse 21 of Chapter 5, Jesus begins His next statement with the warning against committing murder.

Jesus uses the Old Testament reference to the physical act of murder, but He also speaks of murder related to the authority that He gave us by virtue of His New Covenant (Matt. 16:18-19; John 14:12-14; Prov. 18:17[21]; James 3:1-18). This fact is made more evident in verses 22-26 of Matthew Chapter 5; Jesus was indeed contrasting the act of physically killing a person with the power of the tongue.

Back in the Old Testament, only reputable people, such as a king or a prince, had the authority to speak decrees in action. However, when the General of Heaven came to Earth, He extended that authority to us. In Matthew 5:22, Jesus is giving us a warning about the danger attached to the authority of our tongue under His new covenant.

As His Believers, He has given us access to the launch code for the nuclear weapons of Heaven, and we ought not take this lightly (Luke 7:1-[8] 10; Luke 9:51-[54] 56; Mark 11:20-24). Just like the repercussions for a rogue's behaviors in the earthly army, there are repercussions for every word we speak as children of God. Our words can stir up the spirit realm and the armies of Heaven (Ps. 33:6; Eccl. 8:4-6; Jer. 1:9, 5:14; Isa 50:4; Prov. 15:4; 1 Cor. 2:1-13; 1 Peter 4:10-11). With the authority invested in us at Calvary comes great responsibilities; remember the judgment that befell brother Moses when he stroked the stone twice, which cost him the privilege to enter the promised land of Canaan. Remember also the 9[Th] Commandment in Exodus 20:16, "Thou shalt not bear false witness against thy neighbor."

This is the reason why the apostle Paul commands us to bring every thought into captivity to the obedience of Christ (2 Cor. 10:3-5). We ought to be careful of the words that we speak to one another and against others because they will bring condemnations back to us if we misjudge (Prov. 23:6-12; Num. 5:11-31). Just like when someone files a false report in this realm and gets charged, we are also faced with that regulation in spiritual warfare, especially if we are in a leadership position. Moreover, if you are not in a leadership position, you should be careful not to speak against a leader without any proof (1 Tim. 5:17-20; Matt. 18:15-20). The fact that Jesus contrasted the power of the tongue with the actual act of murder shows the serious implication behind the matter (See also Matt. 12:6-[37]). Either speak wisely, or do not speak at all.

Furthermore, we must not forget that the earth was pre-condemned and placed on probation until the Redeemer came to save us from the wages of sin. We were already due for complete annihilation, but the Father commanded that judgment be postponed. Certain things were permitted in the past because the plan of our eternal salvation was still being developed. Now that Jesus has paid for us with His own blood, it is paramount that we extend the same level of compassion towards one another. Not reciprocating that kind of love towards our fellow man is the same as getting placed on probation for a crime that we've committed in the natural realm and getting out of prison just to go repeat the same offense again. In our kingdom, such behaviors will lead to the doubling of the penalty, a penalty for the probationary crime, and one for the new mischief (Compare Isaiah 40:1-8).

Under Christ's appendage, we have been fully integrated unto Heaven's commands according to each one's ability. There is an ascension ministry and a descension ministry – and the proper sequence of growth is: Servant (Ezekiel 18:4), Sonship (Gal. 4:1-7), and then Servant Leadership (Rom. 1:1; 1 Cor. 12:28).

The authority that was reserved only to the Levites regarding ministry has been extended to all those who show themselves approved (Num. 4:1-20; 2 Tim. 2:

[15]-26). The Levites were in charge of the LORD's Tabernacle and the Ark of Testimony, and they were held at a higher level of accountability because of that (Leviticus 10:1-3). Likewise, since we now have the Spirit of Jesus living within us, we are called into accountability for our walk as Christians. The apostles, the prophets, and the pastors are interceders for us here on Earth, as Jesus is our Interceder in Heaven—but we each have to do our part.

In Matthew 5:21-26, the Lord is warning us of the power of the tongue, the danger of self-condemnation that the tongue holds, and our duty concerning the words of our lips as emissary of the Most High. We ought to have the forgiveness of God in our hearts, and we should walk in humility knowing that we have been spared the justified reproof of our sinful nature. Lastly, notice in verse 23, Jesus says that if we are bringing a gift to the altar and remember that our brother has a grudge against us, we have to go to him and make peace with him first. This is the attitude that a child of God should have, and Jesus Himself is the testament (Rom. 5:3-11).

- Protect Your Hearts -

"Whosoever looketh on a woman to lust after her hath committed adultery with her already in his heart" (Matt. 5:28).

Jesus, in Matthew 5 verses 27-30, is once again reinforcing the value of the new status quo. He is reiterating the fact that the battle between good and evil is a spiritual battle for the soul, and we should be careful to protect our hearts. This is why we can no longer think of the actual sexual intercourse as the sin; we have to protect our hearts and minds before it gets to that. This warning is directly connected to the porn addiction that is ruling our societies today. We live under the motto that "sex sales," and that motto is constantly being projected into our psyches in order to keep us sexually aroused at all times. Being constantly sexually aroused makes it easy for us to fall into fornication at a moment's notice. Marriages are ruined, homes are broken, and people even die at times over a moment of passion or a one-night stand. What's more? Masturbation, which normally goes hand in hand with porn addiction, is actually an indoctrination method that Satan has established to help fuel his new "Gay" World Order (Luke 17:28-32; Gen. 19:1-[5]). When a man is pleasuring himself, he is actually programming his mind to the concept of a man pleasuring a man. Holding his own dick in his hand and playing with himself is the precursor that later led many brothers to accept homosexuality as a natural output. The same goes for the ladies concerning lesbianism. This is because the demons behind the porn industry want to pervert the natural order of God, and if we watch porn, we are inviting them to enter our lives to do their bidding.

Jesus then goes on to paint a vivid picture of the importance of protecting our hearts in these last days because the final chapters have been written.

"And if that right eye offend thee, pluck it out, and cast it from thee: for it is profitable for thee that one of thy members should perish, and not that thy whole body should be cast into hell. And if thy right hand offend thee, cut it off, and cast it from thee: for it is profitable for thee that one of thy members should perish, and not that thy whole body should be cast into hell" (Matt. 5:29-30).

The eyes are the windows to the soul. If that window is receiving light from the Sun of righteousness, our vessels will remain bright. If it is receiving polluted light from the world, we will be polluted.

Moreover, the heart is where our soul's desires reside. If our eyes are polluted by the world, the abundance of our hearts will be polluted. By protecting our hearts from the evil of this world, we are in fact preserving it from its influence and adherence (Deut. 2:30; Ex 35:21-35; Proverbs 4:23-27; Luke 6:45; James 4:8).

Our intentions come from our motives, which are driven by the desires of our hearts and souls. If we have nothing but negativity in our hearts, we will have nothing but obscurity to offer to others (Matt. 12:33-37). That's why it is important for us to be conservative with what we watch or participate in because a little leaven leavens the whole lump (1 Cor. 5:6-8). Besides, concerning our sexual desires, if they do not comply with God's precept of one husband and one wife, we can end up violating the tenth commandment, *"Thou shalt not covet thy neighbour's wife"* (Exodus 20:17) and the lust of the flesh will reign over us. Remember, the devil (aka Mister Copycat) likes to plant seeds that he hopes to capitalize on later. When it comes to the lust of the flesh, all it takes is a look, and the fantasy wheel starts turning.

Once the wheel starts turning, it is hard to bring it to a stop. *"For as a man thinketh in his heart, so is he"* (Prov. 23:7). The tree of knowledge has given us mini computers (now called cell phones) to facilitate that fact. Everything can be done on these portable tracking and monitoring devices. I have even noticed that sometimes I could just be speaking with someone about going to the store for a certain item, and my personal monitoring device will instantly start sending me notifications about the nearest store to me without me even searching for it. In addition, when it comes to sexual temptations and addictions, I believe that this **cellular organism** has been our generation's biggest chip in. Lastly, I just don't understand why this new generation of touch screen needs to feed off our electrostatic discharge to be operational. I just wonder sometimes.

Nevertheless, the principle of "as a man thinketh, so he is" is a fact that I have noticed growing up in the ghetto. The thieves were always thinking about stealing or worried about being robbed by one another. The habitual liars always thought we were lying to them. The potheads always thought that we were holding some weed. The pimps always thought that every woman was slutty and could be sexually turned out. The police always assumed the worst about us, and the pastors were always looking for someone to save. I often ask myself what a caring and compassionate society would look like.

Later, in Matthew Chapter 6:23, Jesus corroborates that preeminence with the term, *"If therefore the light that is in thee be darkness, how great is that darkness!"* (See also 1 Tim. 6:9-10.) The writer even ends the statement with an exclamation point so we may understand that this is a declaration, not a question. We must protect our hearts.

- Marriage Is Sacred -

After observing the habits of men and their abuse of the law over 30 plus years, in the next two verses, Jesus, as our general, passes a ruling concerning marriage:

"Whosoever shall put away his wife, saving for the cause of fornication, causeth her to commit adultery: and whosoever marry her that is divorced committeth adultery" (Matt. 5:32).

He had to make that ruling because, as usual, men were taking advantage of any gap in the system. Moses gave them the right to divorce to avoid the wrath of God upon the Israelites' camp because men are going to do what men want to do (Deut. 24:1-4).

By the time Christ entered the scene, they were using it for any made-up causes. In addition, because women in those days had no rights, they could not speak on the matter. So Jesus, The Good Shepherd, exercised wisdom against the rules of men to restore order. In Matthew 19:3-12, He goes on to express His reason for that judgment. Although it was the second time the disciples were hearing about Jesus' ruling concerning divorce, in verse 10, we can see that this ruling also perturbed them. Jesus provided this adultery rule because as a man, we are naturally more inclined to respond to our reptilian side of the brain.

Don't get me wrong; physical attraction is part of communion between a man and a woman too. However, the communion of two hearts, or the joining of the souls between a husband and his wife, is what God wants above all. This caliber of relationship creates a stronger, purer bond. For the body will age and beauty will fade away, but genuine love can withstand the tests of life.

The effect of the reptilian brain is more evident today. For many people, marriage is no longer a sacred thing, and it is more regarded as a convenient thing to do if you are rich, or as a burden if you are poor. Such a lack of passion has also contributed to generations of dysfunctional homes and countless ruined lives. Here in America, we still have policies that discourage the abuse of divorce; policies like child support and alimony help discourage impulsive divorces, but this is not the case for everyone.

While travelling in the Middle East, I noticed in some cities, many women dressed in brown chadaree would sit together by the road with their heads down. They seemed miserable. After inquiring with the interpreter about the meaning of that ritual, I found out these women were disowned as wives by their husbands.

Apparently, in that part of the Middle East, once a husband decides the marriage is over, he would just drop his wife by the roadside to signify to any passerby that she was available to the next man. These poor souls would then gather in support of each other, until they eventually found a new home. The interpreter then explained to me that the reason why the husband dishonored her could be as simple as the wife not performing her wifely duties on a particular day, and whether or not the reason she could not perform was due to illness was irrelevant. The husband did not need to suffer a divorce decree. If he was not satisfied, he just dropped her off by the side of the road and went home to his other wives.

This level of gratuity is why Jesus had to rectify Moses's order; this type of liberty hyperbolized by the spirit of the beast causes men to lose their way. Polygamy was not God's initial plan for man, but He allowed it for a while. As with everything else, we have spoiled that appanage as well (compare Abraham in Gen. 21:9-20, David and 2 Sam 12:1-23).

- Vain Oaths (Read Your Bible) -

"Again, ye have heard that it hath been said by them of old time, Thou shalt not forswear thyself, but shalt perform unto the Lord thine oaths: But I say unto you, Swear not at all; neither by heaven; for it is God's throne: Nor by the earth; for it is his footstool: neither by Jerusalem; for it is the city of the great King. Neither shalt thou swear by thy head, because thou canst not make one hair white or black. But let your communication be, Yea, yea; Nay, nay: for whatsoever is more than these cometh of evil" (Matt. 5:33-37).

After Israel was delivered out of Egypt, God gave them His law and precepts to inform and preserve them from the power of sin. He gave them His judicial code, taught them how to judge, and gave them the sentence they should administer for each crime. He did that because they needed to unlearn all they had learned in Egypt during their 400 years of captivity, which could be considered their basic training, during which time they were broken off and grew tired of the oppression of Egypt. This left them thirsty and ready for the Advanced Individual Training that followed. He wanted to build them up according to his METL (Mission Essential Task List), so He could then send them out to minister to the heathen nations that surrounded them. The LORD divided Israel by tribes for that purpose, and He assigned to each tribe a specific marching position during their travel. This kind of breakdown was the equivalent of the marching formation of our military movements today. God was indeed preparing his people to fight against the heathen nations.

Starting off with the Passover in Genesis Chapter 12, the LORD covered every subject that was pertaining to the growth and development of His chosen people. He instructed them about the principles of His Holiness because the Holy God deserves a holy nation (Lev. 13:16).

In Leviticus 27 and Matthew 5:37, God teaches the Israelites about the importance of letting " *your communication be, yea, yea; Nay, nay: for whatsoever is more than these cometh of evil.*"

Also in Leviticus 27, He warned them of the cost of making vows and the importance of keeping our commitments unto the LORD. In other words, since we are to be holy as God is Holy, and *"God is not a man, that he should lie; neither the son of man, that he should repent:"* neither should we lie or speak vainly (Numbers 23:19; see also Deut. 23:21-23; Num. 30 and Eccl. 5:4-7).

Understandably, the Father knows that we are mere mortals, but He also knows what He has placed within us. He looks at us not based on our outward appearance but what is on the inside. At minimum, He expects us to know His directives so that we can be wise in our decision-making process (Deut. 11:16-21).

By the time we get to the book of Judges, Moses, Joshua, and the elders who outlived Joshua all went to sleep, and the generation that followed forgot about the One True God by worshiping false gods and observing pagan rituals (Judges 2:7-13). They set about to do what they were forbidden to do, and they married and gave their daughters in marriage to these evil nations (Judges 3:5-7). This led to Israel getting cursed and walking in subjugation to foreign nations until God raised a judge to deliver them (Judg. 3:8-11). This went on back and forth for about 400 years. Confusion ran rampant among the children of Israel during that time, and every man did what was right in his own eyes (Judges 17:1-6). It is during that time of ignorance that we see a judge offering his daughter as a burnt offering unto the LORD (Judges 11:29-40). What that judge did in that passage is the epitome of vain oaths, which was brought upon him through ignorance.

Before I move further, let us be fair to God for a minute. As mortal beings, we do not have the insight of what the future may hold, nor do we have control of the present. At any moment, the end may come for each one of us, and as soon as the present gets here, it is gone. For as you were reading the last statement, the present happened, and it just happened again! If we were to be honest with ourselves, we really only have the past as a reminder of what to do, or not to do, and we also have Jesus Christ as our eternal hope for the future. The present is described as the "here and now," and "the time currently existing or in progress." However, on average, 65 million people die each year in the world. That is 178,000 deaths each day, 7,425 each hour, and 120 each minute (These numbers are pre-pandemic). No one is guaranteed a next breath. Only God can truly exist through the space-time continuum, and only He can stop time (Josh. 10:12-14). Therefore, we ought to be confident, but also humble in our walk with Christ, for tomorrow is not promised and only God has all the pieces of the puzzle. It is only by His Grace that we are still here. Our natural predisposition to do evil is the reason why He allows so many terrible things to happen to us in the first place (Gen. 8:20-21).

Many people look at that passage in Judges Chapter 11 and say there is no way that God would allow a person to be sacrificed for Him. In essence, that is the truth, but the truth goes beyond the actual event of Judges 11.

To understand why this event happened in the first place, we must go back to the days of Noah:

"And God blessed Noah and his sons, and said unto them, Be fruitful, and multiply, and replenish the earth. And the fear of you and the dread of you shall be upon every beast of the earth, and upon every fowl of the air, upon all that moveth upon the earth, and upon all the fishes of the sea; into your hand are they delivered. Every moving thing that liveth shall be meat for you; even as the green herb have I given you all things. But flesh with the life thereof, which is the blood thereof, shall ye not eat. **And surely your blood of your lives will I require; at the hand of every beast will I require it, and at the hand of man; at the hand of every man's brother will I require the life of man. Whoso sheddeth man's blood, by man shall his blood be shed: for in the image of God made he man.** *And you, be ye fruitful, and multiply; bring forth abundantly in the earth, and multiply therein.* **And God spoke unto Noah, and to his sons with him, saying, And I behold, I establish my covenant with you, and with your seed after you"** *(Gen. 9:1-9).*

Additionally, we need to remember the instruction God gave to the Israelites concerning all their dwelling places:

"So these things shall be for a statute of judgment unto you throughout your generations in all your dwellings. Whoso killeth any person, the murderer shall be put to death by the mouth of witnesses: but one witness shall not testify against any person to cause him to die. Moreover ye shall take no satisfaction

for the life of a murderer, which is guilty of death: but he shall be surely put to death. And ye shall take no satisfaction for him that is fled to the city of his refuge, that he should come again to dwell in the land, until the death of the priest. **So ye shall not pollute the land wherein ye are: for blood it defileth the land: and the land cannot be cleansed of the blood that is shed therein, but by the blood of him that shed it. Defile not therefore the land which ye shall inhabit, wherein I dwell: for I the LORD dwell among the children of Israel"** *(Num. 35:29-34; see also Deut. 11:22-24).*

And lastly, the wisdom of God concerning wise counsel:

"For by wise counsel thou shalt make thy war: and in multitude of counselors there is safety. Wisdom is too high for a fool: he openeth not his mouth in the gate. He that deviseth to do evil shall be called a mischievous person. **The thought of foolishness is sin: and the scorner is an abomination to men."** *"My son, eat thou honey, because it is good; and the honeycomb, which is sweet to thy taste:* **So shall the knowledge of wisdom be unto thy soul: when thou hast found it, then there shall be a reward, and thy expectation shall not be cut off"** *(Prov. 24:6-9, 13-14).*

The last verses postdate the book of Judges but nevertheless, we can clearly see the warnings concerning the shedding of blood on sacred land and the call for a wise entourage. Moreover, God's attributes in Exodus 34:7 also revealed to us the LORD God's sentiment concerning the iniquity of the fathers at the time:

"Keeping mercy for thousands, forgiving iniquity and transgression and sin, and that will by no means clear the guilty; **visiting the iniquity of the**

fathers upon the children, and upon the children's children, unto the third and to the fourth generation."

Before the fall of man, we were vegan. God did not create us to be bloodthirsty beings, but sin brought about the thirst for blood and our reoccurring demise. God came and freed Israel out of bondage, established a covenant with men, and gave us His precepts to follow. Our predisposition for evil kept forcing His hand over and over again (Deut. 30:15-20).

This last statement may cause some of you to ponder, how can we force the hand of God? Well, it is because our Creator believes in free will, and He created us to have interactions with us as His children. Just like an earthly father, He allows us to partake in the decision-making process of our lives and our destiny. Nevertheless, as God, He just cannot compromise his integrity. It would bring devastating repercussions to all living beings if God would ever allow Himself to be corrupted. When the Scriptures say that it is because of His love that we are not consumed, it means that God often holds His peace – because of His agape love – and searches for ways to appeal our cases for His good pleasure. He can save us from ourselves without showing partiality. This is the reason why He later changed His mind on the matters of "visiting the iniquity of the fathers upon the children" as an absolute standard (Ex. 34:7), and declared "The soul that sinneth, it shall die" in Ezekiel 18:1 [20]-32.

Our Heavenly Advocate does not hold His title in vain. If we had no need for one, the Father would not have sacrificed His Son. He did that so we could have Someone to intercede for us before Him. This is yet another reason for us to be humble and walk in the love of God.

One prime example of the demise of mankind is the current division of society based on ethnic groups. When God made man, He made us to be unified and relatable, regardless of our ethnicities. Following the succession of the flood, we decided that we wanted to build a tower to go to Heaven (Gen. 11:1-4). Therefore, the Father came down, confused our speech, and caused us to scatter upon the face of all the earth (Gen. 11:5-9). He divided us to safeguard us against our own evil impulses. The division was to protect us, but instead, we have grown further apart over the millennia, and we have fought tribal wars ever since. Can you imagine how much closer and relatable this whole world would be if we all spoke a single language and were not so prone to devise evil? Even if the cultures over the millennia would have diversified, we would not have grown so far apart. Speaking with the same tongue would have helped us maintain a better esprit de corps. Instead, we mock and humiliate one another because of our differences. We are our worst enemy, and it has cost us a great deal of blessings.

Like the people in the time of Nimrod, Israel forced the hand of God during the 40 years spent in the wilderness and broke the covenant they had made with God (Josh. 24:1-28); God removed His protection around them and dealt with them archly (Judg. 2:6-19, see also Deut. 28:52-58 and 2 Kings 6:24-29). Israel is set apart because of God's promise to Abraham, not because they were better than the other nations, but because God set them apart to bless them for Himself (Josh. 24:1-15). Just like Abram became Abraham and Saul became Paul, Jacob became Israel through the will of God. The blessing is and has always been Yahushuah (Rom. 9:1-29). God informed Israel beforehand about the consequences of disobedience, and He made it clear to them that they should not take His Words lightly. They were to kill only under His directives because God searches the hearts of men, but killing eventually became a sport for Israel (2 Sam. 2:12-16). God is fair and impartial, and from the beginning, His desire has been to save people from all nations (Gen. 12:1-7; Gal. 3:13-18), but the heart of men kept leading them down the wrong path.

- Misunderstanding -

So going back to Chapter 11 of the book of Judges, the Bible tells us that Judge Jephthah gets chosen and anointed by God to go fight and deliver Israel from the hands of the children of Ammon. As the son of a prostitute (11:1-3), he is so moved to have received such honor, that he makes a vain vow unto the Lord by promising a burnt offering of whatsoever would come out to meet him first when he returns from battle (11:30-31). This vow later causes him to sacrifice his only child, his virgin daughter. In verse 3 of Judges 11, the Bible gives a clue to where the vain gloriousness came from. Vain men who were most likely rejects of society, like brother Jephthah, followed after him (Compare 1 Cor. 15:33; Prov. 1:8-19). These vain men who sympathized with him were without a doubt filling his head with pagan propaganda, and these pagan's teachings mixed with the sporadic teaching of God's Law led him to kill his own daughter (see also Judges 2:3).

There is much conflict about the outcome of Jephthah's daughter within the body of Christ, but I believe he actually burned his child as an offering because he had confused the Lord's precepts for demon's doctrines. God allowed it to happen because He wanted the generations that followed to learn from Jephthah's mistake.

I have also heard of a teaching out of Leviticus 27:29, which claimed people were offered as sacrifices to God for devoted vows beforehand, and Judge Jephthah was simply following that law; he merely did not foresee his daughter being the one who would first come out of his house to meet him. Leviticus 27:29 states, "None devoted, which shall be devoted of men, shall be redeemed; but shall surely be put to death." These teachings claim that God used to accept human sacrifices. But that is not a plausible translation for Leviticus 27:29 because we do not serve a pagan god; we serve the Almighty God.

I disagree with that interpretation because throughout the Scriptures, God made it clear that He despises the idea of men getting sacrificed in His honor (Leviticus 18:21; Deuteronomy 12:30-31, 17:1; Psalms 106:34-40).

The only time God commanded someone to be burned is found in Joshua 7:14-15, and it was not a burnt offering. It was an execution. (See also Psalm 51:16-17, 40:6-8; Deut. 18:1-13; Lev. 21:9; Num. 11:1-3 and John 5:20-21.)

The sacrifice of man is a pagan ritual that was prompted by fallen angels who hate the image of God and wanted to see the image of God suffer. I believe Leviticus 27:29 is referring to people who were condemned to death for certain violations. Those types of violations are recorded in Exodus 21 and Leviticus 20.

One can only speculate about how many times the people of Israel abused that law by offering their slaves, or their hand servants, as a surrogate to the priests in order to save themselves—or a rebellious child—from the death penalty.

However, the fact remains that our God does not take pleasure in any form of "human" sacrifices, and He only commanded Israel to present animals for burnt offerings (Jer. 7:31). They were required at that time because the people in the Old Testament needed to be saved from eternal damnation, and blood was the only currency for sin until the Holy One of Israel purchased our debt in full (John 19:33-34).

The lessons we can take from the story of brother Jephthah are: Know Jesus for yourself, spend time with Him, and memorize His teachings. What are a couple hours among friends, anyway? The time should not even be noticeable. It does not matter if you are the spawn of a prostitute or a well brought-up individual. Be wise and shield your mind from the counsel of scoundrels, and do not make vain oaths you cannot afford. In addition, be confident and humble in the fact that Jesus loves you and died for you (Psalm 53:2; Eccl. 5:1-7; Prov. 18:20-21; James 5:12).

Now, as harsh as the reality of the past may seem, we are facing an even greater judgment. The truth is that in the past, God tolerated certain mistakes because He was not yet abiding within us. For we had not yet received a Spirit transplant; we existed through the Breath of life initially given to Adam at the Garden of Eden (2 Peter 1:2-8, 19-21). In the past, God even gave whole nations for the remission of sin from Israel in order to preserve their lineage (Isaiah 43:3-14), until our Savior came to redeem the earth (John 3:16). There is just nothing else that can be given to redeem us now; the Son of God is the highest and only legal tender for our souls.

In the past, men mainly had the anointing that was borrowed, and the Spirit of God came over His chosen vessels to minister through them as was needed. For example, Judge Othniel and Samson were giving specific anointings to fulfill their duties (Judges 3:10, 13:25, 14:5-6, 15:11-15). This was the custom until Jesus Christ came to give us baptisms with the Holy Ghost (John 1:29-34). So, now we are saved, have the Holy Ghost living within us, and we all have the anointing that remains (*dorea-charisma*) (1 John 2:27); and some have the anointing that is delegated (*doma*) (Ezekiel 44:6-16). To be optimal in our office, we all still need the anointing that is delegated or borrowed, which is The Axe Head Anointing given by Jesus Christ.

Although God has been patient with us, the final hour is ending. This is why the Bible is conjuring us to give all diligence to our faith in Christ, so we may continue to grow and not be barren (refer back to 2 Peter 1).

This is also why we are commanded not to grieve or quench the Spirit. We, as Christians, are under a finer microscope because more has been invested in us (Luke 10:17-24). We have the finished work of Christ on the Cross as the foundation of our faith, plus the Holy Ghost and the Holy Scriptures as our guides. There are just no valid excuses to be made. The current atmosphere is a declaration of the sad reality of this realm; it shows us that there is no stability in the system of men. Neither is there any eternal hope in the anti-Christ's system of the beast that will eventually become official (James 5:1-12). Our One and only hope is the Son of God, and His name is Jesus Christ. He sits at the right hand of God (Matt 5:34; Acts 7:55-56; Eph. 1:17-23), the earth is His footstool (Matt. 5:35), and we have no control on what tomorrow holds (Matt. 5:36).

Therefore, "let your communication be, Yea, yea; Nay, nay: for whatsoever is more than these cometh of evil" (Matt. 5:37).

CHAPTER ELEVEN

JOHN 14:6

Don't Drop the Baton

As stated before throughout this book, the struggles that we are facing in this current age are not new, and all the patriarchs before us shared similar pain. Abraham was told to leave his family to go to a place he had never seen. Noah preached about the coming flood [for about 120 years] during a time of pure wickedness, to no avail. David was crowned king by God but still had to run and hide. He had to wait fifteen years before he could get on the throne. Daniel was serving as a eunuch while in captivity in Babylon, and John the Baptist was decapitated for telling the truth. The list of the saints who suffered goes on and on. Nevertheless, just as God was with them through their journeys, we are not alone in these last days. Jesus is with us, and the heavens stand in support of us.

In Hebrews 11, the Bible gives us the definition of faith and the exposé of its application by the patriarchs before us. The key verse in that chapter is verse 6:

"But without faith it is impossible to please him: for he that cometh to God must believe that he is, and that he is a rewarder of them that diligently seek him."

This is a call for commitment. Irrespective of where we are in our travels, we have to remain confident that God is real and that our travails are not in vain. Furthermore, throughout the entire book of Hebrews, the writer is reminding us of the superiority of Christ over the Judaic system. He wants to reassure the people of the Church of the Hebrews that they are not being persecuted for nothing. They are to take courage to know that we, as Believers, are walking towards an eternal kingdom. Conversely, in Chapter 11, the author goes down memory lane to elaborate certain facts.

The first thing he elaborated is the fact that faith is the **substance** of things not seen but hoped for. Secondly, he speaks of the sovereignty of God perambulating the afterlife and the fact that everyone's righteousness follows them. Then he speaks of Enoch being translated, or transported, from this realm to the realm eternal without seeing death, and the importance of having faith in order to please God. The writer then proceeds to remind us we are travelers in a foreign land, and God is not ashamed to be called the God of those who understand that factuality and continue to endure. For this very purpose, Jesus, the Son of God, was born a man, died, then rose again on the third day victorious. Afterwards, Jesus went to sit at the right hand of the Father to intercede for us and to prepare a place for us that we can all live one day by His side.

The word *substance* in the Webster's Dictionary means many things, but the one meaning that stood out to me during my study is: "***Ultimate reality that underlies all outward manifestations and change.***" In other words, in regards to Christianity, faith is the foundation of our lives, the underlines of all outward manifestations and change. Faith is not particular to Christianity alone, but the promises of the Bible are only for those who have faith in GOD through Christ Jesus.

Paul then goes on to elaborate the reality that not all of God's promises will be fulfilled in this realm. He talks about how many Believers, just like Moses, had to have enough faith to reject the favors of this world for an unseen world that is to come. A world that no man has seen, which beauty no one can even imagine. A perfect world made with eternal beauty. A new world made for those who please God and fulfill their purpose unto Him that calleth.

By faith, says the litterateur, the walls of Jericho (or the challenges of this life) fell down after the Israelites went around it for about **seven days**.

Addendum: Seven in Biblical numerology is the number for completeness, perfection, finished work and rest. The eschatology of number seven in this verse is that we are guaranteed all things only at the completion of this journey. Those promises will be fulfilled during the millennium reign of the Saints with Christ (Rev. 20:4-6; Isaiah 56:1-8). This does not mean that we should not pursue happiness while here, but even if we only receive sorrows in this lifetime, we ought to remain righteous until the end.

In addition, often a blessing may be right before us, but in that respect is something God has commanded us to do that we haven't done yet. This lack of perception and commitment causes our blessing to be held back (Heb. 3:8-19, 4:1-13). The lack of perception can be resolved by simply inquiring an answer from Jesus through prayer and fasting (see the book of Daniel). The lack of commitment, however, requires a change of heart and disposition (James 4:7-8).

By faith, we are told that Rehab the prostitute is counted among the Saints for believing in God and for her bravery towards Israel (Joshua 2:8-14). By faith, many were tortured, not accepting any compromise, so that they may see the resurrection. Some were mocked, scourged, imprisoned, stoned to death, sawn in half, and much more. They endured this for the sake of the evangel of Jesus Christ, whom they did not get to see or hear (Matt. 13:16-17; John 6:63).

According to the Text, all of them are commanded for their faith, but none of them have yet received their eternal inheritance. For this journey is a relay race, and we are the current runners on the track, perhaps even the last runners on this journey. As they wait for the last stragglers at the finish line, they are watching us. They are cheering for us with all expectation of joy and satisfaction to see us make it to the end. I command you again today to be strong and know we are not alone. We have Heaven as our support, and Jesus is with us all the way. *"If God be for us, who can be against us?"* (Romans 8:31).

- Endure Daily -

Concerning vengeance, The Bible tells us under the New Covenant, we have to be a blessing and not a curse, even to those who persecute us.

"Bless them which persecute you: bless, and curse not. Rejoice with them that do rejoice, and weep with them that weep. Recompense to no man evil for evil. Provide things honest in the sight of all men. If it be possible, as much as lieth in you, live peaceably with all men. **Dearly beloved, avenge not yourselves, but rather give place unto wrath: for it is written, Vengeance is mine; I will repay, said the Lord. Therefore if thine enemy hunger, feed him; if he thirst, give him drink: for in so doing thou shalt heap coals of fire on his head. Be not overcome of evil, but overcome evil with good"** *(Romans 12:14-21; see also Matt. 5:38-42; Psalms 4:4-5; Psalms 63 and Eph. 6:23-24).*

In the Old Testament, our ancestors were given the power to kill pagan nations before God, but we no longer live in that timeline. The Old Testament's stories are merely there as life lessons, as a witness of God's love and patience, as a road map to the kingdom of God, and as a testimony of the Son of God's preeminence. In the New Covenant, we must bear the daily affronts of this world, while proclaiming the message of the Kingdom of God.

To be honest, as a veteran, this is the hardest part of the gospel for me. In the army, we were taught that what makes the green grass green is, "Blood! Blood! Bright red blood!" Now as a Christian, I have to find the courage to walk away from situations that I sometimes feel require my undivided – knuckles' – attention.

The example of the possessed man from the mall is my main reminder of the implication, or danger, of giving in to violence. The Lord also gave me the following reference to strengthen my disposition to be gentle:

Our Creator, our loving Father, our Savior, is much more. He is also the Lord of Armies, JEHOVAH-SABAOTH. As the Lord of Armies, He leads the battles against the forces of darkness and has prepared the instruments of war for that purpose (Job 38:22-23) to maintain discipline. He has established military protocols to govern His mighty angels (Ps. 103:19-22). Now the plan of salvation was established before our creation (1 Peter 1:18-21; Eph. 1:3-6), but the execution of that plan was calculated and executed through various phases. Let us look at what God did through a military operation's perspective.

Following the fall, God first established people for Himself out of the seed of Abraham. He then invaded the earth with His mighty power, which He demonstrated in Egypt. Afterwards, He commanded His established, earthly army to seek and destroy His enemies so the earth would know the God of Israel is all-powerful, and there is no other God besides Him. This was the norm until He fulfilled His Zeal towards us through Jesus Christ, the Son of God. He now commands us to go and win the hearts and minds of all people without merging with their customs or walking according to this beast's system.

This way of operating transpired over to our realm. What God did would be the equivalent of the United States Military invading Afghanistan by first bombing their high-value targets, then sending boots on the ground to seek and destroy the remaining combatants. Then followed by Karzai's 12 diplomatic-policy approach to winning the trust of the people under the label of "winning of the hearts and minds."

To reiterate, through Israel, God first dispatched (or established) His garrison. He started with bombarding the land through a show of force in the Old Testament, and then He sent boots on the ground from the wilderness to the Promised Land in order to rid the land of the enemy's stronghold. God then sent His Chosen One to reconcile the earth with a show of love and to establish the New Covenant of the Kingdom. Under this current decree, we are a garrison of light sent to proclaim the Kingdom of Heaven through the precepts of Jesus Christ. By proclaiming the principles of justice, love, and liberty through the Son of God, we regain the hearts of the children of the country in which we are stationed. We are now commissioned with the proclamation of the ministry of reconciliation through the Son of God. Furthermore, just as God led the battle of guts and blood against the heathen back then (2 Chr. 20), He leads the battle of spiritual warfare today (Heb. 1:1-3). Jesus as The Lord of Hosts commands us now to turn the other cheek (Matt 5:39) and to bless those who persecute us. Paul corroborates that fact in Romans 8:36 by reminding us that we are as sheep sent to the slaughter (compare context to Ps. 44).

In Romans 8:36, Paul is quoting King David from Psalms 44, who declared that fact during a time of defeat and persecution. In the passage, David is once again crying out to the Lord about Israel's condition, but he is also making it clear that despite all of the afflictions, Israel had remained faithful to God's covenant (Ps. 44:17-22). Likewise today, tribulations and sorrows should not separate the sheep from the Shepherd.

I would be lying if I claimed I am excited about the prospect of being, "as a sheep for the slaughter," but this is what the Bible tells us on the matter of Christianity. Although some messages are more difficult to digest than others, I am not going to attempt to facilitate my own salvation. I prefer to follow God's Word until the end.

On the matter of turning the other cheek, particularly in regards to the tribulation to come, I don't believe Jesus is saying we should volunteer to be punching bags, but we ought not fight back or seek revenge. Instead, we should walk away or even run from danger if we can. Some of you reading this message will be of those who survive until the end (Matt. 24:22; John 4:34, 6:38-40, 7:30, 10:10-40, 18:11; Acts 16:19). The reason Jesus painted such dreadful pictures in Matthew 5:39 and in Matthew 5:44 is because of the vivid reality of the last tribulation. *"Resist not evil: but whosoever shall smite thee on thy right cheek, turn to him the other also. Love your enemies, bless them that curse you, do good to them that hate you, and pray for them which despitefully use you, and persecute you."* He is not saying that we should seek pain or death to honor Him, but we must be aware of the reality (or cost) of discipleship to Him in this realm.

These types of messages are frowned upon in the church these days because we have gotten too comfortable, but the Bible speaks for itself (Matthew 24:9-10; Mark. 13:19-23). In John 16:1-4, Jesus also tells us that we will eventually be outcast. By the end, people will put us to death thinking they are honoring God.

The time for the chariot battles has passed. We are under new orders now. We have been commanded to walk in the likeness of Christ and to preach His gospel with love. Although it is not an easy task, who am I to argue with the King?

Notwithstanding, if the idea of being a sheep sent to the slaughter still disturbs you, perhaps this next revelation will help when that time comes.

In Revelation 14:9-11, the Bible tells us that all who worship the beast, his image, and whosoever receives the mark of his name will be tormented forever and ever. They will have no rest day nor night. According to verse 10, the condemned will be tormented in the presence of the holy angels, and the Lamb. What this means is there will be two prophecies fulfilled on that terrible day. First, our Father will be fulfilling His promise to our Lord, while simultaneously avenging us of our tormentors (Psalm 110:1 and Rev. 6:9-11; also Rev. 16:4-7; Matt. 23:33-36).

God is so merciful and such a loving Father that regardless of the fact that we are all sinners and mankind tortured and killed His only begotten Son, it is not enough for Him to torment the unbelievers for eternity. He allows for the innocents and the righteous in Christ to be abused, tortured, and killed as well, so that He can justify Himself on the day of torment for the wicked. Although God does not have to report to anyone, He still wants to be fair and impartial to all His creation; yes, even the wicked.

He has set up His revenge for the wicked so that they can be tormented fairly. When they are being ripped apart repeatedly according to each one's demises on their day of torment and they begin to plead with God for mercy, He can reject their pleas without any self-reproach. God will be remorseless because He will have the agonies of His Son and of all the Saints before Him as a recollection. For there are more than two Books, God also has prepared the Books of remembrance for Himself, and nothing will escape His divine judgment (Ps. 56:1-8; Daniel 7:9-10; Malachi 3:13-4:3; Rev. 20:7-12). The Lord even keeps the tears of the righteous in a bottle so He can quench the thirst of the heathen on their day of reckoning (Isaiah 2:1-22, 10:1-4; 1 Th. 5:1-11; Daniel 4:34-37). See what great trust the Father has placed in us that we should be His light, His messengers, His love, and for a lack of a better word, His alibi. What a great honor it is to be counted as one who can endure for the Eternal God as Jesus endured all things and is seated at the right side of GOD.

Now I must reiterate that I am not saying we should look for an opportunity to be made martyrs. What I am conveying here is that Revelation 13:9-[10] is pertaining to our generation. Because we are the generation that is to endure the official mark of the beast and this *"calls for patient endurance and faithfulness on the part of God's people (NIV)."*

After all the wickedness I have witnessed in this world, I do not want to even conceive of the madness that will take place in the lake of fire. I personally do not have any business down there. I do not want to know anything about this place called the lake of fire. My excitement is returned unto me knowing that if I suffer for the Gospel of Christ as He suffered for me, I will be counted worthy to be at the Marriage Supper of the Lamb. This is the reason behind this extended breakdown, but please do not be an overzealous Christian (Proverbs 19:2), for our patient endurance and faithfulness comes only from the LORD, and my cross is not your cross.

Vengeance is the Lord, and we do not live in the Old Testament days anymore. Winning the heart and mind of God's people is the new battle. JEHOVAH SABAOTH Himself has changed the status quo. Anyone operating outside of the Commander-In-Chief's order is a

rogue Soldier and will not be rewarded profitably (Matt. 7:21-23; Rom. 8:31-39).

- Love -

"Love your enemies, bless them that curse you, do good to them that hate you, and pray for them which despitefully use you, and persecute you" (Matt. 5:44).

Love is the core of the Gospel of Jesus Christ, and our entire existence extrapolated from His passion towards the world (John 3:16). To love only our loved ones, or those who do us good, is not a proper forthcoming expression of God's children. It all goes back to our worship. For if we are in Christ and Christ is in us, then our behaviors should replicate our Heavenly Father's behaviors towards all men. The Father makes His sun rise on the evil and on the good, and He sends the rain for the just and on the unjust. Again, this does not mean that we condone their evil deeds, but we reach out to the world with love and compassion. It means that we simply preach the Gospel of Christ as written because the Word of God can fend for Himself (Heb. 4:12).

As Christians, we can sometimes look at things in a conceited or selfish way; ergo, let's review the publican remark in the Text:

"For if ye love them which love you, what reward have ye? do not even the publicans the same? And if ye salute your brethren only, what do ye more than others? **Do not even the publicans so? Be ye therefore perfect, even as your Father which is in heaven is perfect**" (Matt. 5:46-48).

Per the Bible, the only selfishness the Gospel allows is in our conviction that Immanuel, born a man, is the Son of God and our redeemer (1 John 4:1-4; Gal. 1:8-12; Jos. 24:15). It's all about Him. Remember the ten virgins.

We must be just to God; the whole Bible speaks of God's love, for God's love is displayed from Genesis to the Apocalypse. What I mean by that is even before He had formed the earth, God already ran every scenario through His omniscient mind. He knew there was a 90 percent chance that man would rebel against Him, follow the devil, and He would have to sacrifice His only begotten Son to save us from the pit of eternal death one day. However, He was willing to take that risk for us because He is fierce, and He wants to one day meet you face-to-face; He loves the idea of interacting with us and acknowledging the consciousness of each one soul (Isa. 1:18-19).

What the Father is saying to us in Isaiah 1:18-19 is: "I would love to talk to you; let us talk it out," and in some instances He is saying, "We have to talk it out!" He is also saying to us, "Come let me show you the way. Let me show you who you are, for your identity can only be found in the Trinity." Can you imagine God reaching out to animated dust particles? This is just amazing to me, and who are we that we should contend with Him?

God also knew for all that He did, the majority of us would still follow the broad path of eternal perdition (Matt. 7:13-14). Nevertheless, the vista of great multitudes of souls marching in one day through the Pearly Gates was worth the ultimate sacrifice to Him. This is why He chose to endure the nature of men throughout the ages (Isaiah 46:1-[9-10] 11).

As the omnipotent God, He could have destroyed the last earth, gathered all the fallen angels and the devil at once, cast them into the lake of fire, and He would have been justified. Then He could have just remade man without the gift of free will. We would have never known what had taken place before our new birth or experienced what it means to have a conscious soul. Similar to zombies, we would have served Him through eternity without a thought.

Conversely, the Creator made all things good, and He longs for true worshipers who worship Him in Spirit and in truth for His loving kindness. He cherishes a cheerful giver. Despite our acquired infirmities, His desires toward us had to be fulfilled because of His Agape Love for mankind. The sternness of His actions is to be commanded, not questioned. Had He not stopped us at the tower of Babel, "as it was in the days of Noah," would have come long ago, long before there was any hope for redemption. If it wasn't for God's love and mercy and the Lamb of God who bought our debt with His own blood, instead of a great multitude, only a trickle of men would be saved (Rev. 7:9-17).

Through Jesus Christ, we are reborn from deity into destiny. Without His divine interventions and chastising, we would have reached critical mass before our current timeline long ago (see Gen. 11:1-9). The Tower of Babel is just one instance that we know of. The truth is, God has been protecting us from self-destruction for millennia now, while simultaneously healing us, preserving us, delivering us, and finally redeeming us for Himself.

Philanthropists spending millions trying to find the Lost City of Atlantis just don't get it. Atlantis is said to have been built by Egyptians after the great plagues befell them. Some even speculate that the reason they built the city on water is because of their "infinite wisdom." They believed the God of Israel was only the God of the earth, and they assumed they would be safe on the ocean (1 Kings 20:23[28]). However, our God is the omnipresent God.

He watched them build their new city on the ocean using the knowledge they received from the fallen ones. The Omnipotent Father then flicked His finger and sunk it at the bottom of the ocean (1 King 20:28-30). The city holds forbidden knowledge, and the money, time, and energy would better serve these archeologists if they invested their efforts towards doing charity work. The same goes to the gentleman looking for the Ark of the Covenant in Nova Scotia. He has wasted decades and millions of dollars in vain trying to outmaneuver the One who holds all the pieces of the puzzle (Rev. 11:19).

Those who are passing judgment against God are either ignorant or blind; ignorance can be redeemed, but woe unto those cursed with spiritual blindness (Mark 4:11-12).

Under such unbearable truth as children of God, we have no other choice but to reciprocate the Father's kindness to our enemies. Praise be the name of The LORD God Almighty. For to us, knowledge is given to understand the mystery of the kingdom of God. For us, we are given the Spirit of God to guide us into all truth pertaining to the kingdom of God, and to us is given the Kingdom of God through Jesus Christ. The love of God cannot be measured, only acknowledged and reciprocated.

Even if I had ten lifetimes, I could not do any justice to what is already written about God's Love in the Bible. I beseech each one of you to read the Bible for yourselves and ask the Father for wisdom. Search my spirit by the Spirit of God so that you will get confirmation for your own selves concerning all that I have written in this book. The time of our realm is ending, so let us not delay but rather be as the apostle John commanded us:

"Beloved, let us love one another: for love is of God; and every one that loveth is born of God, and knoweth God. He that loveth not knoweth not God; for God is love. In this was manifested the love of God toward us, because that God sent his only begotten Son into the world, that we might live through him. Herein is love, not that we loved God, but that he loved us, and sent his Son to be the propitiation for our sins. Beloved, if God so loved us, we ought also

to love one another. No man hath seen God at any time. If we love one another, God dwelleth in us, and his love is perfected in us. Hereby know we that we dwell in him, and he in us, because he hath given us of his Spirit. And we have seen and do testify that the Father sent the Son to be the Savior of the world. Whosoever shall confess that Jesus is the Son of God, God dwelleth in him, and he in God. And we have known and believed the love that God hath to us. God is love; and he that dwelleth in love dwelleth in God, and God in him. Herein is our love made perfect, that we may have boldness in the day of judgment: because as he is, so are we in this world. There is no fear in love; but perfect love casteth out fear: because fear hath torment. He that feareth is not made perfect in love. We love him, because he first loved us. If a man says, I love God, and hateth his brother, he is a liar: for he that loveth not his brother whom he hath seen, how can he love God whom he hath not seen? And this commandment have we from him, That he who loveth God love his brother also" (1 John 4:7-21).

- Be Humble Even In Your Giving -

"Therefore when thou doest thine alms, do not sound a trumpet before thee, as the hypocrites do in the synagogues and in the streets, that they may have glory of men. Verily I say unto you, They have their reward" (Matt. 6:2-3).

Matthew 6:1-4 is an antibiotic against boastfulness, self-gratifications, and hypocrisies displayed in Acts 5:1-11. In that passage, Jesus provides us with the remedy for a pathogen that has been ravaging our generations for quite some time now. It's the need to be honored by men (John 12:42-43) and to be seen doing good so that we can receive recognition from men. This virus has created a raw wave of so-called philanthropists who can't seem to do any charity work outside of the cameras. They have to be validated for every "good deed" so they may have the glory of men. Jesus declared in that passage that these types of people already have their rewards for their "good deeds;" a finite, irrelevant and perishable reward coming from one dead man unto another. Honor in our current timeline does not even demand any tangible substance, and this new vector has now evolved to "kun flu" cheering rallies, which former U.S. President Trump used to mock China during the early stages of the COVID-19 pandemic, and this promoted even more division in the minds of the constituents.

These modern day philanthropists like to go on the Tell-lie-vision to boost their self-proclaimed values and hold the populace hypnotized by the worth of their hypocritical good deeds. Jesus labeled them hypocrites in the Text because their alms are not real. It is all based on how much recognition they can get from it. Most of the time, in fact, when a rich person is seen on TV giving donations, it is because they know they will receive a tax cut for it later. It is all a shame, and the people who make the real sacrifices are hardly ever noticed. But do not be fooled by them; the directives about giving alms are clear. Do it out of the goodness of your heart without expecting any rewards in return, then will our Father in Heaven take notice. For God looks inward, and He is not Someone that can be duped; and besides, good people are not going to Heaven, only people who are saved are going to Heaven because there is none good but the Father (Mark 10:18). Therefore, good deeds alone have no eternal value in themselves unless they glorify the Holy Spirit who is the Spirit of truth (Luke 1:39-47).

The world being under these various hypocrites' spell is bad enough, but regrettably, this is also the same condition of many of our churches today. The Temple of God is being overrun by modern day Pharisees, who unlike their counterpart, are much harder to spot. They do not have only the outward appearance of a righteous person, but they also have certain gifts of the Spirit. However, they operate without the elemental element of the Gospel of Christ, which is charity (1 Cor. 13). The one that is most common among them is the gift of ministry or the ability to speak with the tongues of men and of angels. These days, Pharisees can sell milk to a cow. The alms from these men are tainted because for every dollar they give, they rob the children of God of a thousand. These evil men and women sell holy water for a healing that never comes, and I actually saw a pastor offer to sell outlines of his feet on TV in exchange for a donation.

These monetary blessings are already ours to claim in Jesus' name. Any types of good deeds from these types of people are scripted.

If you are not walking in the Spirit of God daily, they'll have you paying for their private jets, their mansions, and their fancy dog's collar. Never mind the current pandemic or the economic crisis, they are now asking for your stimulus check too because these mansions are not going to compensate themselves.

It is a very sad situation for them. I would think that seeing the current state of the whole world and the signs of the end would encourage them to repent of their evil deeds and change their ways. Instead, they are digging in even more. This is the extent of the mark of the beast. Even the man with the Bible in his hand anointed by the Spirit of God cannot find his way back to God; he is as a prophet getting ministered to by a mule (2 Peter 2:10-22).

"Woe unto them! For they have gone in the way of Cain, and ran greedily after the error of Balaam for reward, and perished in the gainsaying of Korah" (Jude 1:11).

The error of Balaam in the Text has to do with more than the love of money. Balaam was also a lover of recognition, and he wanted to be acknowledged for his spiritual gift as a prophet. He wanted to be admired and receive the honor of men, which is just as bad as someone given alms for recognition in return. This is a common trait of the pride of life. Although it does feel good to receive compliments for doing good deeds and using our gifts for the Gospel, it should not be the motivation for our actions. At the same time, you should not feel bad for being noticed in your good works. However, functioning under the predisposition of quid pro quo is hypocritical and will not be rewarded with God's blessings. We breathe because we exist; we do not exist to breathe. Our existence is only because of God's Grace, Love, and Mercy, so we ought not neglect to give Him the honor and praise in all that we do, including our giving.

Concerning the Pharisees, I have once heard someone say, "Well, Jesus said they are seated in the seat of Moses and the Prophets, so we must do as they said but not live as they live." To that person I say, "Well, Moses and the Prophets were fulfilled in Jesus; all authority has been given over to Him, and He commands us now to let our light shine. This is why after Jesus ascended into Heaven, His disciples spoke boldly against the Scribes and Pharisees and refused to compromise their faith" (see Acts 4:1-31; John 16:1-3; Acts 23:1-33 and Matt. 10:16).

It must be noted that not all the Pharisees in the time of Jesus rejected His Gospel. In fact, Jesus was actually buried by two Pharisees (Acts 6:7; Luke 23:50-56; John 3:1-21, 12:42-43, 19:38-42). Our brother Paul was also a Pharisee (Acts 23:6), and he was also a killer of Christians; but one encounter with Jesus changed his life forever.

Although I speak boldly against their customs and doctrines, I am in no way saying all Pharisees will be condemned to Hell. Only God knows who will be chosen, and I am still optimistic for them. However, the hour is late in the day, and the tabooing of the Gospel is getting old. The Bible speaks to us clearly, and so should we speak to all.

I want to clarify myself once again before we move on. I am here to let my light shine, and I am in no way saying that you should speak as I am (Matt. 19:11). It took me years of pondering in the Spirit on these matters before I felt compelled to speak out. If it is not your calling to confront evil face on, do not engage. Nor am I suggesting that anyone should impulsively leave their assembly because of the modern-day Pharisees.

Think of your assembly in this way. While serving in the military overseas, my unit travelled a lot. It was part of our mission's requirement to move through various provinces. During those excursions, we stopped at various bases. Some were state-of-the-art combat stations with all the amenities of a modern-age city, while some barely had enough resources to function at optimal capacity. Nevertheless, regardless of where we slept overnight, it was always safer to sleep within the defense perimeter of the base. We ate what they had to offer. We followed the rules of the battle base, and many times, we even merged what little resources we had to help them be more efficient.

Going outside of the perimeter wires just to wander around was not a safe option for anyone in uniform. We endured and enjoyed the case-by-case layout of each resting station until our deployment was completed, and then we went home.

These experiences as a soldier are what keep me going today. I cannot say I am part of every church function anymore, but I go every Sunday to honor my Creator. I haven't completely given up on the house of prayer just yet. However, I am mentally ready for the "Great Apostasy."

If you are in a place where you are still getting some rhema words or perhaps even some state-of-the-art rhema, but there happened to be some discrepancies in the clergy, do not be so quick to give up on your congregation. Inquire of the Lord first; for all you know, you may hold the missing piece—or gift—needed to bring spiritual balance or even order to your congregation. Any given day, the abomination of desolation will make its grand entrance. The true Believers will have to take a walk from the general church assembly, or assimilate to beast worship. So, do not be surprised, and be ready to move. We will eventually be living our Christian life preaching the Gospel under constant systematic persecution, just as the apostles did in their days.

Some people can easily be deterred, and I am sent from the LORD Yahushuah Hamashiach only to educate and encourage, not to create confusion or panic. Only God knows what calling He has proposed for you, so ask Him! The words I speak come to me from the Holy Spirit and the Holy Scriptures. These two Deities are available to all saints. In the meantime, be humble, even in your giving, so that you do not invite the spirit of the beast to entice you and turn you into a modern-day Pharisees and hypocrite.

- The Creator Is Our Loving Father -

Jesus was born the Son of Man and as a man. He was raised as a carpenter. According to Luke 2:21-24 and Leviticus 12, His adopted parents Joseph and Mary were poor individuals. The gold and the oils that were instituted as an offering by the wise men must have been very welcome by them. It was well needed at that time because they were on the run from King Herod of Israel.

Another side note: Historians and theologians alike have determined the gifts the three wise men had brought to Jesus were the equivalent of a small fortune. Some even say it could have been as much as ¾ millions of dollars worth in

Jesus' days. If this were true (and I believe there is much truth to it), that would mean three things:

First: When the Father gives His children an assignment, all that is needed is provided for the mission, not just spiritually, but naturally and financially as well. The financial support will not just appear in our bank accounts, but it is already released. We just have to learn to be obedient to the guidance of the Holy Spirit (Isa. 60:6; Matt. 1:18-25; Luke 2:1-5; Matt. 2:11).

Second: The place where the released blessing is to be received may not be our favorite place to be. It may be under siege by a wicked king (Matt. 2:1, 16), or you may find yourself in a manger's situation (Luke 2:7). We may have to be in an uncomfortable situation to see the provisions set aside for us (Luke 2:6). It helps to be humble on this journey, to place God first, and to *"seek ye first the kingdom of God, and his righteousness; and all these things shall be added unto you"* (Matt. 6:33). The Father knows all we need for the tasks at hand. We need only to trust Him. People building their own blessings off the back of someone else either have a lack of faith, or a lack of discernment and patience. Either way, they have the wrong motivation.

Third: This would also mean the wealth our Lord and Savior received at birth from the Magi was donated to and shared with others. This would be the only explanation for a millionaire Prophet to be raised as a carpenter and to live a meeker life as the Son of Man (Isaiah 53:2; John 1:46; Matt. 8:19-[20]). Withal, concerning earthly things, it also implies that Jesus Himself exercised the principle of "being blessed so you can be a blessing to others." That would mean Jesus took the wealth that the Father bestowed upon Him and gave alms, but He never sought to be acknowledged by men for His good deeds.

"For we have not a high priest which cannot be touched with the feeling of our infirmities; but was in all points tempted like as we are, yet without sin"
(Hebrews 4:15; see also Matt. 19:16-[21] 24).

Conclusively, the false prophets (prosperity preachers) proclaiming Jesus would not have been riding a mule if He were living among us in the flesh today have failed to understand the finished work of Christ. For as soon as Jesus was born, He was being persecuted by King Herod (Matt. 2:1-16; John 15:20). He was found by the Magi in a manger, not in a million-dollar mansion (Matt. 6:19-34, 8:20). The provision that was sent through the Magi by the Father to Christ for the mission did not overrule His sensory processing abilities. Jesus knew even as a child the purpose of God for His life (Luke 2:41-50). He did not ride on a fancy chariot during His ministry (or a private jet). Jesus was on His feet most of His time here with us in the flesh, and He once rode on an ass (Matt. 21:1-7). Jesus' whole focus during His time with us was to glorify the Father by preaching the gospel of redemption and salvation through the Son of God (John 4:34-38, 6:38-40; Isa. 44:2; Jer. 1:5-7). By establishing these principles through His own personal life, Jesus has given us the footprint of Christendom. It does not mean that we cannot be successful in this life, but if the Son of God suffered, we must not be expecting prosperity only during our time here. We should be free from the burden of materialism, for our home is not this world; we are sent from the Father to walk in the likeness of the Son and to fulfill our calling. And our calling often requires much sorrow in order to be brought forth to the surface, in order for our light to be seen; and the greater the calling, the greater the sorrows must be.

Okay, where was I? Yes, as stated in Hebrews 4:15, Jesus was tempted in everything for our sake. This means as the Creator, what He already knew of mankind's nature, He had to learn again from the Son of Man's perspective.

Therefore, the Master is not asking us to do anything that He has not endured Himself. This declaration also gives a new meaning to 2 Cor. 8:9 and Phil. 2:6-8. I believe these verses mean that Jesus was willingly brought up in an underprivileged household so He could experience the righteousness and faithfulness of the Father as a man for Himself (Psalms 37:16-37). Jesus not only abnegated His position as the Son of God and the Jewel of Heaven, but also as the Son of Man when He renounced monetary wealth. I believe verses 5 to 34 of Matthew Chapter 6 are testaments that Jesus, as the Son of Man, experienced this earthly life for Himself because as our General, He leads by example. Hence, in Matthew 19:21, when Jesus told the rich young man to go sell all that he had in order to feed the poor and follow Him, Jesus was actually telling the rich young man to do something that He experienced for himself. Jesus renounced all things of this world and followed the Father's instruction for our sake, and by faith, He went to the grave but rose again on the third day. He now sits at the right hand of God the Father forever more.

Jesus grew up watching the interaction of men from various backgrounds. He secretly observed them as the Son of God, taking mental notes and keeping records of our expressed nature. He saw us spiritually naked and exposed at our most vulnerable moments with all of our qualities and flaws. With the discerning anointing of the Holy Spirit, the General then made His assessment.

Concerning prayer, Jesus said, *"And when thou prayest, thou shalt not be as the hypocrites are: for they love to pray standing in the synagogues and in the corners of the streets, that they may be seen of men. Verily I say unto you, They have their reward. But thou, when thou prayest, enter into thy closet, and when thou hast shut thy door, pray to thy Father which is in secret; and thy Father which seeth in secret shall reward thee openly. **But when ye pray, use not*** *vain repetitions, as the heathen do: for they think that they shall be heard for their much speaking. Be not ye therefore like unto them: for your Father knoweth what things ye have need of, before ye ask him*" (Matt. 6:5-8).

Among many things, the Bible is a love letter from our loving Father. He has declared His love and desires for us before the beginning of time (2 Tim. 1:9-10; Eph. 1:4-6; Titus 1:1-3). As children of God through Christ Jesus, we ought to come and speak to Him as such. Jesus wants us to acknowledge that when we come to the Father in prayer, He commands us to differentiate with the hypocrites who use vain repetition, stand before men, and proclaim their so-called relationship with the Father. These hypocrites have a double mind to do evil. They stand before men to be glorified, while simultaneously speaking vain repetitive words in an attempt to tickle the ears of God. Their true goal is to attempt to trick God and men; they are beyond conceited.

Our prayers to God should be as a child interacting with his or her dad. Except that our Father, which art in Heaven, is also GOD, the Creator of all things. Therefore, the highest level of reverence is due to His Name (Psalms 33; Luke 11:1-4). Just like a regular child would recognize his dad as papa, no matter how strict his father may be, we should have that same outlook towards our Father and our God (Matt. 18:2-4; Hebrews 12:5-14).

Upon completing His recon, Jesus concluded all outward display of holiness not inspired by the Holy Ghost was hypocritical in essence. Instead, we ought to be conservative in our daily walk with God so the spirit of hypocrisy may not find room to dwell in us (compare 1 Cor. 14:1-6 to 2 Sam. 6:13-23). Similar to the spirit of jealousy and the spirit of error, the spirit of hypocrisy brings mischief and discord (Numbers 5:14-30; 1 John 4:6; Matt. 15:1-20; 1 Peter 2:1-3). These spirits of discord are the reason why most churches do not have any real power nowadays. Too many of them have learned to have their church services with or without God, and most are either ruled by democracy or autocracy.

In addition, Jesuit priests have tainted the doctrines of Jesus Christ in the church. Most of today's theologies are based on religious systems of belief. True theocracy requires a constant connection to God. For the *logos* is being constantly refined by the *rhema* because this war is a full-scale military operation, and the Commander in Chief is actively engaged. And so should we be in our prayers and worship. Moreover, there are too many macho ministers in the kingdom these days preaching long messages with no real substance. Only big words and fancy quotes.

Riddle me this, ye poets:

How can the founder of the church not be invited, or be left out of His own gospel?

I once heard a man of God speaking words of wisdom on a radio station. During the message, he stopped to reveal an important clue to his ministry. He shared with his congregation his preparation steps for each service. He informed them that for each message he presented to them, he spent on average 12 to 14 hours in his study secluded from the world with his head in the Bible. He fasted and prayed to Jesus for guidance on what to say to the people of God. He told them he had to do it this way because he is simply a vessel of God, and his job is to get new wine from the wine dresser to pour into the cups of the Lord's hosts. I believe this should be the attitude of all preachers across the board. The church is the Lord's, and so should be the message therein, as our God is an interactive God.

Even the Son of God, throughout His ministry, would regularly look for a quiet place to interact with the Father. He did that in order to recharge His Spirit so that the Holy Spirit would be in the forefront of His ministry.

For the spirit is willing but the flesh is weak (Matt. 26:38-41).

Jesus is sharing with us His personal experience as the Son of Man, experiences that He witnessed and lived through His prayer life with the Father. Simultaneously, He declared to us that these experiences are available to us, as well as through Him, but only after we repent of dead works and forgive men for their trespasses.

In verse 8 of Matthew 6, Jesus tells us **not** to be like the hypocrites when we pray, for our Father knows what we **have need** for before we even ask. Ergo, if we have no need for what we are praying for, or if it would become a yoke for us, He may not answer (Matt. 7:9-11).

Concerning fasting, Jesus said, *"Moreover when ye fast, be not, as the hypocrites, of a sad countenance: for they disfigure their faces, that they may appear unto men to fast. Verily I say unto you, They have their reward. But thou, when thou fastest, anoint thine head, and wash thy face"* (Matt. 6:16-17).

Here we see the same word again, "hypocrites." Once again, the reproach against those who seek the honor of men. The reoccurring of these reproaches is to emphasize the importance of being transparent before God and the importance of honoring God rather than men. Jesus commands us to anoint our head and to wash our faces while we fast because the Father is in control, and He knows what we have need for. He simply expects us to be proactive in our walk with Him because since we are the children of God, and we are holy as He is Holy, we ought to be as He is in all things. God desires for us to adopt His attributes. As our loving Father, He welcomes and enjoys the concept of interaction. He is also delighted by the concept of our growth and development in Him, through Him, and by Him (Ex. 14:13-16; 1 Sam. 16:6-12; Heb. 12:22-[23]). Moreover, just as in the days of Daniel, the angels of darkness may be impeding the answer to our prayer request at times. As the old folks used to say, "Sometimes you have to pray your way through."

Remember, this is a full-scale military operation. As soldiers of God's army, we have to do our parts, and sometimes, the mission may require 21 days of perseverance in prayers and fasting.

In Exodus 14:15, God is not rebuking Moses for calling on His name because the Red Sea represented the time for faith in action. God had already declared Moses to be "as a god" into Aaron, and as the old saying goes, "His word is bond." Furthermore, God finished demonstrating His great power in Egypt through the rod that was in Moses' hands. He simply wanted to see Moses take some initiatives and play his position as the herald of the LORD. If corrections needed to be made, just like with the prophet Samuel, God would have made them.

With the prophet Samuel, the Father was teaching His prophet the danger of visual fixation on the physical stature or athletic prowess of men (1 Sam. 9:1-2, 15:35, 16:6-7). In the previous verses referenced, we can see that prophet Samuel had an eye for physical beauty. He used words that emphasized the outer appearance of Saul in 1 Samuel 9:2 when he first met him, without even knowing the nature of Saul. Samuel was so attached to Saul that he mourned the judgment of the Lord against Saul for a while (see 1 Samuel 15:35 and 16:1). Then later, the prophet was again moved when he saw Eliab, the son of Jesse, for the first time because of his stature, which led God to correct Samuel for his inclination towards outer appearance in 1 Samuel 16:6-7. God wanted to rid prophet Samuel of that inclination. Both Moses and Samuel were being schooled by God in both instances. The Father loves to teach us His ways because His ways are perfect, and they bring us into order (Ps. 19:7-14, 33). Once we learn to apply the ways of the Lord into our lives concerning our specific calling, we can walk in the likeness of Christ.

God is omnipotent, omniscient, and omnipresent. He is all that we can ever desire and more, and He wants us to understand, acknowledge, and apply that fact by staying in communication with Him through prayers. Fasting helps us get closer to God when we pray because the spirit is strengthened when we fast. We can also hear God's voice more clearly in order to learn His ways and walk in Christ's footsteps (see Deut. 13).

Our Father, who art in Heaven, is like a prominent man with many children who desires to see each child excel to the fullest with their imputed abilities. Our Loving Father is like a doctor who wants to see his sons follow in his steps and become great surgeons in various medical fields in order to carry his legacy. He is like a musician instructing his children in the art of music with the expectation to one day see them perform a great symphony on the big stage. Although His purpose may not always be clear, we can wholeheartedly trust Him (Prov. 25:2).

Although the purpose of our fasting may be specific to a current dilemma in our lives, the Father who already knows our needs uses it to enlighten us of His vision for the future; fasting tamest the flesh and sharpens the spirit. This is why we ought not parade around disfigured during fasting, but rather, we should be excited with anticipation about the response to come from Heaven concerning our dilemma and the growth and development our fasting will reap.

It all goes back to the virtues that we have lost at the garden (Gen. 3:8[19]; Daniel 12:3; Rev. 16:8-9). According to Genesis 3:19, I do not believe men knew about sweating before the fall. I believe we were as bright as the sun in the garden, but our disobedience caused the flesh to leap over our spirits and our soul to expose our naked flesh. This is one of the reasons why God had to make new garments from animal's skin to cover our new, corrupted, naked body before excommunicating us out of the garden. Before then, the glory of the LORD was their covering, and they could not see their shame or nakedness under the brightness of God's glory (Luke 2:9). Because of that, the essence of the Creator now lives within the wall of the flesh behind the soul. When we receive Jesus Christ as our Savior, we get a spiritual transplant, and we get a new life (fresh charge) in Christ. However, it is up to us to apply ourselves through prayer, fasting, and the reading of the Word to develop our inner and true self, which is the spirit man (compare Mark 6:46-52 to Job 9:8-11 and Gen. 1:1-2; see also Matt. 17:15-21).

God's mysterious transcendence is manifested in Mark 6:48, Matthew 17:1-2, and Luke 24:36-43. Jesus Christ is an indication of the power of God living within us. This is not to say we can transfigure or walk on water as we see fit. We are much more than bread and meat, and we ought to spend time in fasting and prayers to understand our true worth in the Lord (Matt. 4:1-4; John 6:63; 1 Cor. 1:27-31).

Yes, one could make an argument of the matter if one so chooses, but to what avail? We have eaten the forbidden fruit and are under a curse. For the snake still goes up on its belly, and God has done all of the leg work and redeemed us for Himself without violating His own protocols. Therefore, we ought to just be glad and apply ourselves through the principles of praying, fasting, and studying our Bible so that we can defeat our adversary (the devil) in spiritual battles. The end of our burden is at an end, and He has promised to wipe away all our tears and make everything anew. Let us therefore rejoice in our fasting and give Him praises.

Our General, throughout all of His ministry, was re-establishing the connection between God and man (Luke 3:23-[38]). He wanted to remind us of our true essence—first with words and parables, followed by signs of wonders, and finally sealed by His own Blood at the Cross. Even before the time of His crucifixion, He wanted to establish these fundamental principles so that following His resurrection, we would be convinced of these facts. For our faith is strengthened by the fact that our Savior is risen as He prophesied.

Just like when God speaks to us with dreams and visions, Jesus painted pictures with His Words to elaborate the Father's thought towards us. That is because we are visual beings. This is the reason why within His marching orders (Matthew 5-7), Jesus is also reiterating the type of relationship that we ought to have with Father God in the first place (see also Isa. 58:1-14).

Now more than ever, it is clearly apparent that we should live by those principles. We need to stay connected to the source of our power to be effective against the current state of the world. They are the foundations for us to live by as children of God, and we should not forget that we are travelers in this foreign land. We are behind enemy lines. As such, our treasures should be where our home is.

Concerning treasure, Jesus said, *"Lay not up for yourselves treasure upon earth, where moth and rust doth corrupt, and where thieves break through and steal: But lay up for yourselves treasures in heaven, where neither moth nor rust doth corrupt, and where thieves do not break through nor steal: **For where your treasure is, there will your heart be also**"* (Matt. 6:19-21).

Heaven is where our home is. In fact, we are merely spirit beings going through a temporary physical experience in this realm. We are not forbidden to excel in this realm; however, this is not our home, and as brother Paul said, *"All things are not expedient"* (1 Cor. 6:12-13, 10:21-23). Moreover, the place that the Lord has gone to prepare for us is for the incorruptible body that we will inherit upon completion of our journey. This "ashes to ashes and dust to dust" vessel cannot follow. Additionally, Heaven is full of treasure rooms. The righteous deeds for the Lord unlock the doors of these treasure rooms in Heaven. When we get there, the Lord Himself will preside over the unwrapping and presentation of each gift. The lack of commitment from us here, however, will be rewarded accordingly in the afterlife as well.

In verse 22 of Matthew 6, Jesus declares:

"If that eye be single - **or if that eye would be clear, sound, and healthy with the connotation generous** *- then thy whole body shall be full of light."*

This statement from the Lord is directly connected to verses 18 to 21 concerning the location of our treasures and what should be the desires of our heart (compare Isa. 58:6-10). He is in effect revealing to us what the atmosphere of Heaven is and ordering us to be heralds of this empathic climate here on Earth. He commands us to live by this ambiance by being conservative with our outlook on life and maintaining a sound, healthy, and generous eye to look to our fellow men with a caring and loving eye, and to extend the love of God towards all (Luke 14:7-14).

By doing this, people shall know that we are truly children of God. For our God is the omnipotent God, and His children will not starve to death (Mark 6:32-44; Ps. 37:25-31; Matt. 6:25-34). If we are doing His will and walking the path of righteousness, we will have no wants. His blessing will overflow to our brethren as well (2 Sam. 6:13-[19]).

Just think about this for a minute. Regarding the estimate of the gold from the three wise men, and the example that our Lord and Savior established for us with His own personal life:

"Jesus The Wealthy," gave away His wealth to the needy so that He can dedicate His time to the gospel of GOD. He makes Himself poor so that **we** can receive the fullness of His life as a dedication to our salvation. He goes around from town to town preaching the gospel, often with no food to eat, and no shelter (Mark. 11:12; Matt. 8:20). However, in Matthew 14:13-21 and 15:29-39, thru faith, "Jesus The Poor" fed 5000 thousand people the first time, and 4000 people on a second occasion; and all this without a dime. In fact, He had **12** baskets full of leftovers the first time, and 7 baskets of leftovers the second time (Mark 8:14-21).

There are a few things that may cause us to suffer as Christians. The most common is unforgiveness. The second is not repenting for our sins. The third is asking with doubt in our heart, and lastly, the times of trials (or chastising). Moreover, withholding your tithes and offering will also deny you His blessings. I believe that if we truly had a heart towards Christ, the men of God (the pastors) wouldn't even have to preach about tithes so much (Ex. 36:5-7).

Ultimately, God is a Man of His word. If we are walking in His will, we will have more than enough to maintain our living expenses, maintain the House of God, and feed the needy. Many of us cannot help our local churches or neighbors because of the excessive lifestyle that we are straining to live by. The consumerism spirit has too many of us Elects chasing the finite and perishable objects of this world (Matt. 6:24).

Furthermore, Heaven's ambiance does not have room for the type of empathy this world promotes where evil is condoned, all belief systems are tolerated, and transgenderism is celebrated as progress. There can be only one God and one Kingdom (Matt. 6:9-10). Jesus is the blueprint of Heaven; the type of love that Jesus Himself lived by glorifies the kingdom of Heaven. For during His time on Earth, Jesus did not condone but empathized with the poor, prostitutes, tax collectors, spiritually and physically sick, Samaritan woman, Canaanite woman, Roman Centurion, and whoever was seeking after the Father with a pure and faithful heart (Matt. 9:10-13).

In Matthew 15:21-28, we can see how the faith of the Gentile woman healed her daughter. Jesus was reluctant to help her at first because His mission was to restore the house of Israel, and Paul had already been chosen to be a light for the Gentiles. The Lord said to her, "It is not good to cast the children's bread to the dogs" because just like in Luke 8:43-48, He was being conservative in how He disbursed His anointing (Luke 4:18-19, 14:25-35; Lev. 25:8-24). Although the Father gave the Son the Spirit without measure (John 3:33-35), the Lord had to be conservative and live by the same principle of discipleship that He warned us about in Luke 14. In order to fulfill His task and reset the clock on our behalf, He regulated His own anointing according to the Father's task to Him.

Simultaneously, the light of the body is the eye, and the Light of the eye is Christ. For our eyes to be light, we must first receive the Light, which is Christ (John 14:6), then we must maintain a positive charge to the Source of light. Lastly, He must be our only light source. Any other source of energy that fuels our life is of the devil, and he can only supply darkness because there is no light in him. Only the greatest darkness will you find in him (trust me I know). The devil, as stated throughout this parchment, likes to use materialism and the love of this world as a means of distraction in exchange for our worship (Matt. 4:8-11).

In verses 23-24 of Matthew Chapter 6, Jesus is comparing the darkness of an evil eye to mammon. The word mammon is the Aramaic word for riches. In that passage, Jesus is using it as an example of a life-goal opposed to God, not just money. *"Ye cannot serve God and mammon,"* which means we must choose which kingdom we want to be part of. Anything from the evil eye, which promotes darkness, is to be rebuked from our souls. The lust of the flesh, the lust of the eyes, the pride of life, or any other lust for this temporary world is equivalent to worshiping the beast and receiving his mark.

I am going to go on a limb here and say that it is not by coincidence that the devil uses the Eye of Horus, or the all-seeing eye, as his main symbol. I also believe the warning from Jesus about having an evil eye, or an eye predisposed for the glory of this world, it is a double-edged sword-word from the Lord.

Therefore, Jesus tells us to take no thought for our life as the Gentiles do, for they live for this realm. They do not have the prospect of an eternal kingdom as we do. They do not have the understanding that all they are chasing after as validation for their existence are just old fables from the defeated fallen angel. He is a professional illusionist, and he is constantly remastering his spells to meet each generation. Or as the Preacher said:

"Vanity of vanities, saith the Preacher, vanity of vanities; all is vanity. What profit hath a man of all his labor which he taketh under the sun? One generation passeth away, and another generation cometh: but the earth abideth forever. The sun also ariseth, and the sun goeth down, and hasteth to his place where he arose. The wind goeth toward the south, and turneth about unto the north; it whirleth about

continually, and the wind returneth again according to his circuits. All the rivers run into the sea; yet the sea is not full; unto the place from whence the rivers come, thither they return again. All things are full of labor; man cannot utter it: the eye is not satisfied with seeing, nor the ear filled with hearing. **The thing that hath been, it is that which shall be; and that which is done is that which shall be done: and there is no new thing under the sun. Is there any thing whereof it may be said, See, this is new? It hath been already of old time, which was before us.** *There is no remembrance of former things; neither shall there be any remembrance of things that are to come with those that shall come after" (Read Eccl. 1:2-11).*

So, let us first seek the kingdom of God and his righteousness. All these things shall be added unto us. There is no real profit in this realm because when we die, we can't take any of it with us. Only the righteousness of Christ manifested through our lives will have their weight in precious jewels in the afterlife (Matt. 6:33).

Now, the kingdom of God is to be distinguished from the kingdom of Heaven proclaimed by John the Baptist in Matthew 3:2-[3]. The kingdom of God is all the kingdom reunified under Christ, as it was before the beginning of time. It is the kingdom that was before Lucifer's rebellion. The kingdom of God is the fulfillment of *"Thy will be done in earth, as it is in heaven,"* as later explained by Paul in 1 Corinthians 15:22-28 (see also Rev. 11:15, 20:6; Psalms 103:19; Daniel 4:24-26 and Luke 17:20-21). John the Baptist was in effect proclaiming Christ as the Jewel of Heaven and the Great Light of Heaven sent to unify God and men. When John the Baptist was taken out the battlefield, our General - Jesus - picked up his baton to carry His own proclamation of salvation (Matt. 4:12-17).

Side note of Luke 17:20-21: *"... The kingdom of God cometh not with observation: neither shall they say, Lo here! or, lo there! for, behold, the kingdom of God is within you."* That is, the kingdom of God is a spiritual kingdom that will be manifested at the appointed time.

The Holy Spirit, which lives within us, is the seal and the guide to the kingdom of God. The spirit realm can see our seal (Acts 16:16-17). When all things are made clear, we will see the kingdom of God with our own eyes (2 Kings 6:15-17 and Numbers 22:21-34).

It is as if God placed a seal on our spirits so we cannot see or hear the astral realm without His approval (Gen. 28:12-13; John 1:50-51). Nevertheless, to those sealed by His Spirit and bonded for Heaven, we are as Christ was in the flesh, a piece of Heaven on Earth.

Furthermore, even those who are outside of Christ's covenant have the knowledge of God through the spirit of the land because the law of nature testifies of God and of His magnificence. If they would only listen to the conscience of their hearts, they would see the teaching of Nashaw concerning pseudoscience and a globe earth just doesn't make any sense (Rom. 2:12-16). This is why at the last judgment, no one will be able to say I did not know because *"the heavens declare the glory of God; and the firmament showeth his handiwork"* (Psalms 19: [1]-6).

Side note #2: At the great gathering mentioned in Matthew 24:31, the angels of the Lord are the ones coming to gather us. There will be no magic trick for the gathering of the saints. (Remember the watchers in Daniel 4:13-17, the Bible says that they were watching over the kingdom of king Nebuchadnezzar, and through the counsel of the Most High, a decree was made against Nebuchadnezzar for his insubordination). Nebuchadnezzar lost his mind and kingdom for seven years and was later restored (Daniel 4:19-37). Just like the heathen king, we have watchers and guardian angels assigned to us, and the Lord has many angels with various ranks and powers to serve His purposes.

At the gathering, there will be no hocus-pocus. The angels will appear unto us and gather our souls from this realm into the eternal kingdom, just as they went into the city of Sodom and Gomorrah and rescued Lot and his family out of destruction (Gen. 19:15-26). When that time comes, God will place in our hearts recognition of His messengers as they appear unto us. Moreover, when that day comes, we need to be wiser than our brother Lot—and his wife—because we will be Heaven bound. Nothing besides our souls can traverse over to the realm Universal, so why bother with the material things of this world? We won't have any use for them where we're going anyway (Luke 17:28-32; Matt. 24:32-44).

- Conclusion of Chapter Eleven -

*"Take therefore no thought for the morrow: for the morrow shall take thought for the things of itself. **Sufficient unto the day is the evil thereof***" (Matt. 6:34).

The world is full of stressful scenarios. "What if this and what if that" has been at the center of the news lately, also referred to as *whataboutism*. The Father in His infinite wisdom has already made provision for us in all things. When we look for Him earnestly, we will find Him. He has never left His throne, and His sovereignty has never been challenged. He has to maintain order, be fair, impartial in judgment, and He has nothing but good will towards us. It is now up to us to draw near to God. We have to look at life from His predestined perspective. Worrying about "what if," only opens up space for the spirit of doubt to occupy our minds. Jesus has revealed to us all things that pertain to our current timeline in the Bible, the "time of the end." Whichever prophecies are still sealed will be revealed in due time (Daniel 12:1-[4]; Rev. 10:4-11, Rev. 11:1-14; James 1:5-7). The only thing we have to do is place all of our faith in The KING OF KINGS and LORD OF LORDS. He will carry us through.

- Who Are We to Judge? -

"Judge not, that ye be not judged. For with what judgment ye judge, ye shall be judged: and with what measure ye mete, it shall be measured to you again" (Matt. 7:1-2).

This command is linked directly to the judgment of condemnations towards one another. The Lord is not saying that we should be silent to evil, but we ought not be quick to pass condemnation against another, unless otherwise anointed to (2 Sam. 12:1-10). We should simply let the Word of God do its bidding. It is one of our detrimental compromises to point the finger at someone else's flaws and cover our own blemishes. It's almost like we feel vindicated by being the accuser of another. This hypocritical expression of vengefulness comes from a vindictive spirit. This spirit uses reverse psychology to motivate us to be negative towards one another. Instead of uplifting each other's morale, we are quick to criticize our own. This fact is made even more evident in our entertainment today. This spirit also promotes disloyalty, fear, and cowardliness (Gen. 3:12). We all have sinned and are not in a position to condemn anyone; the only one righteous enough to declare condemnation is Jesus Christ (James 4:10-12). This is why it is important that we speak from the Spirit/spirit, and we do not judge from the flesh, which looks outwardly, or from the soul who passes conceited judgments.

However, in the first verse of The Similitudes, Jesus declared that we are the salt of the earth. Salt is used for taste and to preserve food in today's markets, but in Biblical times, they had no refrigerators. Therefore, its primary use was to preserve. Salt is said to have two levels of preservatives in the food industry. First, it dries out food by drawing water out. This osmosis process helps prevent the growth of bacteria which needs water to survive. Second, it kills most microbes through the process of osmolarity. This preservative aptitude is what our Savior is commanding us to display. He wants us to use our salt (our anointing) to draw the water of demonic doctrines out of our society, so we can prevent the growth of corruptive bacteria in our communities. Notwithstanding, it is not our job to judge the meat for being meat. It is our duty to recognize the spoiling fate of the meat, and to the best of our abilities, preserve and kill the microbes that are attempting to destroy its molecules. Nevertheless, the only way we can do that is by retaining our flavor, which is our savor or anointing.

Although we should refrain from the ministry of condemnation, we are authorized to condemn the sin but not the sinner, only after we have removed the beam out of our own eye.

This is the reason why I use "we" and "our" in many of my observations. Whether or not I have ever committed that sin does not matter. I speak from a watchman's point of view under the decree of the porter's ministry (Ezekiel 33:1-16; John 10:1-5). God is the Judge. My remarks come from a place as a sinner who feels compelled to speak these words of wisdom to the whole world because the back-alley ministry is getting old. I hesitated for too long to blare this on the rooftop, and I am starting to feel the guilt of cowardliness upon my soul.

Therefore, judging the condition of our societies (church, governments, and communities) is not a sin. We should only operate through the Spirit of God, which observes the actions of men and responds according to the will of God through the love of God. We must speak only from the Spirit of God, not from the flesh which judges outwardly or the soul which uses counterfeit authority to manipulate, intimidate, and exploit the living. Our spirit must take oversight over our soul. Ergo the warning:

"For in the same way you judges others, you will be judged, and with the measure you use, it will be measured to you" (Matt. 7:2 NIV).

The following verses are some examples of the proper ways to approach a covenant brother or sister who's at fault - Lev. 19:17-18; Prov. 18:13-14, 19:11; 2 Tim. 3:16-17; Gal. 6:1-5; Titus 3:8-11; Rom 16:17-18; Matt. 18:15-17 and 1 Cor. 5:9-13.

Although salt cannot stop the decay of the meat, it can slow it down and preserve it for a while longer. Moreover, we can speak against wickedness because Jesus has been given authority over the world. He has overcome the power of the world and conquered sin and death. The official union of the kingdom of man with the kingdom of God will be shortly. As the conqueror, Jesus has all power over both realms, and His commission compels us to speak against evil (Ezek. 3:18-27; James 4:17; 2 Tim. 4:1-5; Heb. 13:12-13; Matt. 10:16).

In verse 6 of Matthew 7, Jesus ends the segment about judging with a warning against giving what is holy unto the dogs and casting our pearls before swine.

"Give not that which is holy unto the dogs, neither cast ye your pearls before swine lest they trample them under their feet, and turn again and rend you."

According to the Zondervan Bible Dictionary, dogs in Bible times were generally outcast and known for their ravenous and ruthless nature, prone to prowling and filthy habits (Prov. 26:11), and swine, although they had the divided hoof, they were considered unclean (Lev. 11:7; see also Matt. 8:31-32).

In addition, ancient Hebrews believed that swine were actually demons. I'm not sure about pigs being demons (maybe that would explain some of my early behaviors in life), but it is not by coincidence Jesus used these two animals; these animals are the spiritual equivalent of those labeled fornicator, coveters, idolaters, or drunkard in 1 Cor. 5:11. They are to be given a fair chance to redemption (Matt. 18:15-35), but if there is no improvement in his or her character, we ought to disassociate with them.

Moreover, concerning the warning against the dogs and the swine, Jesus is also saying we ought to be careful not to rebuke a Pharisee, a warlock, or a witch in his or her domain. In other words, if you are in a place where the ruling party is corrupt, and they have the people hypnotized by some kind of spell, be careful not to take a stand against them publicly. Similar to the dogs and the swine in Bible times, they will prowl and return to trample you under their feet (Prov. 23:6-9). This is because many religious, political, and judicial establishments operate under the principle of the "good old boys," these are folks with the same educational and social background who make decisions based on either autocracy or democracy.

An autocratic church is ruled by the pastor. Their philosophy and doctrines are what rules the ministry of the church, they will only agree with those who think like them, and there is little to no connection with Heaven. It's a one-man show, and no matter how righteous you may be, they will only listen to those who agree with them, and will stand with their customs over God's truth.

A democratic church, on the other hand, is led by the people. They rule over the presbytery with an iron fist. The pastor and elders do as the congregation desires, and the family with the highest offering—or the family that has been there the longest—gets to tilt the scale as it sees fit. To make headway in that environment, you have to practice lickspittle and carry extra mouthwash. This type may also see a flicker of Light from time to time, but they are correspondingly hindering their connection to Heaven and interfering with God's plan for His Church by choosing the people's word over God's word.

Theocracy, however, is the ideal disposition for an assembly to have because of its principles of a church, which is God-led from every aspect. This does not mean there will not be conflicts, but with Jesus at the wheel, prayer, worship, order, and disciplines are constant dispositions. With that also comes the power to cast out demons, heal the sick, and even raise the dead. These powers are available for all theocratic churches.

Congruently, when we are obedient to God's rules, our labors are not in vain (Matt. 5:38-42; 1 Cor. 6:7-8; Daniel 1:5-16 and Matt. 5:2-12). Always consort with Christ in your heart in all matters. He alone can direct our paths, and not every disagreement is worth the fruit of our lips. Remember the promises He gave us in Matthew 18:18-20; there is more power in unity (Ecc. 4:9-12).

Some of you may ask, "How can, in the same chapter, Jesus says let the relentless sinner be as a "heathen man and a publican" (Matt. 18:17), yet warn us of the danger of being delivered to the tormentors if we do not forgive everyone from our hearts their trespasses" (verses 34-35)?

Well, it is because once again, we are only authorized to condemn the sin, not the sinner. We are not supposed to hold grudges or be judgmental towards our brothers and sisters who fall short in their walk with Christ, for the journey is full of trials and dangers. Unfortunately, many will fall (James 4:1-12).

If you were a soldier on the frontline surrounded by enemy combatants fighting valiantly, and all of sudden, the soldier covering your flank got taken out, you wouldn't just turn towards him and start yelling at his corpse. Neither would you just stop fighting or cover your position. Instead, you will have to cover down and adjust your fighting position. This is simply what our General is inferring to. Just like in physical warfare, this battle between Good and evil will have many casualties and many "Private Snafus". If we can recover our comrades, then we must. If there is no possibility, then we just have to fulfill the mission without them. Likewise, in this relay race, we must keep our eyes on the Prize and not lose sight of the goal. Jesus is the Prize, and Heaven is the goal. This is just the reality of war. Some make it back with a few scratches. Some make it back with missing limbs, while others don't get to come home alive (Matt. 18:7-14). Who are we to judge the turn of events? We are to be grateful that we are still in the fight and still here. For where there is life, there is hope.

- Ask of God -

Next, Jesus reiterates to ask of God as we would ask our earthly fathers (minus the insubordination).

> "***Ask***, *and it shall be given you;* ***seek***, *and ye shall find;* ***knock***, *and it shall be opened unto you: For every one that asketh receiveth; and he that seeketh findeth; and to him that knocketh it shall be opened. Or what man is there of you, whom if his son ask bread, will he give him a stone? Or if he ask a fish, will he give him a serpent?* **If you then, being evil, know to give good gifts unto your children, how much more shall your Father which is in heaven give good things to them that ask him**" *(Matt. 7:7-11)?*

Although Jesus has extended His rulership to us (Matt. 18:18) and more importantly, made us heirs to His kingdom (Luke 10:20), Jesus commands us to ask, seek, and knock because our authority requires the application of our faith.

This is in effect another declaration of the atmosphere of Heaven, for our Father is not one to promote laziness or self-entitlement. He knows what we have need of before we even ask, but He is preparing us for the eternal kingdom. He wants our interaction with Him here on Earth to reflect the kingdom of Heaven (Zech. 1:8-13). Our brothers, the angels have their own set of instructions (Ex. 23:20-21; Heb. 1:13-14; Rev. 1:1, 22:8-9), and we have ours. Ultimately, under Christ, we are one big family (Heb. 2:1-[11]). In that passage (Matt. 7:7-11), Jesus is once again giving us directives and declaring unto us the power that our memberships to His kingdom hold. For our God is not an uppity God sitting in Heaven pouting and wondering where's our prayer request. He desires true fellowship with us. This is the reason for the principle of "ask, seek, and knock". In other words, He is saying I know what you need, but I want us to have a personal relationship. I want us to talk. Once we understand that principle, then our relationship with the Father can be solidified through our prayers, praises, and worship, which in turn are rewarded with His blessings (Psalms 103). On the other hand, ignoring His desire for interaction with us could in fact lead to reproach (Ps. 50:22-23), and even curses (Mal. 2:2). I guess we could compare it to a prenuptial agreement: Be truthful to our relationship, and let us spend time together in communion. All that is Mine is My Son's, and ye are therefore heirs of all things through Him. That is the best prenuptial agreement I have ever heard of, especially since God is so easy to love (His ways are not our ways). Things may seem confusing at times, but His love, faithfulness, and devotion to His relationship to us are beyond measure. Our worship for the Father should therefore be spontaneous. Our reconciliation to the Creator was signed by His divine Blood, and the veil that separated us from our Father has been ripped in half from the top down.

"Seeing then that we have a great high priest, that is passed into the heavens, Jesus the Son of God, let us hold fast our profession. For we have not a high

*priest which cannot be touched with the feeling of our infirmities; but was in all points tempted like as we are, yet without sin. **Let us therefore come boldly unto the throne of grace, that we may obtain mercy, and find grace to help in time of need*** (Hebrews 4:14-16).

Therefore, again I say, we now have to do our part. Just as faith without work is dead, faith in action shall receive answers. It shall find a solution to the problem at hand, and it shall see doors open to provide new opportunities through the will of God. Likewise, our faith in action (through the Holy Ghost) is the vehicle that leads us to the Wedding Supper of the Lamb. For our name being in the Book of Life is as a reservation that needs to be picked-up in person, and no one else can pick it up for us.

Moreover, some prayer requests may require persistence and supplication from us (see Daniel 10:1-14). Added, we should also note that whatever we ask must be according to the will of the Father. In John 14:12-14, Jesus worked out this factor. What we ask of God in the name of Jesus cannot be selfish in nature or based solely on the desires of the flesh. God made the flesh to be a part of His image, so we ought to take care of the vessel as well. It is the spirit that quickens; the flesh profits nothing.

In John 15:1-11, Jesus goes even deeper into what that promise implies. He reiterates that this privilege is for those who abide in Him and keep His commandments, and the intent of these blessings is to testify of the Father's love.

"If ye abide in me, and my words abide in you, ye shall ask what ye will, and it shall be done unto you. **Herein is my Father glorified, that ye bear much fruit; so shall ye be my disciples. As the Father hath loved me, so have**

I loved you: continue ye in my love. If ye keep my commandments, ye shall abide in my love; even as I have kept my Father's commandments, and abide in his love. These things have I spoken unto you, that my joy might remain in you, and that your joy might be full" (John 15:7-11).

What Jesus means by that is as children of God who are obedient to His commandments, we are pruned periodically so that fruit, more fruit, and much fruit may come forth. For as God loves a cheerful giver, He also loves a productive child. So that the world may know that, He abides in us, and we in Him. It is not that God needs us to be glorified, for He is the personification of glory all by Himself. However, we were made for that purpose. As children of the Most High, when we align ourselves with our purpose, His glory can flow through us, and His Holy Name will be praised through us. This attitude of the Father is demonstrated in the parable of the prodigal son in Luke 15:11-[22-23] 32, and in the details of the Priest's Garment in Exodus 28 (17-22), (36), (41-43). God wants to share His legacy with us, exactly like an earthly father enjoys compliments regarding his children when they do well. Our Father in Heaven takes pleasure in seeing us grow and excel in His Spirit (Job 1:8, 42:10-17).

For example: When you are a prayer warrior and people testify of prayers answered through you, God gets the glory, and you are blessed through fellowship or partnership with Him through the application of your faith towards your fellow men. When you can interpret dreams and people testify of answers received and clarity of thought achieved through your interpretations, God is glorified. You are then blessed for being a worthy vessel. When you are a **true prophet of God** who prophesies, and the prophecy comes to pass according to the words spoken from your mouth, God is glorified. You are then blessed for you are of the lineage of Elijah, the prophet of the LORD. These are some examples of "fruit," "more fruit" and "much fruit," which glorify the Father.

Lastly, when we place God's kingdom first, all that we need is then added into our lives as demonstrated earlier in the rendering of "Jesus The Wealthy" and "Jesus The Poor." Jesus would not lie to us, so if we are asking a certain thing and not receiving it, we are either not ready to handle that blessing, or we just don't need it. For example, asking for a bigger house for the benefit of the new addition to the family is an acceptable prayer request. At the same time, if we are on a minimum wage job, God will not bless us with that bigger house until He has blessed us with the means to financially maintain it. God is not an enabler; He is a practical God (Rev. 19:17-21). He does not honor impulsive behaviors. As children of God, we ought to understand that basic principle. Sometimes the problem with us is that we did not heed the warning, or we have failed to fulfill the previous decree concerning a certain matter (see Gen. 12-13; Ex. 4:24-31; 1 Kings 17:1-[13] 16;). Moreover, I would be remiss to not mention the story of King Solomon and the blessings he received after asking God for wisdom instead of selfish treasures (1 Kings 3:5-15; Prov. 4:5-9).

I believe if ten percent of the Body of Christ would come together for the sake of the land and agree on the same thing **according to His will**, it will be done. Never mind the secret societies of this world; they cannot stop the Hand of God from exerting His will. I only mentioned them in this book because there have been so many conspiracy theories since this pandemic started. I just wanted to make a connection between the factuality of the hidden hand with the reality that our Creator, our Lord and Savior, the Alpha and Omega, holds all the cards (Rom. 13:1-8). Jesus promises us in Matthew 21:21-22, that whatsoever we ask in His name in prayer without doubting, we shall receive. What would be a better time than now to take Jesus up on that offer? The time of men is at an end, but no one knows the exact hour. Why not hope and pray for another extension? The worst that can happen is the Father will say no, in which case, we ought to be glad we are about to go home soon.

If God so chooses, we shall see the plagues that have been befalling us recently recant. We can make America a true Christian Nation and slow down the decay of our society. Furthermore, we will have to tear down the pillars of Baal and stop the Moloch's sacrifices, which bring plagues to the earth, and we must restore the Christian values as intended. Let us not allow this great country to go down before its predestined time. Let us ask, seek, and knock on Heaven's doors.

"For every one that asketh receiveth; and he that seeketh findeth; and to him that knocketh it shall be opened" (Matt. 7:8).

They say America owes $28.43 trillion in debt. I say put it on my Father's tab. He is good for it, and He'll have this taken care of in no time at all.

But it all starts with first finding the love of God and allowing it to get manifested through us with the love for righteousness and the love for our neighbor. This is the "Golden Rule."

"Therefore all things whatsoever ye would that men should do to you, do ye even so to them: for this is the law and the prophets" (Matt. 7:12).

This is the only way into the kingdom of God. There is no other algorithm for salvation that can preserve us from this bestial system and save us from eternal damnation. In addition, as bitter as this may feel to be told we should express love unto others in this current atmosphere, love is the only remedy for this dying world. Love will shame the devil and bring peace to the land; for how long does not matter because we do not have any control over time either way. Let's fight for the "present", and God willing, when tomorrow gets here, let's fight the good fight some more.

"Enter ye in at the strait gate: for wide is the gate, and broad is the way, that leadeth to destruction, and many there be which go in thereat: Because strait is the gate, and narrow is the way, which leadeth unto life, and few there be that find it" (Matt. 7:13-14).

- Search the spirit by the Spirit -

After we have done all that we can do in the Spirit, we must remember God gets the final say in all things. He works in mysterious ways, so we must stand firm and wait (Eph. 6:12-13). Since we know that all things are only guaranteed at the end of this journey, we should not be discontent with God if things do not get better moving forward. Instead, let us take advantage of "the calm before the storm" to sharpen our faith.

Therefore, beware that we are in the last hour. More and more false prophets will emerge. They will come to you wrapped in sheep's clothing, proclaiming to be from the Lord Himself. But by their fruit you should know them.

"Even so every good tree bringeth forth good fruit; but a corrupt tree bringeth forth evil fruit. A good tree cannot bring forth evil fruit, neither can a corrupt tree bring forth good fruit" (Matt. 7:17-18).

Again I say, beware; for we are in that last hour, and there is more evil now than ever before. Search this book with the Spirit of God, and search even your spirit by the Spirit of God (Matt. 24:23-26; John 16:13-15; 1 John 4:6). Ask for His discernment, and you shall receive it.

There is only one true way into the kingdom, and not everyone who proclaims to be saved will enter the kingdom of Heaven. Only those of us who walk with Him on a daily basis and fulfill our calling, according to His purpose, will receive an eternal membership into the "Church City" called The New Jerusalem and the Church Of the Firstborn (Heb. 12:22-23). For wonderful works outside of God's will is the same as a ring in the nose of a pig because:

"Behold to obey is better than sacrifice, and to hearken than the fat of rams. For rebellion is as the sin of witchcraft, and stubbornness is as iniquity and idolatry" (1 Samuel 15:22-23).

All the workers of iniquity will be rebuked for their disobedience and stubbornness at the final judgment. There will be no drug deals, and there is no such thing as purgatory. So today is the day to choose wisely. The options are simple. Do we want the foundation of our faith to be solidified as doers of the Word, or do we marginalize our faith as hearers?

*"Therefore whosoever heareth these sayings of mine, and doeth them, **I will liken him unto a wise man, which built his house upon a rock: And the rain descended, and the floods came, and the winds blew, and beat upon that house; and it fell not; for it was founded upon a rock.** And every one that heareth these sayings of mine, and doeth them not, shall be likened unto a foolish man, which built his house upon the sand: And the rain descended, and the floods came, and the winds blew, and beat upon that house; and it fell: and great was the fall of it" (Matt. 7:24-27).*

Notwithstanding, I won't lie to you, battle buddy. I cannot say I always turn the other cheek or that it is a joy to love my enemies and do good to those who hate me. The truth is, I can't do any of these things on my own anyway; it's just not in my nature. It is only through the Spirit of Jesus Christ, which dwells in me and keeps me day by day, that I am able to stand strong. The more we spend time together, the easier it is for me to be a complying child and be more sanctified (Phil. 4:13; John 14:10).

We must diminish, and the Spirit of Christ living within us must grow. This is the only way. Once we reach the point of complete surrender to Christ, we shall then be as one submerged in the river of life (Ezekiel 47:1-12; Rev. 22:1-2). Then shall the healing power of God operate at optimal capacity through all those bearing their cross, as in the days of the apostles (John 4:10-[26]; John 7:38-39; Mark 16:17-18; Acts 5:12-16, 9:36-42; 19:11-12). I truly believe due to our current state, these signs of wonders will soon be a daily occurrence in our churches.

I believe you have grasped the meaning of the Sermon on the Mount that Jesus gave to us in Matthew Chapters 5 to 7. He gave us this message as the remedy for all our troubles here on Earth. The overall point of the sermon is that we shall trust God with all our heart, mind, and soul. I encourage each one of us who are saved, having been blessed with the Holy Spirit, to read our Bible daily so we can receive more revelations from the Word for ourselves. I also encourage those who want to be saved and sealed by the Holy Spirit to come to Jesus and repent of their sins. The pastor's job is to educate us on the Father's vision for the body of Christ as a whole, but we each have been called into ministry (Ezekiel 14:12-20). Some of us may even, one day, be anointed to follow in the footsteps of the overseers. Some of us have been anointed with a gift – motivational gifts – that will provide some vital support to the kingdom of Christ.

At the conclusion of the Sermon on the Mount (Matt. 7:28-29), the Text tells us the throng was astonished at Jesus' teaching. Even though the purpose of the remedy was not clear to the multitudes of the time, they recognized one thing for sure by the end of the sermon. They recognized Jesus was speaking as one having authority over the scribes. Jesus was in effect proclaiming His sovereignty over all things even before completing His mission. On that day, He provided mankind with the answers for all the issues of the world. He provided the remedy for the earth's condition for the past, present, and future generations.

CHAPTER TWELVE

JOHN 14:6

Jesus Is the Primordial Assurance

The primordial assurance is the love of God manifested through Jesus Christ at Calvary; through Him were all things made and nothing that exists, exists outside of Him. He wrapped Himself with humility and came to Earth some two thousand years ago to set the record straight and give us a way out of eternal damnation. Jesus is the only means we can overrule the influence of this corrupt world over our lives.

The truth is if the world had been applying those directives given to us on the mount the last two thousand years, our society would have never achieved its current condition. You should notice I said the world and not precisely the church. This is because according to the Text, Jesus spoke these words in front of multitudes of people (Matt. 4:23-5:2).

To the world, He spoke in many parables because they were not permitted to understand certain things, at least not until He had restored Israel first. He spoke this message plainly to the whole of them. How many were Jews, how many were Romans, or slaves, or free? The Bible does not say, but according to Zondervan's Bible Dictionary:

"The Decapolis was composed of ten cities; they were initially given to the tribe of Manasseh, but later became occupied by Greeks and Romans (65 B.C.)."

This would mean that our Lord and Savior gave these instructions to the Jews, the Greeks, and the Romans.

The Great Commission was given to those who are saved, but these were the words He gave to all in attendance that day. In other words, Jesus planted the seed of remedy for our current state within the Jews and the Gentiles alike. No one from that day can say they were not given fair warnings and no one in our generation can say God is to blame for our decay.

It is men who have sinned against God; therefore, we now reap the plagues of our labour. However, just like with chemotherapy, it is better to attack the cancer in its late stage than to just let it metastasize (spread) and die, because not every stage 4 cancer diagnostics are terminal. Besides, since our General was deliberate enough to plant the seed for the remedy of the mark of the beast to a diverse multitude, we, the Church, are to take advantage of His labor. You will be surprised to know how many people I have met in this so-called "evolved generation" who think Hell is just a hoax. People are more prone to believe in science fiction, black holes and green little aliens than in a loving caring Creator. They spend years studying the Marvel Comics library of superheroes and memorizing the Star Wars Aurebesh alphabet so they can fit in and validate their existence within the illusion of this realm. The fear of God is not present because there is little to no awareness that there is a God to begin with or that Jesus is not just a folk story. He's the only way to eternal salvation. This is because most of the porters are preoccupied with the world; we are just too busy chasing after the newest trends and the latest handbag to care. The name porter in the Bible represents a "gate-keeper"—a person stationed at an entrance or gate to admit and filter out those entering (see 1 Chronicles 26:1-19). Porter in modern terms also means a burden carrier. In relation to Christendom, the term porter represents members of the church according to each one's position. From the pastors, elders, deacons, ushers, down to the parking lot attendees, we are all members of the porter's ministry. This title has been extended to all Christians under the new covenant established by Christ because we are each one a temple for the Holy Spirit, and we have to guard our hearts and minds at all times. Through our walk with Christ and living a sanctified life daily, our prayers have the power to shut down all demonic portals and draw people to the eternal truth of the gospel of Jesus Christ. The house of the Lord (the church) is supposed to operate as a well-oiled military unit both in the church and outside the church; that is what it takes to keep our light shining through this dark world.

The lust of the flesh (gluttony, homosexuality, adultery, or fornication), the lust of the eyes (private jets ministry, covetousness, envy), the pride of life (greed, soul-authority, egotism, Christian identity, or Black Hebrews Israelites) has become too predominant in too many of our churches. We need to return to our first love, which is our commitment to the primordial Assurance of our faith and to the true and infrangible, agape-fueled gospel of Jesus Christ.

The lack of love brings demises and curses to the land, but charity can remove multitudes of sins and postpone the decree of Heaven for many more generations. God is not eager to kill men. He has all of eternity to do that. Nor is He a bloodthirsty Father. He does not sit in Heaven waiting for us to fail so that He can send pestilence and bad omen towards us. The latter are the outcome of our iniquities. His desires have always been good towards us. His desire is that as many as would receive Jesus, would receive eternal life (Ezek. 33:11-29; 2 Peter 3:1-9).

It is the devil and his minions who are after bringing judgment of death upon mankind. His human overlords are under the delusion they're going to get a special seat at his table, and it is true. What Satan has failed to tell them is that his table is going to be set in the lake of fire. Let those who have ears to hear, wake up. Moreover, the rest of those who serve him in deliberate commitment are born to damnation. They are like the son of perdition, born to accomplish the wrath of God through the prophecies (Pr. 16:4). We ought to pray for them, but blind sympathy for their condition is not recommended. These three chapters of Matthew (5-7) are linked to a singular message; denounce the devil and the system of his beast and adore God (Rom. 8:1-[18], 31).

Illusion is a false impression that leads to delusion or false belief, and through sigils, infiltrations, decentralization, mass projections, and other means, the enemy and his overlords have been working against the Church of Christ. Their aim is to usher in their concept of a perfect world. To accomplish their goal, they have been slowly and methodically suppressing the light of the Church of Christ. They've been doing that because the army of gloom knows darkness prevails when the light is missing. Darkness will occupy the space allocated for the light (Pr. 29:2). Let me make it plain. The light from the pulpit and God's Elects is supposed to be the first line of defense. Without it, the porter's ministry is to no avail, and the enemy can run rampant all over the Church. If the Church is subdued, what is of the world? If the world is overruled by evil **before its appointed time**, then we have failed, and the blame is on the Church. No preacher can blame the fate of our society on politics or even the secret societies (2 Cor. 4:1-7; Eph. 4:27). The power to bind and to loose was given to us, not them!

The armies of Heaven are at our commands, as long as we use our weapons wisely and for the glory of Jesus' name and the advancement of His kingdom through the guidance of the Holy Ghost (Ps. 103:20). We have the power to command the invisible into the visible according to each one's calling, for The LORD God Almighty has already given His angels charge over us. Whether it is one regiment or ten thousand, it does not matter because one angel is all it shall take to bind the devil (Rev. 20:13). It is time that we begin to apply the authority invested in us at Calvary and stop these trolls from terrorizing our Churches, our governments, and our homes. Speak and fear not the reproach of this condemned world. Preach and warn the people of the incumbent attacks from the enemy, evangelize, and rally-up the call to order for the souls of the heathens and backsliders alike.

The Lord is not pressed for time because *"...one day is with the Lord as a thousand years, and a thousand years as one day"* (2 Peter 3:8).

Some may ask, "But to what end? What is the purpose of applying these principles now, for the prophecies were written and the days will come to an end?" And that is true, but it is also written:

"Charity suffereth long, and is kind; charity envieth not; charity vaunteth not itself, is not puffed up. Doth not behave itself unseemly, seeketh not her own, is not easily provoked, thinketh no evil; Rejoice not in iniquity, but rejoiceth in the truth; Beareth all things, believeth all things, **hopeth all things, endureth all things. Charity never faileth: but whether there be prophecies, they shall fail; whether there be tongues, they shall** cease; **whether there be knowledge, it shall vanish away. For we know in part, and we prophesy in part**" (1 Cor. 13:4-9; see also Daniel 9:27 and Matt. 24:15-[22]).

- What About the Devil? -

What about him? He is on a short leash, and his time is near. The devil has never been a challenge to the Creator; he is more like a stubborn child being taught a lesson (Rev 20:1-3). We are not supposed to taunt him because that is not the way of a child of God. We're not to be afraid of him either or empathize with his demise. For want of a better depiction: Satan is like the stubborn older brother who's been kicked out of the family circle for doing drugs and breaking the rules of the house. If he comes by when parents are not around and asks to come in, you say Papa said not to let you in the house (house here represents our temple: mind, body, and soul - James 4:7). When he tries to bully his way in, we put on the whole armour of God (Eph. 6:10-18). If he starts reminding us of the time we peed in the bed (bringing up our past), we bring up his future resting place in the lake of fire. We ought to know the Word of God, so we can defeat him in spiritual warfare. It is part of our duties as Christians to put him back in his place and to destroy the work of Satan by letting our light shine in the midst of the darkness, but the rest is in the hands of Jesus Christ (Job 12:12-16). I say all that because the devil will sometimes try to get us caught up in philosophical or intellectual debates with him about the disposition of our faith. Most Christians, when we are cornered by the devil with those types of attacks, tend to engage in debates with him, but we cannot win by debating with Satan. We must do as Jesus did when He got tempted while in the wilderness (Matt. 4:4-11): maintain a sanctified life, go to the Scriptures, and state the truth; Satan cannot handle the truth. A philosophical debate is the same trap Satan used in the Garden of Eden with Eve. We don't owe the devil any explanation for our faith. We simply rejoice in the Object and objectives of our faith (Luke 10:19-28) because God has everything under control.

Last Note: If you are praying for a loved one and nothing seems to change or improves, do not quit. Some people will not come to God until they hit rock bottom. God knows us intimately, and He will sometimes allocate torments in order to expedite the process of salvation so that the individual may not take root in his iniquity (Gen. 15:13-[16]; Ezekiel 16:2-3).

I truly hope these words find you in good spirit, or at least leave you empowered in the Lord. Satan knows if we know our real strength, we could paralyze his plans and cause the land to flourish and prosper. The Scriptures tell us that our power is in the **Blood of the Lamb** and the **word of our testimony** (Rev. 12:11). The Blood of the Lamb represents Jesus, the word of our testimony represents our faith in action, and the object of our faith is Jesus. The Father's greatest weapon is His Word (Ps. 119:8-9), and He has given us access to Him (John 3:16). We ought to bear witness of His magnificence so our testimony may lift Him up and men may draw to Him. Moreover, let us not settle for the finite and the temporal anymore. The eternal kingdom is where the real treasures are. Over there is no mold, no pain, and no sorrows.

"Fret not thyself because of evildoers, neither be thou envious against the workers of iniquity. For they shall soon be cut down like the grass, and wither as the green herb. Trust in the LORD, and do good; so shalt thou dwell in the land, and verily thou shalt be fed. Delight thyself also in the LORD; and he shall give thee the desires of thine heart. Commit thy way unto the LORD; trust also in him; and he shall bring it to pass. And he shall bring forth thy righteousness as the light, and thy judgment as the noonday. Rest in the LORD, and wait patiently for him: fret not thyself because of him who prospereth in his way, because of the man who bringeth wicked devices to pass. Cease from anger, and forsake wrath: fret not thyself in any wise to do evil. For evildoers shall be cut off: but those that wait upon the LORD, they shall inherit the earth. For yet a little while, and the wicked shall not be: yea, thou shalt diligently consider his

place, and it shall not be. But the meek shall inherit the earth; and shall delight themselves in the abundance of peace" (Psalms 37:1-11 KJV).

The idea that this world can one day become a man-made utopia is something that is just ludicrous. Moreover, we cannot escape the inevitable, and we cannot stop the end of times from coming. Think of it this way; if the end of times does not come, there is no need for the second coming. That would mean Christ's torture and death would have been in vain. This is just unacceptable. The only options left are life-eternal or death-eternal? If God so chooses, we may still get a little more time here on Earth to fulfill His calling. However, we, the church, will have to first take a solid stand.

Peradventure you are not yet saved and still have any doubt about

His assurance; perhaps a review of the life of Jesus Christ may help:

- THE RESUMÉ OF JESUS CHRIST –

Address: JEHOVAH SHAMMAH, Psalms 46, John 16:13, Matthew 28:20, 1 Cor. 3:16.

Phone: El ROI, Psalms 139:7-12, Romans 10:12-13, 1 John 1:9.

Website: ADONAI, The Bible. Keywords: Christ, Lord, Savior (Ps. 23), Creator (Psalms 8), Son of God and Jesus (John 3:16, Isaiah. 9:6).

Objective:

I am the Creator and Savior of the world. My name is Jesus Christ. Some prefer to call Me by my Hebrew name, Yahushuah Hamashiach, and many have received me as their Lord. I have sent you my resume because I am seeking to deliver you, to heal you, to make you free, to empower and save you in this last hour. Please consider the signs of the time, and if you are not saved yet, give Me a chance to redeem you before it's too late.

Qualifications:

I am the only true God, and my origin can be traced through your history. I have fulfilled all the prophecies concerning my physical birth, death, and resurrection.

1. **Prophecy:** Genesis 3:14-15, "And the LORD God said to the Serpent, Because thou hast done this, thou art cursed above all cattle... And I will put enmity between thee and the woman, and between thy seed and her seed: it shall bruise thy head, and thou shalt bruise his heel."

2. **Fulfillment:** <u>Galatians 4:4,</u> "But when the fullness of the time was come, God sent forth his Son, made of a woman, made under the law."

3. **Prophecy:** <u>Malachi 3:1,</u> "Behold, I will send my messenger, and he shall prepare the way before me: and the Lord, whom ye seek, shall suddenly come to his temple, even the messenger of the covenant, whom ye delight in: behold, he shall come, saith he shall come, saith the LORD of hosts."

4. **Fulfillment:** <u>Matthew 11:7-10,</u> "... For this is he, of whom it is written, Behold, I send my messenger before thy face, which shall prepare thy way before thee."

5. **Prophecy:** <u>Isaiah 7:14,</u> "Therefore the Lord himself shall give you a sign; Behold, a virgin shall conceive, and bear a son, and shall call his name Immanuel."

6. **Fulfillment:** <u>Matthew 1:18-23,</u> "Now the birth of Jesus Christ was on this wise: When as his mother Mary was espoused to Joseph, before they came together, she was found with child of the Holy Ghost... And she shall bring forth a son, and thou shalt call his name JESUS: for he shall save his people from their sins. Now all that was done, that it might be fulfilled which was spoken of the Lord by the prophet, saying, Behold, a virgin shall be with child, and shall bring forth a son, and they shall call his name Emmanuel, which being interpreted is, God with us."

7. **Prophecy:** <u>Isaiah 9:7,</u> "Of increase of his government and peace there shall be no end, upon the throne of David, and upon his Kingdom, to order it, and to establish it with judgment and with justice from henceforth even forever. The zeal of the LORD of hosts will perform this."

8. Fulfillment: <u>Matt. 1:1,</u> "The book of the generation of Jesus Christ, the son of David, the son of Abraham."

9. Prophecy: <u>Psalms 72:17,</u> "His name shall endure forever: his name shall be continued as long as the sun: and men shall be blessed in him: all nations shall call him blessed."

10. Fulfillment: <u>Galatians 3:16,</u> "Now to Abraham and his seed were the promises made. He saith not, And to seeds, as of many; but as of one, And to thy seed, which is Christ."

11. Prophecy: <u>Micah 5:2,</u> "But thou, Bethlehem Ephratah, though thou be little among the thousands of Judah, yet out of thee shall he come forth unto me that is to be ruler in Israel; whose goings forth have been from of old, from everlasting."

12. Fulfillment: <u>Matt. 2:1-2,</u> "Now when Jesus was born in Bethlehem of Judea in the days of Herod the king, behold, there came wise men from the east to Jerusalem."

13. Prophecy: <u>Psalms 72:10-11,</u> "The king of Tarshish and of the isles shall bring presents: the kings of Sheba and Seba shall offer gifts. Yea, all kings shall fall down before him: all nations shall serve him."

14. Fulfillment: <u>Matthew 2:1-11,</u> "Now when Jesus was born in Bethlehem of Judea in the days of Herod the king, behold, there came wise men from the east to Jerusalem... And when they were come into the house, they saw the young child with Mary his mother, and fell down, and worshiped him: and when they had opened their treasures, they presented unto him gifts of gold, and frankincense, and myrrh."

15. Prophecy: <u>Hosea 11:1,</u> "When Israel was a child, then I loved him, and called my son out of Egypt."

16. Fulfillment: <u>Matthew 2:13-15,</u> "Arise, and take the young child and his mother, and flee into Egypt... When he arose, he took the young child and his mother by night, and departed into Egypt: And was there until the death of Herod: that it may be fulfilled which was spoken of the Lord by the prophet, saying, Out of Egypt have I called my son."

17. Prophecy: <u>Isaiah: 61:1-2,</u> "The Spirit of the Lord GOD is upon me; because the LORD hath anointed me to preach good tidings unto the meek; he hath sent me to bind up the brokenhearted, to proclaim liberty to the captives, and the opening of the prison to them that are bound; To proclaim the acceptable year of the LORD, and the day of vengeance of our God; to comfort all that mourn."

18. Fulfillment: <u>Luke 4:18-19 [21],</u> "The Spirit of the Lord is upon me, because he hath anointed me to preach the gospel to the poor; he hath sent me to heal the brokenhearted, to preach deliverance to the captives, and recovering of sight to the blind, to set at liberty them that are bruised, To preach the acceptable year of the Lord."

19. Prophecy: <u>Isaiah 35:4-6,</u> "Say to them that are of a fearful heart, Be strong, fear not: behold, your God will come with vengeance, even God with a recompense; he will come and save you. Then the eyes of the blind shall be opened, and the ears of the deaf shall be unstopped. Then shall the lame man leap as a hart, and the tongue of the dumb sing..."

20. Fulfillment: <u>Matt. 11:4-5,</u> "...The blind receive their sight, and the lame walk, the dead are raised up, and the poor have the gospel preached to them."

21. Prophecy: <u>Psalms 72:12-14,</u> "For he shall deliver the needy when he crieth: the poor also, and him that hath no helper. He shall spare the poor and needy, and shall save the souls of the needy. He shall redeem their soul from deceit and violence: and precious shall their blood be in his sight."

22. Fulfillment: <u>Matthew 4:23-25,</u> "And Jesus went about all Galilee, teaching in their synagogues, and preaching the gospel of the kingdom, and healing all manner of sickness and disease among the people. And his fame went throughout all Syria: and they brought unto him all sick people that were taken with divers diseases and torments, and those which were possessed with devils, lunatic, and those that had palsy; and he healed them..."

23. Prophecy: <u>Psalm 69:9,</u> "For the zeal of thine house hath eaten me up; and the reproaches of them that reproached thee are fallen upon me."

24. Fulfillment: <u>John 2:17,</u> "And his disciples remembered that it was written, The zeal of thine house hath eaten me up."

25. Prophecy: <u>Zechariah 9:9,</u> "Rejoice greatly, O daughter of Zion; shout, O daughter of Jerusalem: behold, thy King cometh unto thee: he is just, and having salvation; lowly, and upon an ass, and upon a colt the foal of an ass."

26. Fulfillment: <u>Mark 11:1-10,</u> "And they brought the colt to Jesus, and cast their garments on him; and he sat upon it."

27. Prophecy: <u>Jer. 31:31,</u> Behold, the days come, saith the LORD, that I will make a new covenant with the house of Israel, and with the house of Judah."

28. Fulfillment: <u>Luke 22:15-20,</u> "... And he took bread, and gave thanks, and broke it, and gave unto them, saying, This is my body which is given for you: this do in remembrance of me. Likewise also the cup after supper, saying, This cup is the new testament in my blood, which is shed for you."

29. Prophecy: <u>Zechariah 11:12-13,</u> "... And the LORD said unto me, Cast it unto the potter: a goodly price that I was prised at of them. And I took the thirty pieces of silver, and cast them to the potter in the house of the LORD."

30. Fulfillment: <u>Matthew 27:7-10,</u> "... And they took counsel, and bought with them the potter's field, to bury strangers in. Wherefore that field was called, The field of blood, unto this day. Then was fulfilled that which was spoken by Jeremiah the prophet, saying, And they took the thirty pieces of silver, the price of him that was valued, whom they of the children of Israel did value; And gave them for the potter's field, as the Lord appointed me."

31. Prophecy: <u>Micah 5:1,</u> "Now gather thyself in troops, O daughter of troops: he hath laid siege against us: they shall smite the judge of Israel with a rod upon the cheek."

32. Fulfillment: <u>Matthew 27:30,</u> "And they spit upon him, and took the reed, and smote him on the head."

33. Prophecy: <u>Psalm 69:20-22,</u> "Reproach hath broken my heart; and I am full of heaviness: and I looked for some to take pity, but there was none;

and for comforters, but I found none. They gave me also gall for my meat; and in my thirst they gave me vinegar to drink."

34. Fulfillment: <u>Matthew 27:34,</u> "They gave him vinegar to drink mingled with gall: and when he had tasted thereof, he would not drink."

35. Prophecy: <u>Psalms 34:20,</u> "He keepeth all his bones: not one of them is broken."

36. Fulfillment: <u>John 19:32-33,</u> "But when they came to Jesus, and saw that he was dead already, they broke not his legs."

37. Prophecy: <u>Psalm 22:16,</u> "For dogs have compassed me: the assembly of the wicked have enclosed me: they pierced my hands and my feet."

38. Fulfillment: <u>John 20:27-28,</u> "Then saith he to Thomas, reach hither thy finger, and behold my hands; and reach hither thy hand, and thrust it into my side: and be not faithless, but believing. And Thomas answered and said unto him, My Lord and my God."

39. Prophecy: <u>Psalm 22:18,</u> "They part my garments among them, and cast lots upon my vesture."

40. Fulfillment: <u>Matthew 27:35,</u> "And they crucified him, and parted his garments, casting lots: that it might be fulfilled which was spoken by the prophet, They parted my garments among them, and upon my vesture did they cast lots."

41. Prophecy: <u>Psalms 31:5,</u> "Into thine hand I commit my spirit: thou hast redeemed me, O LORD God of truth.

42. Fulfillment: <u>Luke 23:46</u> "And when Jesus had cried with a loud voice, he said, Father, into thy hands I commend my spirit: and having said this, he gave up the ghost."

43. Prophecy: <u>Deut. 21:23,</u> "His body shall not remain all night upon the tree, but thou shalt in any wise bury him that day; (for he that is hanged is accursed of God;) that thy land be not defiled, which the LORD thy God giveth thee for an inheritance."

44. Fulfillment: <u>Gal. 3:13,</u> "Christ hath redeemed us from the curse of the law, being made a curse for us: for it is written, Cursed is every one that hangeth on a tree.

45. Prophecy: <u>Psalms 110:4,</u> "The LORD hath sworn, and will not repent, Thou art a priest forever after the order of Melchizedek."

46. Fulfillment: <u>Hebrews 6:20,</u> "Whiter the forerunner is for us entered, even Jesus, made a high priest forever after the order of Melchizedek."

47. Prophecy: <u>Isaiah 42:6,</u> "I the LORD have called thee in righteousness, and will hold thine hand, and will keep thee, and give thee for a covenant of the people, for a light of the Gentiles."

48. Fulfillment: <u>Acts 26:22-23,</u> "That Christ should suffer, and that he should be the first to rise from the dead, and should show light unto the people, and to the Gentiles."

49. Prophecy: <u>Psalms 16:10</u> "For thou wilt not leave my soul in hell; neither wilt thou suffer thine Holy One to see corruption.

50. Fulfillment: <u>John 20:13-14</u> "And they say unto her, Woman, why weepest thou? She saith unto them, Because they have taken away my Lord, and I know not where they have laid him. And when she had thus said, she turned herself back, and saw Jesus standing, and knew not that it was Jesus."

51. Prophecy: <u>Psalms 49:15</u> "But God will redeem my soul from the power of the grave: for he shall receive me. Selah."

52. Fulfillment (1): <u>Acts 2:22-24</u> "Whom God hath raised up, having loosed the pains of death: because it was not possible that he should be holden of it."

53. Fulfillment (2): <u>Acts 1:3,</u> "To whom also he showed himself alive after his passion by many infallible proofs, being seen of them forty days, and speaking of the things pertaining to the kingdom of God:"

54. Prophecy: <u>Psalms 68:18,</u> "Thou hast ascended on high, thou hast led captivity captive: thou hast received gifts for men; yea, for the rebellious also, that the LORD God might dwell among them."

55. Fulfillment (1): Mark 16:19, "So then after the Lord had spoken unto them, he was received up into heaven, and sat on the right hand of God."

56. Fulfillment (2): Ephesians 4:7-15, "But unto every one of us is given grace according to the measure of the gift of Christ. **Wherefore he saith, When he ascended up on high, he led captivity captive, and gave gifts unto men**. (Now that he ascended, what is it but that he also descended first into the lower parts of the earth? He that descended is the same also that ascended up far above all heavens, that he might fill all things.) And he gave some, apostles; and some, prophets; and some, pastors and teachers; For the perfecting of the saints, for the work of the ministry, for the edifying of the body of Christ: That we henceforth be no more children, tossed to and fro, and carried about with every wind of doctrine, by the sleight of men, and cunning craftiness, whereby they lie in wait to deceive; But speaking the truth in love, may grow up into him in all things, which is the head, even Christ:"

All these are just some of the many prophecies you can read about Me in the Bible. The truth is, I am the most decorated General in my Father's Army. My previous awards include: King of Peace, The Angel of The LORD, The Good Shepherd, and The Word Of GOD, just to name a few.

References:

Believers from all generations can testify of my reliability concerning my divine healing power, deliverance, restorations, and supernatural guidance.

In Summation:

The above summary shows that I am more than qualified to be your Lord and Savior, so I want you to try Me today for yourself. I will not fail you.

Summary

The Holy Ghost inspired this book, and it was written in order to connect the checkpoints in the figure of life, or the vertices of life, if you may, concerning our origin, our fault, redemption, and the eternal judgment to come. The perennial vertex in the algebra of life is and has always been Jesus Christ. He is the Alpha and Omega, and the beginning and the end. There is no hope and no future outside of Him.

All of the events that have befallen earth since creation are the direct result of the conflict between the loving Father—GOD—and a disobedient, stubborn child by the name of Satan. We merely found ourselves in the crossfire. Nevertheless, our loving Father is fearsome, and He is not weary. We have nothing to fear but God Himself, for He is mighty and all-powerful. He is great in power and wonders, and He is greatly to be feared. The fear of God should not be mistaken with the fear of man. The fear of God brings reverence, wisdom and prosperity to the hearts of men. As one should know not to put their hand in a lion's mouth, one should know to respect the Creator.

The prophecy of the end of times has long been proclaimed, and the prophecy will be fulfilled accordingly. However, no one but God knows the hour and the day. This is why I remain optimistic. At the same time, let us not be too comfortable, so we will not be turned into pillars of salt like Lot's wife.

Moreover, the concept of getting a computer chip inserted under my skin against my will does not sit well with me because clay and iron cannot mix (Daniel 2:42-44). Therefore, the attempt of mixing nanotechnology with our biological DNA is an abomination against God, and it is repeating the days of Noah. However, it was paramount for me to point out that the true mark of the beast is the disposition of our hearts and minds. Our worship is what the devil is really after; therefore, we have to protect our hearts and minds. And our worship must be to Jesus alone. I believe this nanotechnology vaccine is actually demonic in nature and made to alter our faith from the inside out. The devil is in effect trying to copy God's way of operating within us through His Holy Spirit. This is why now more than ever before, we must learn to walk in the Spirit. The Holy Spirit is our heavenly seal and our right of passage from this condemned world into the New Jerusalem. God Himself established the enemy's operating range. Although he is a crafty opponent, he cannot operate outside of the Father's rules of engagement. So again I say, we have nothing to fear from Satan because he is on a short leash. The devil and his entire overlords are on borrowed time because **no one can stop the Hand of God**.

God allowed our natural man to leap forward after the fall in order to save us and still bless multitudes of us with eternal life as He proposed to do at the garden (Rom. 8:18-[20] 30). Some may say it is not fair, but the Blood of the Lamb of God says otherwise. For if God was willing to take the form of a man to live among us, to suffer with us, and give His life for us in order to make a way back to Him, His judgments are then beyond fairness. God is the Universum of all things, and His integrity sustains all the realms in fairness and justice. He cannot deviate from righteousness because that would make Him a fraud, and this would challenge the existence of all things. We simply cannot argue with His methods because there is more at stake than our finite existence. Instead, we ought to be thankful that He made a way for us to still be redeemed. Besides, we are in our current state because we kept forcing His hand by constantly playing the harlot with false gods and idols.

The remedy for all the issues of man was given some two thousand years ago in the passage of the Sermon on the Mount, and this remedy was endorsed by Jesus' life and His ultimate sacrifice at the Cross. If we listened and followed the instructions He gave us back then, our society would not be so saturated with darkness, and the devil would not be so excited today to see his schemes coming to fruition. Nevertheless, we are the power to shut and open Heaven, according to God's will. The enemy may huff, puff, and even growl. In Jesus' name, he is already defeated, and we walk in victory. Let us no longer be ignorant and stubborn of the facts of life, but let us rather press forward with all that we are and bring honor and praises to our LORD and Savior. He is the KING OF KINGS and LORD OF LORDS, and His Kingdom will endure forever.

I bless and applaud you Father for your patience. I glorify you for your love and ultimate sacrifice Big Brother, and I shall swim in your fullness Holy Spirit.

I am compelling each one of us today, saved and unsaved, to review our outlook on life, understand His vision for our world, receive and/or not lose our spiritual seal, and renew our strength in Him. In Jesus' Mighty Name. Amen and Amen.

To Israel

To my Hebrews family: I know who we are, and I am aware of the fact that 1619 to 2019 equals 400 years. However, the King has commanded us to reach out with love to the best of our ability. This is why I cannot let the revelation concerning my true identity hinder my good sense of judgment. Truth be told, we are who we are because God said so, not because of any personal merit (Ezekiel 63). I know that it is not an easy task to express mercy towards Edom, but if we ought to be called children of God, we must at least try. Furthermore, the curse of Deuteronomy 28 was brought upon us by our own action. We were chosen out of all the other nations to prepare the way for the LORD, but we continuously played the harlot with Him. We were rejected as a result of that. Brother Elijah, a prophet, had to stand in the gap instead to fulfill the task initially given to the twelve tribes to prepare the way of the Lord - one man to fill the shoes of a nation - but he did it with the help of the Lord.

I understand that we will soon be restored, and the world should know that the LORD has always loved us. This is the only reason we are still here. I believe this is the reason why the spirit of Israel has been so driven towards reparation and equality lately. Although I am against the constant violence and the burning of our communities, I will not speak any more on that matter. I feel you, and I understand your frustration about racism.

However, I must remind you that the first 400-year sentence given to our ancestors for the purging of their iniquity was extended to 430 years (Gen. 15:13-[16]; Ex. 12:40-41). The reason why is unclear, but we must be aware and understand that Jehovah will be the One leading us out again. For it is written:

*"And the LORD shall bring thee into Egypt again with ships, by the way whereof I spoke unto thee, Thou shalt see it no more again: and there ye shall be sold unto your enemies for bondmen and bondwomen, **and no man shall buy you**"* (Deut. 28:68).

The term *"no man shall buy you"* means that the strength of man will not restore Israel. The strength of the Divine is what will bring Israel out of Egypt. I don't know how, when, or who among us will be chosen to walk in the steps of Moses and Joshua. However, Yahushuah will be the one directing our exodus again, and many strangers will join our ranks this time (Isaiah 14:1). So let us be wise and inquire of the LORD so that we do not follow after King Saul who failed to wait on the word of the Lord and was rejected as king. The will of God will be done regardless of the opposition or the opinion of man. I love you, brothers and sisters. You are beautiful just the way you were made. Whether you choose to call God by His Latin name or His Hebrew name, my prayers go to you all. I can't wait to see you all at the camp of the saints in the beloved city in Israel.

BE BLESSED.

- NOTES -

Dictionaries used for phraseology and context:

Chapter 1

1. Bryant, Al. *Zondervan Compact Bible Dictionary.* Zondervan Pub. House, 1994.

2. Webster, *Merriam. Merriam-Webster*, Inc. Encyclopedia Britannica, Inc., 1964.

3. Ibojie, Joe, et al. *Illustrated Dictionary of Dream Symbols: a Biblical Guide to Your Dreams and Visions.* Destiny Image Europe, 2005.

4. Longman, Dictionary. "A Man/Woman Etc. after My Own Heart." *LDOCE*, 2020, www.ldoceonline.com/dictionary/a-man-womanetc-after-my-own-heart.

Chapter 2

1. Munroe, Myles. "Chapter 3. Who Are You?" *Understanding Your Potential*: Discovering the Hidden You, by Myles Munroe, Destiny Image Publishers, 1992.

2. Darby, Stephen. "The Religion of the Days of Noah - YouTube." *DestinedMinistry.com*, 15 July 2018, www.youtube.com/watch?v=3zVAkhNhTZI.

3. Ginsburg, Ruth Bader, and Ruth Bader Ginsburg. *Sex Bias in the U.S. Code: a Report of the U.S. Commission on Civil Rights*, U.S. Government Printing Office, 1977, page 102.

4. Fairchild, Mary. "What Caused the Great Schism of 1054?" *Learn Religions*, 2019, www.learnreligions.com/the-great-schism-of-10544691893.

5. Cahill, Edward. "Document Illustration; the Anti-Christian Character of Freemasonry; Its Policy and Methods; Its Religion; Its Universal Oneness; Its Influence in High Finance." *Freemasonry and the AntiChristian Movement.* M.H. Gill and Son, 1959.

6. Merton, Holmes Whittier. *Heliocentric Astrology, or, Essentials of Astronomy and Solar Mentality: with Tables of Ephemeris to 1910.* F, Warne & Co., 1899.

7. Discoveries, Amazing. "Paganism and Catholicism: The Mother-Son Sun Worship System." *Amazing Discoveries*, 27 May 2009, amazingdiscoveries.org/S-deception_paganism_Catholic_Nimrod_Mary.

8. Wenz, John. "10 Of America's Must-See UFO Destinations." *Popular Mechanics*, Popular Mechanics, 25 May 2018, www.popularmechanics.com/culture/g3059/ufo-road-trip/.

9. Adams, Kathy. "Why Is Las Vegas Called Sin City?" *10Best*, 8 June 2017, getaway.10best.com/12803289/why-is-las-vegas-called-sin-city.

10. Hub, Bible. "Nashaw - Strong Hebrew Concordance." *Strong's Hebrew: 5378. נָשָׁא (Nasha) -- to Beguile, Deceive*, 2020, www.biblehub.com/hebrew/5378.htm.

11. Minium, Alice. "50 Reasons Why You Should Believe The Earth Is Flat." *The Odyssey Online*, The Odyssey Online, 5 Aug. 2020, www.theodysseyonline.com/heres-all-the-proof-you-need-that-the-earthis-flat.

12. Wikipedia, Wikipedia. "History of Science Fiction Films." *Wikipedia*, Wikimedia Foundation, 6 Nov. 2020, en.wikipedia.org/wiki/History_of_science_fiction_films.

13. Kaysing, Bill. *We Never Went to the Moon: America's Thirty Billion Dollar Swindle*. New Saucerian Press, 2017.

14. Bernays, Edward L., and Mark Crispin. Miller. *Propaganda*. IG Publishing, 2005.

15. Darlow, Mark. *Staging the French Revolution Cultural Politics and the Paris Opéra, 1789-1794*. Oxford University Press, 2012.

16. Morgan, Edward, et al. "10 FACTS You Must Know About The Jesuits!" *Prepare For Change*, 5 Nov. 2019, prepareforchange.net/2019/11/05/10-facts-you-must-know-about-thejesuits/.

17. Wikipedia, Wikipedia. "Probability Theory." *Wikipedia*, Wikimedia Foundation, 2 Oct. 2020, en.wikipedia.org/wiki/Probability_theory.

18. "Section 105." *Nietzsche: the Gay Science*, by Bernard Arthur Owen. Williams and Josefine Nauckhoff, Cambridge University Press, 2001.

19. How, Earth. "Theory of Evolution: Charles Darwin and Natural Selection." *Earth How*, 22 June 2020, earthhow.com/theory-ofevolution/.

20. Prince, Derek. "Derek Prince - The Enemies We Face (Part 1-4) - YouTube." *YouTube*, 2017, www.youtube.com/watch?v=FaculokYqLc.

21. Nation, United. "Universal Declaration of Human Rights." *United Nations*, United Nations, 2020, www.un.org/en/universal-declarationhuman-rights/index.html.

22. Wikipedia, Wikipedia. *The Vatican and The Jesuits*, 2020, www.bibliotecapleyades.net/vatican/esp_vatican37.htm.

23. Mingst, Karen. "United Nations." *Encyclopædia Britannica*, Encyclopædia Britannica, Inc., 2020, www.britannica.com/topic/UnitedNations.

24. Maclaren, Sean. "A Very Brief History Of America: How The Jesuits Have Distorted Our Own Past." *Sean Maclaren*, 8 June 2015, seanmaclarenbooks.com/a-very-brief-history-of-america-how-the-jesuitshave-distorted-our-own-past/.

25. Wikipedia, Wikipedia. "Historical Columbia." *Wikipedia*, Wikimedia Foundation, 21 July 2020, en.wikipedia.org/wiki/Historical_Columbia.

26. Julia, Chen "Columbia, Allegory Of America," ObscureHistories.com, 6 December, 2015, https://www.obscurehistories.com/columbia.

27. Staff, WIVB. "Queen of Heaven Carnival Happening This Weekend in West Seneca." *News 4 Buffalo*, News 4 Buffalo, 13 July 2019, www.wivb.com/news/local-news/queen-of-heaven-carnival-happeningthis-weekend-in-west-seneca/.

28. Nelson, Kris. "Tell-Lie-Vision - How Fake the 'Real' News Is." *Evolve Consciousness*, 17 Dec. 2017, evolveconsciousness.org/tell-lie-vision-fakereal-news/.

Chapter 3

1. Kremer, Ken. "SpaceX Delays Upcoming 1st Dragon Launch to ISS." *Phys.org*, Phys.org, 17 Jan. 2012, phys.org/news/2012-01-spacexupcoming-1st-dragon-iss.html.

2. Times, NY. "SpaceX Launch: Highlights From NASA Astronauts' Trip to Orbit." *The New York Times*, The New York Times, 30 May 2020, www.nytimes.com/2020/05/30/science/spacex-launch-nasa.html.

3. Earth, Google. "How Many Square Miles Is the Earth?" *Reference*, IAC Publishing, 2020, www.reference.com/science/many-square-miles-earth9a828fe84c9dab10.

4. Williams, Pete. "In Narrow Ruling, Supreme Court Gives Victory to Baker Who Refused to Make Cake for Gay Wedding." *NBCNews.com*, NBCUniversal News Group, 14 Dec. 2018, www.nbcnews.com/politics/supreme-court/narrow-ruling-supreme-courtgives-victory-baker-who-refused-make-n872946.

5. Jones, Molly. *The First Amendment: Freedom of Speech, the Press, and Religion*. Rosen Central, 2011.

6. News, CBC. "Canada's Gender Identity Rights Bill C-16 Explained." *CBCnews*, CBC/Radio Canada, 2017, www.cbc.ca/cbcdocspov/features/canadas-gender-identity-rights-bill-c16-explained.

Chapter 4

1. Kirkness, Jordan. "This Is All Stolen Land: Native Americans Want

2. More than California's Apology." *The Guardian*, Guardian News and Media, 21 June 2019, www.theguardian.com/us-news/2019/jun/20/california-native-americans-governor-apologyreparations.

3. Agency, Guardian staff. "Trump Administration Revokes Tribe's Reservation Status in 'Power Grab'." *The Guardian*, Guardian News and Media, 31 Mar.

2020, www.theguardian.com/us-news/2020/mar/31/trump-administration-revokes-mashpee-wampanoagtribe-reservation-status.

4. Windsor, Rudolph R. *From Babylon to Timbuktu: a History of the Ancient Black Races Including the Black Hebrews*. Bnpublishing.com, 2018.

5. Darby, Stephen. "Persecution of True Israel - YouTube." *DestinedMinistry.com*, 2017. www.youtube.com/watch?v=OiRgpM6UyRU

6. Jones, Jae. "Branding of Slaves: Brutal Act Used for Identification Purposes and Severe Punishment." Black Then, 8 Feb. 2020, blackthen.com//branding-of-slaves-brutal-act-used-for-identificationpurposes-and-severe-punisment/.

7. Exposed.Org, Thug. "CULT HAND-SIGNS & ALCHEMY...))) EXPOSED...NEW WORLD ORDER" *YouTube*, 2020, www.youtube.com/watch?v=LG2MSidRZdo.

8. Rayford, Johnson L. "Thug, Drug & Tattoo Ancient History/Thuggee Tribe-South" *ThugExposed.Org*, 2011, www.youtube.com/watch?v=9lXejmEexiw.

Chapter 5

1. Chokshi, Niraj. "Teenagers Recorded a Drowning Man and Laughed." *The New York Times*, The New York Times, 21 July 2017, www.nytimes.com/2017/07/21/us/video-drowning-teens-florida.html.

2. Rosenblatt, Kalhan, and Rima Abdelkader. "California Woman Livestreamed Dying Teen Sister on Instagram After Car Crash." *NBCNews.com*, NBCUniversal News Group, 26 July 2017, www.nbcnews.com/news/us-news/california-woman-livestreamed-dyingteen-sister-instagram-after-car-crash-n785846.

Chapter 6

1. MacGuill, Dan. "Did 41 Senators Vote to Let Babies Scream Until They Die If Born Alive?" *Snopes.com*, 25 Feb. 2020, www.snopes.com/fact-check/41-senators-vote-babies-born-alive/.

2. Ortlieb Updated March 24, Tracy Collins. "Abortion Laws by State: These Are Your Rights." *Parents*, 24 Mar. 2020, www.parents.com/pregnancy/abortion-laws-by-state-these-are-yourright/.

3. Admin. *The Nate Max Project*, 19 Mar. 2017, www.thenatemaxproject.com/2017/03/19/list-of-companies-using-fetalcells-from-aborted-babies-to-flavour-products/.

4. Clark, Dartunorro. "End Child Marriage in the U.S.? You Might Be Surprised at Who's Opposed." *NBCNews.com*, NBCUniversal News Group, 8 Sept. 2019, www.nbcnews.com/politics/politics-news/end-childmarriage-u-s-you-might-be-surprised-who-n1050471.

5. Belanger, Ashley. "What Most People Get Wrong About Religion And Child Marriage." *Teen Vogue*, 1 Jan. 2020, www.teenvogue.com/story/child-marriage-and-religion-in-the-unitedstates.

6. News, CBS. "Florida Church with Naked Paint Parties Loses Tax Exempt Status." *CBS News*, CBS Interactive, 11 Mar. 2015, www.cbsnews.com/news/florida-church-with-naked-paint-parties-losestax-exempt-status/.

7. Line, Date. "DateLine TV Jehovah's Witnesses Pedophile's - YouTube." *DateLine TV*, 4 June 2018, www.youtube.com/watch?v=fJq1XtJNzA8.

Chapter 7

1. Lyric, Lewin. "The Future Is Female." *CNN*, Cable News Network, 2018,www.cnn.com/interactive/2018/01/politics/womens-marchcnnphotos/.

2. Contributor, Wikipedia. "Shooting of Charles Kinsey." *Wikipedia*, Wikimedia Foundation, 17 Oct. 2020, en.wikipedia.org/wiki/Shooting_of_Charles_Kinsey.

3. Point, Columbia. "The Federal Government Takes on Physical Fitness." *The Federal Government Takes on Physical Fitness | JFK Library*, 2020,www.jfklibrary.org/learn/about-jfk/jfk-in-history/physicalfitness.

4. Cook, Lindsey. "Study: Americans 24 Pounds Fatter Than in 1960." *U.S. News & World Report*, U.S. News & World Report, 2014, www.usnews.com/news/blogs/data-mine/2014/09/04/study-americans24-pounds-fatter-than-in-1960.

Chapter 8

1. United Church of God. "Israel's Golden Age." *United Church of God*, 16 Feb. 2011, www.ucg.org/bible-study-tools/booklets/the-united-statesand-britain-in-bible-prophecy/israels-golden-age.

2. Chappell, Bill, and Richard Gonzales. "Brandt Jean's Act Of Grace Toward His Brother's Killer Sparks A Debate Over Forgiving." *NPR*, NPR, 3 Oct. 2019, www.npr.org/2019/10/03/766866875/brandt-jeans-act-ofgrace-toward-his-brother-s-killer-sparks-a-debate-over-forgi.

3. Denver, CBS. "Mother Sharletta Evans 'Adopts' Man Who Killed Her Son." *CBS Denver*, CBS Denver, 8 Nov. 2019,

4. denver.cbslocal.com/2019/11/08/sharletta-evans-casson-raymondjohnson/.

5. CNNwire. "Father Forgives and Hugs Man Involved in His Son's Killing." *fox8.Com*, fox8.Com, 9 Nov. 2017, fox8.com/news/fatherforgives-and-hugs-man-involved-in-his-sons-killing/.

6. Schoenberg, Nara. "Mom Forgives the Man Who Murdered Her Daughter, Answers His Letters from Prison." *Chicagotribune.com*, 26 Dec. 2017, www.chicagotribune.com/lifestyles/sc-fam-mother-forgivesmurderer-0116-story.html.

7. Gordon, Michael. "This Is What She Wanted Me to Do - A Mother Forgives Daughter's Killer." *Star*, Fort Worth Star-Telegram, 2016, www.star-telegram.com/news/nationworld/national/article80162857.html.

8. Khamisa, Azim. "Azim Khamisa and Ples Felix." *The Forgiveness Project*, 16 Apr. 2020, www.theforgivenessproject.com/stories/azimkhamisa-ples-felix/.

Chapter 10

1. Team, WLC. "Lunar Sabbath." *Bible Prophecy | Online Bible Studies | Videos | WLC*, 2020, www.worldslastchance.com/yahuwahs-calendar/thelunar-sabbath.html.

2. Windam, Jarvis. "The Postponement Rules." *The Postponement Rules in the Calculated Hebrew Calendar Was Never a Part of the Calendar God Gave to His People*, 2020, www.ironsharpeningiron.com/postponements3.htm.

3. WLC. "Constantine I & Hillel II: Two Men Who Deceived the Whole World." *Bible Prophecy | Online Bible Studies | Videos | WLC*, 2020, www.worldslastchance.com/yahuwahs-calendar/constantine-hillel-twomen-who-deceived-the-whole-world.html.

Chapter 11

1. Patel, Piyush. "How Does Salt Help Preserve Certain Food Items (Particularly Meat)?" Science ABC, 14 Jan. 2020, www.scienceabc.com/eyeopeners/salt-help-preserve-certain-food-itemslike-meat.html.

About the Author

Michael Jedaiah is a native of the Caribbean and a veteran of the United States Army. He has served in both Operation Iraqi Freedom and Operation Enduring Freedom. He has served as Team Leader and later as Squad Leader at Fort Hood, Texas. He was discharged honorably after proudly serving his adopted country and is now managing his own music production studio. He recently graduated from the "Sonship – School Of The Firstborn" program at Christian House Of Prayer in Killeen, Texas. Throughout his life, Michael Jedaiah had the privilege to travel to France, Germany, Amsterdam, England, and the Middle East. He enjoyed meeting people of various cultures and backgrounds.

This is the author's first book. It is compiled with a lifetime of experiences, observations obtained through the gift of discernment, and revelations from the Holy Spirit. Michael Jedaiah has served as an usher, and most recently as a youth counselor at Parts Of Many, an outreach program for troubled teens sponsored by Grace Christian Center in Killeen, Texas. You can email Michael Jedaiah at michaeljedaiah78@gmail.com.

Made in the USA
Columbia, SC
31 October 2021